The Key To
Spiritual and Psychic
Development

Table Tipping

"An exciting and direct communication tool for connecting with your Spirit Guides and Higher Self for personal and Universal knowledge."

Angela M. Mattey

Tam Enterprises publishing Co.
Phoenix, Arizona U.S.A.

ISBN 1-882836-00-6
Library of Congress Catalog Card Number 92-91268

Book design, illustrations and cover: Angela M. Mattey

Printed in the United States by:
TAM ENTERPRISES
P.O. BOX 55451
PHOENIX, ARIZ. 85078

This book has been written from my truths as I have received and experienced them over the years. Each person because we are all individual must receive their own truths which may not be mine. Table tipping is just one tool to use to give you insight. I make no claim or guarantees as to the accuracy of the information you receive from its use even though you follow the procedures suggested in this book accurately. The use of table tipping is not intended for making your life's decisions.

Whenever I refer to a person as male gender in general references within this book, I am doing it for the convenience of not having to use the words he or she in each instance. I am referring to all humanity when I use the term he. In reference to the God Force, I use the term He for the convenience of the term only, I do not believe that the Source of the God Force is personified or essentially masculine. Throughout the book I often refer to the God Source with such terms as the All, the Universal All, the Source or the Ultimate Mind, all of which will be capitalized in respect for their Divine meaning.

Grateful acknowledgment is made to the following for permission to reprint previously published material:
Parker Publishing Co., Inc.: Excerpt from PSYCHO-KINESIS: *Moving Matter With The Mind* by Adrian U. Clark. Copyright 1973, reprinted by permission of Parker Publishing Company, Inc. West Nyack, N.Y.

FRONTISPIECE

AUTHOR'S STATEMENT OF INTRODUCTION

I have reached the realization that we are here in this physical life experience to honor our soul and whole spiritual Self by not only allowing its growth, but by empowering its own personal evolution and its universal role in the evolution of all human spirituality during this period of earth history. In order to achieve spiritual evolution, we must learn who we are on all levels and develop a deep working awareness of our whole self; physically, emotionally, mentally, psychically and spiritually. As we expand our spiritual and psychic consciousness I believe we are actively working within the divine plan of the next level of human spiritual evolution.

I am thankfully acknowledging the value of spiritual table tipping as an evolved form of a traditional mystical physical tool process because of its role as a powerful and concrete step in my development towards my balance, wholeness and secure connection with my inner knowingness. It expanded my consciousness due to the unique fact it is a group tool unlike other physical tools such as the tarot cards or a pendulum. When you meditate and are at one with your Godself through a tarot card, you are still caught up in your own energy field and its filters. Whereas when you tune in within a group energy field, such as exists in the table tipping process, your energy field is amplified and its focus is strengthened by the other persons present allowing for more powerful spiritual connections than you could personally achieve. You will discover that, by virtue of the blend of all of the sitters' energies, you have raised your personal awareness and energy level to an impersonal level of universal awareness and energy. This energy expansion allows you to step out of your personal concerns and become an activated and aware player within the universal game plan of evolution. Also, because of their presence and interaction, the other sitters and their spiritual energies will be able to tune in to spirit's answers with a neutrality that is unavailable to you.

AUTHOR'S STATEMENT OF INTRODUCTION

Due to its physical level of reality the table performs as a perfect bridge between the third and other more subtle dimensions creating a powerful reflective support of your own present chosen existence as a bridge and multidimensional blend of a physical body, a soul and a Higher Self.

Today's world and its fast paced high energy changes demands of us to be; balanced, in the universal flow of energy, attuned with a deep ever expanding awareness to our Higher Selves and in harmony with all the essence levels of the God Source in order to survive in joy and in empowerment enabling us to manifest our good. Because I believe spiritual table tipping to be an important and very practical step available to you for opening your consciousness to your whole Self helping you to joyously live your evolution within the world's present demands, I have written this book. It is an easy to use manual, teaching you proven techniques for successful spiritual tipping, thus opening the doorway for creating the activity of directly communicating with your spirit guides, teachers, Higher Self and all of the other realms of creation giving you the link to them that acknowledges your flow with the oneness of all.

DEDICATION

This book is dedicated to my patient loving husband, Thomas, who has willingly shared me with so many incarnate friendly beings as well as spiritual entities while I studied and quested for knowledge and understanding of my spiritual self. I am in sincere appreciation of my Chief Spiritual Guide and many lifetimes companion, Christopher, who enacts the role of ambassador during table tipping sessions. During these times, Chris collects together spiritual information and beings crossing many dimensions to enhance my education. This metaphysical journey has led to many very dear and special friendships with relatives, students, mentors, clients and loving, patient, spiritual helpers from many dimensions. Through these relationships this book became a physical reality. I extend my humble gratitude and love to them all for their assistance.

CONTENTS

CONTENTS:

CONTENTS :

CONTENTS :

ILLUSTRATIONS :

FIGURES :

CHAPTER DESIGNS :

All Motifs Demonstrate the Power of Spiritual Table Tipping to FacilitateYour Personal and Universal Growth.

PREFACE

Since 1980 I have been researching and experiencing a phenomenon know as Table tipping or Table tilting. In the late fall of that year my husband and I purchased a large motor yacht which we decided to berth in the San Diego Harbor basin area of beautiful Southern California. We spent many more hours and days than we ever dreamed of on that yacht as it became our second home. It was during this time I was exposed to the awareness expanding adventure of table tipping as there were classes devoted to this subject in the San Diego area. Presented with a particular emphasis on its being a spiritual tool, table tipping was to be focused on getting to know your spirit guides and teachers and helping you to a conscious awareness of your spiritual plan for this lifetime.

There were many table tipping sessions on board our yacht every month. Each one created more excitement and touched a deeper level of an unexplainable joy within me as if I was getting in touch with my spiritual roots. I noticed that my psychic abilities were evolving rapidly and smoothly. I had uncovered an apparently endless source of spiritual knowledge and esoteric truth. It seemed each session expanded my awareness mentally, emotionally and spiritually. I discovered I was raising my spiritual frequency or vibration through emotional, mental and spiritual healings coming through the table into my being from spirit. I was changing my perceptions about life. A beautifully balanced and contented attitude about my role and direction began to form.

Since I was a child I have had an awareness of a spiritual guide. I could see and feel him. Because I was raised Roman Catholic I had a belief system that included Guardian Angels and I always thought of this guide as my Guardian Angel. One day when I was six my "angel" told me his name was Christopher. From that day forward it felt comfortable to

1

rely on him for his gentle strength and truthful guidance. Through table tipping I was now learning all about and reacquainting myself with my angel as a spiritual guide. I was able to explore some of out past lives together and to learn why he chose to be with me spiritually all through my physical life this time.

When my deceased mother came on the table to teach me about the spiritual qualities of color I had a great deal of resistance towards believing that she, my mother, was really present. I demanded that she tell me facts about her life of which I was unaware and that only my father who is still living could verify. The unfolding of this incident was one of my strongest proofs that there was life after death and that I was indeed communicating with my deceased mother through the tool of table tipping. Further details of this incident will be explained later in this book when I discuss techniques on how to properly perform spiritual table tipping.

I had a definite fear about fire that I was able to explore. Through my guide Christopher I came to understand the causes of this anxiety and was able to create total freedom from that almost phobic level of fear.

These exciting, revealing and healing experiences are just three of the powerful and obvious rewards I received through table tipping. My personal energy was expanding to such a degree that I started experiencing more powerful connections in meditation and in dream. I could feel myself opening and evolving spiritually. I was blending my spirituality into my every day life with a different level of ease. Table tipping reinforces an inner sense of calm because of your deeper knowing that your spiritual self is immortal and that the physical body is just a tool through which it can experience. You will learn that physical death is natural; it is not necessary for the physical body to be permanent. It is only a package through which the soul personality can express itself. The soul needs the experiences of the physical world for impressions and imprints to accumulate wisdom. The spiritual self needs several soul-lives within different physical bodies to develop its perfection from different vantage points. We all understand that if three people witness an accident, due to their unique personalities, all three will perceive the same accident differently. Our spiritual self needs different physical life existences for an accumulation of our personal soul perceptions of each life to evolve through our lessons and Karmas.

The principle of a group getting together around a table to collect and exchange ideas is ancient, but the popularity of the cooperation of the physical table in the conversation by its movement traces back to the late 1800's. Although there are vague references to the practice of using moving physical objects for communication all through recorded history, most written reports concerning the phenomenon of table tipping, turning, tilting or rapping are from the late nineteenth century. Historically, interest in table tipping always increases during times of earth, political or economic crisis. Peak eras of table tipping occurred during World Wars I and II. Its purpose then was centered around finding those who were missing and contacting the dead. It was common to consult the dead for reasons such as unfinished family business and a chance for a last good-bye and/or any parting message which war did not allow. If you research the history of table tipping you will discover it involves some famous past figures. However, table tipping as I utilize it is not centered upon the same techniques as the historic Spiritualism rituals used, because their intent was only to contact the dead. It is also important to note that we are not singularly focusing on the phenomenon in spiritual table tipping.

Now we are realizing a return of the desire to table tip with an entirely new approach and direction of intention. The New Age has set the stage for an awareness of Spirit Guides, Higher Self, Spiritual teachers and angels plus an openness to assistance from spirit (of all higher planes and dimensions) to allow each one of us to travel our spiritual path as co-creators with God.

Spiritual table tipping is a **group energy tool** which makes it timely, appropriate and effective due to the present placement of our soul impression or experience in the cycles of human evolution. The human soul has grown through the ancient cycle of a herd consciousness level of soul impression, as well as the need for individuality of the soul as an impression. At present, our cycle within the evolutionary plan is to grow as an individual working within a group expressing in a harmonious spiritual impression. Thus, when one works with the table, the soul experiences how to be individual and still flow with the group as a whole unit of energy. There are times when this whole unit of group energy can raise each individual's energy level so that the group itself can connect with powerful spiritual energies and perform projects with spirit that an individual could not easily perform. This group energy field creates a bonded oneness that opens the way for universal work and the ability to be impersonal enough to work within the universal plan of creation. Powerful healings that are personal and impersonal are accomplished within this enhanced energy field experience.

I have written this book so that you can utilize spiritual table tipping as a basic physical tool to work with your personal awareness expansion or the group's spiritual expansion in an impersonal manner for universal work. You will discover spiritual table tipping to be a new, exciting and a warmly engaging tool to use for; spiritual growth, awareness expansion, developing of your intuitive senses, raising your vibration allowing you to embrace your own balanced power.

I assembled the text with the intention of sharing with you all the secrets you need to be an effective table tipper. I explore the many purposes for table tipping in detail. I present each technique thoroughly, since I was an elementary school teacher for ten years, so that you can have immediate success with your table tipping sessions. You will be pleased and no doubt surprised at the rapid psychic growth that will occur because you are table tipping effectively. I will explain to you the type of table to use and the proper methods and procedures for use of your new spiritual table. I assure you that table tipping in this enhanced format will open the way to adventure plus an awareness and energy expansion opportunity beyond your grandest imaginings. Your spiritual growth will blossom in a direct and understandable manner. You will eventually attain a reliable level of spiritual self confidence that will open the way for trust in your own inner knowing enabling you to sense the subtle guidance from your spiritual helpers. You will be able to bridge the dimensions within yourself because you have grown and gained a freedom from feeling alone on your path. You will be able to experience your oneness with the All as the result of your group energy work.

My dream is that eventually all that you achieve with the table you will be able to do without the table. Then you will develop your own perfectly flowing gift of intuition and inner knowing. That would be your beautiful reward for your spiritual table tipping efforts!

God bless you! A great joy wells up inside of my being as I realize that by your own choice to read and apply the principles of this book you have discovered an effective way to experience the heights and the depths of yourself thus opening the pathway to a powerful transformation. Enjoy the expansion of your awareness and consciousness, plus your discovery of the direct support of all of your spiritual team members. Have fun with your wondrous growth!

Angela M. Mattey

Over the years, I have tipped in numerous class and personal situations. Throughout this book I will be referring to people, places and incidents that in some cases are very personal in nature. The names and locations of these instances have been changed to ensure the personal privacy of those involved. I thank all my students, clients, dear friends, spirit and family members for the support and information they have provided through the table tipping experiences presented in this book.

Special thanks to Ann Allison, Jenny McKenzie, Linda Roessler and Dr. William J. Mayer for their observations comments, support and editorial assistance with this book.

PART ONE :

THE TABLE, SPIRIT AND YOU

COMPREHENDING SPIRITUAL TABLE TIPPING

"TRUST IN THE SMALL VOICE OF YOUR HEART FOR IT SPEAKS FROM THE SEAT OF YOUR SOUL"

CHRISTOPHER

CHAPTER ONE

What Is Table Tipping?

TABLE TIPPING IS the physical and spiritual phenomenon that occurs when people sit around a table placing their fingertips on its surface with singular concentration to connect with spiritual energies for the purpose of interdimensional communication. One person in the seated group is the director or coordinator of the questions and the leader or spokesperson for the group. For best results there must be this type of organization. It is best if the question that is proposed is directed towards a specific spiritual energy or entity for clarity. Mental, emotional and intentional cooperation of all the sitters is very important. All persons at the table should concentrate on the question at hand and open their minds to its answer. The best effects come from the unified desire and focus of every person seated at the table

Sitting around the table creates an energy circle. This process, through special techniques, can amplify each person's psychic and spiritual abilities to send and receive information or energy. This same energy circle can be used to raise each person's energy when it is focused upon information gathering from the Universal realms. Consider the comparison of how much electricity one battery can generate by itself versus the amplification of electrical power produced when several batteries are connected on one circuit. The teamwork effort of an energy circle is exciting and rewarding. As a group you can reach spiritual levels and dimensions that otherwise might be unattainable to one person.

The traditional practices utilized in old-fashioned table tipping included very little, if any, reliance upon each sitter's inner knowing or attunement with spirit through Clairvoyance, Clairaudience, Clairsentience or any of the other possibly active soul or psychic senses. The sitters based all of their information gathering only upon the physical movement of the table itself. The emphasis was placed upon the excitement of the phenomenon of the table's antics. If you observe a seance that is performed with all the persons centered around a table, you become very aware that the medium who speaks for spirit is utilizing the support of the combined energies of the persons in the energy circle formed around the table to make contact with other dimensions. In the past, the focus of these sessions has been to reach physically deceased souls or the "dead" for information.

The new or spiritual table tipping experience actively utilizes the energy circle concept in its highest form through a special emphasis upon a meditation technique, other practices and a united spiritual intention. The focus of the spiritual energy circle is to communicate with beings that are of the light of God and to raise the sitters vibration above the mental levels avoiding subconscious prattle and interference. This spiritual energy circle creates the opportunity for all persons seated at the table to be open for healing on all levels and the expansion of each person's vibration on a personal level. In its highest form, the expansion of the group's energy circle establishes the necessary etheric atmosphere for many powerful possibilities. Each person can enhance their personal psychic abilities. Each person can raise their vibrations quickly and safely for a stronger personal bond that can develop into a deep inner knowingness with spirit guides and their own Higher Self. It will expand the group's energy field into a unit of power that reaches into the rarer and more advanced realities providing direct communication with mastered, beautified, transformed universal beings. This level of use of the table's energy circle provides an expansive view of creation. It takes the individual sitter beyond himself, his ego and his personal needs into exciting and beautifully moving personal and group interactive experiences with Divine levels of existence. The sitters can actually witness the God force through a deeper understanding of the All. The personal meaning derived from these powerful experiences cannot be put into words. The expansion of personal vibration that results from the touching of the God force at these levels activates the energies necessary for direct quantum leaps of spiritual growth for the group and each sitter personally.

Once the participants are seated and have agreed upon the process of proper techniques (chap. 5, pg. 51) there is no doubt that the table will move. Sometimes it gently rocks to and fro. Other times it spins and dances with great energy. One table we used had a top that screwed onto the pedestal by turning it until it was secure. One night a spirit who came on to this table simply unscrewed the top until it was almost disconnected from the pedestal. We were all amazed at this activity until the spirit informed us that it was a Joy Guide who wanted to demonstrate to us not to take ourselves so seriously.

The movement of the table will vary and is usually very individual. It is affected by the sitters and the spirit being with whom they are communicating. Nevertheless, some entities seem to have a special way they move the table giving their communication a personalized signature. One of my friend's guides vibrates the table and then moves it back and forth. It is so unique that when it happens during our sittings we giggle and say, "Hello John, we know it's you." This special signature movement saves a lot of time and effort that would be exerted in identifying the spirit present at the table. I am convinced that is why spirit purposely identifies itself through its own special movement. Spiritual entities are always anxious to get on with communicating and expressing themselves. When you are familiar with distinguishing their personally characteristic maneuver, you will know which spiritual friend is communicating with you by observing the movement positions of the table.

There have been many theories about what makes the table move. Some believe it is totally spirit's energy, others are of the opinion that the people themselves use a subconscious or psycho-kinetic energy to move the table. In a text entitled PSYCHO-KINESIS - *MOVING MATTER WITH THE MIND* by Adrian V. Clark the author states, "Jim Henry who was in public information with the National Aeronautics and Space Administration for several years has conducted many table rocking sessions, since he was ten years old, to obtain information which has led him to be Director of the Chamber of Commerce in New Orleans. He has found that any group can control a table to obtain a higher source of knowledge if they are "believers." [1] Mr. Clark refers to table tipping or movement as useful but does not claim spiritual involvement. There are many texts that casually mention table tipping, but they have not arrived at an agreement as to the cause or the source of energy creating the movement.

My belief is that when sitters relax and focus their energies together within the power of the spiritual energy circle, the movement is a combined energy effort on the part of spirit and the sitters blended in a vibrational flow. This conclusion is justified by personal experience. I have witnessed, felt and seen psychically many color and vibrational exchanges happening, during the table tipping experience in the so-called invisible dimension that surrounds us at all times. I believe that the table moves side to side, spins around, dances, thumps and even walks without physical, conscious, mental or willful intent on the part of the persons sitting at the table. When you are participating in this wondrously powerful experience you, too, become aware that spirit is in command of the table.

If I notice that someone has any form of physical,

conscious or willful effort involved in the movement in any way I ask them to remove their hands from the surface of the table. That type of action works against the purpose of using the tool. It automatically invalidates the information received.

Table tipping is a socially fascinating way to learn old wisdom and unusual knowledge from cooperating spirits from many different planes or dimensions. The more experienced you become with this tool, the greater the chances you will open up to the possibilities of hierarchical beings participating in your quest for information. There is no limit to the levels of awareness you can achieve. You will notice continuous growth in your capacities to hear, see, feel and know spirit through dedication to the higher knowing available to you by the use of table tipping.

In view of the fact you are learning about yourself and any truth you wish to embrace, this tool is effective because it is accomplished in the presence of others. The information you receive is "honest". By this I mean that others not as emotionally involved with your problems are witnessing the answers given by spirit and allowing their objectivity to balance your personal view. You will discover when you ask spirit to answer questions about which you are anxious you will sometimes have difficulty psychically hearing or seeing spirit with clarity. These instances occur when you hear any information that does not correlate with your wishes. When this happens you create a barrier between yourself and the pertinent information coming from spirit. Others around the table will not be involved in the fog of illusions your emotions create giving them clear objectivity to the information.

Another asset of this social or group-oriented tool is that it offers a chance to validate information you have received in the form of a hunch, a vision or in a meditational or dream experience. An example I experienced was that for a long time Christopher appeared to me dressed in white with a cape that was red on one side and black on the other. Sometimes, he would show the red on the outside and at other times the black.

I used the table to ask him why he wore the cape differently at times. He told me that he was sending visual signals to me for answers to my questions and thoughts. He said that I could use the red and the black as significators of **Yes** and **No**. Red for **No** and black for **Yes**. This was exciting and a terrific breakthrough for I always saw him but could not always hear him. Now I had an accurate means of getting answers from him even when I was not table tipping.

As the years passed, I achieved considerable spiritual self-growth through diligent meditation work and table tipping in order to understand how to live my lessons. Then I started to notice a change in my guide Christopher's appearance and energy. One day, while table tipping with my sister-in-law, she also observed the difference in his energy and color. I was excited about the verification, because after so much time of seeing him in certain colors and energies I was concerned why there was a change and reluctant to believe my own intuitive perceptions.

I was not at all comfortable with the change. So we asked Christopher, since he had come to the table, if there was a purpose for his change in appearance. He told us that whenever a human soul evolves on the earth plane there is a corresponding growth with the spirit guides who work with that soul. I realized then that I had successfully achieved another level of spiritual self-growth. Christopher reports that all of us on the earth plane have universal and personal helping spirits. We learned there was a strong interaction between the spiritual entities, called guides, and ourselves for the growth of all is totally intertwined. I have learned that each and every symbol and color I perceive has a specific part in bringing the whole message through from spirit. I understood that I had to be aware of all details, like a good detective, for all were clues to the truth I was seeking. Whenever these clues were not understandable to me I could ask for their interpretation and true meaning through the use of the table.

Table tipping is a specific experience that allows you to directly ask questions of and receive immediate response from spiritual energies residing in other dimensions. It is a third dimensional tool that crosses you into the fourth and other dimensions. Which dimension or spiritual level you communicate with is directed by the content of your questions, your personal energies, the energy of the group and **most of all your intentions**.

NOTES

1. Adrian V, Clark, PSYCHO-KINESIS *Moving Matter With Your Mind*, (West Nyack, New York: Parker Publishing Co., Inc., 1973.) Page 54.

*"OBSERVE WITH RESPECT AND CARE THOSE
WHO SEEM TO VIBRATE OPPOSITE TO YOU,
FOR THEY ARE OFTEN YOUR BALANCING
MIRROR."*

CHRISTOPHER

CHAPTER TWO

Why Table Tipping?

PERSONALLY, I STARTED to do table tipping to expand my knowledge about my past lives and to learn more about my spirit guides. I wanted some assistance with personal spiritual decisions I had to make about the art businesses I operated at the time.

These curiosities of mine led to the knowledge that table tipping was the best thing that ever happened to my psychic spiritual abilities. I realized that these abilities were developing at a rapid and exciting rate. My clairvoyance became stronger and more reliable and my telepathic capacities more than doubled in a short period of time. I realized that the table was awakening and exercising all my awarenesses to be in tune with my soul, my Higher Self and the spiritual guides and teachers that had always been around my being. They had always been there trying to assist me but my awareness of them was not opened. In more technical language, the table experiences had raised my vibrations to cycle closer to their frequencies thereby allowing us to communicate telepathically even though we exist in different dimensions.

Once I was directly communicating with my wonderful spiritual friends, I was discovering knowledge from my own soul and Higher Self, as well as, from my guides about my purpose for this incarnation and what lessons and karmas I was working through this time. I found out, to my delight, that my own fulfillment blossomed from communicating with the angels, spirit guides, higher beings and the universal All that was available to me through the table tipping sessions. All the information from these beings was joyfully given and along with it helpful ideas on how to apply it for my growth. The only key I needed to open this door to such knowledge was a sincere heart, an intention to be on my spiritual path and to gratefully apply it in my everyday life. In other words I was learning to participate with the All.

A pertinent purpose for experiencing table tipping is to be aware that when you are using the table you will be exercising all the psychic and spiritual senses as well as developing an acute awareness of the physical body's senses. Just as we have five physical senses we have spiritual counterparts. I believe that these subtle spiritual senses are both psychic and spiritual. The word psychic comes from the Greek word psychiokos which means psyche or soul, thus these psychic senses come into activity as natural sensitivities of the soul. You can develop the psychic senses of sight (Clairvoyance), of hearing (Clairaudience), of feeling (Clairsentience), of knowing in your mind (Telepathy), of taste (Clairsavorance) and of smell (Clairscentience).

It is important that you be aware that any of these spiritual faculties can be at work. It may be only one at a time or several functioning at once. What is necessary is that you be aware that these faculties exist and allow them to function. It is of considerable importance to concentrate on the heart area rather than always "being in your head." Step away from your mental aspects and combine the heart with the solar plexus area to openly let these "senses" flow and function.

There will be much more information about developing your psychic and spiritual senses thus creating a direct rapport with your inner knowing in Part II, chapter 10.

Another special reason for utilizing table tipping is to collect information effectively. The table tipping process has proved wonderful to use as a follow-up or verification of information I have received through dreams, visions, meditation, inspirational writing or channeling. Table tipping keeps me balanced in my quality of reception or clarity when gathering data. It expands my awareness challenging me to view the bigger picture. Its group approach makes it is easier to separate my ego personality from the information being received in order to allow the precise truth to reach me. This happens because of the presence of the other sitters and the input from spirit through them. The effectiveness of the table tipping process comes to fruition when each person relates to the others any vision, symbol, thoughts telepathically heard, sensations felt or wisdom they just "know" as soon as they receive it. It is as if you have immensely amplified your capacities for reception in the united effort of all the physical and spiritual soul vibrations working as a team.

Because the table is a social tool it can be a positive and forceful evidential tool. Other persons present with you can obtain answers to your questions without knowing about or being influenced by the background situations pertaining to the question. When their answers coincide with previous information that you have gained through meditation or any other process, the confirmation is happily accepted.

A simple example of how this works is demonstrated by a personal experience that occurred two years ago. Each time I reached into my spice cabinet while I was cooking, the Cream of Tartar container would roll out of place and tumble down to the countertop in front of me. Occasionally, it moved with such force it landed on the kitchen floor even though I always placed it in a secure spot on the shelf. This action curiously repeated itself many times during a two week period. Throughout this time I had been feeling unusually exhausted and complained to my chiropractor. Speaking from a background of naturopathic medicine he stated, "You know, you might be low in potassium and not getting enough of it into your system. An old-time remedy is to take a 1/2 tsp. of Cream of Tartar in juice or water each morning for about two weeks." I did just that.

A few days later, a friend and I were table tipping when my Health Guide came on the table and told my friend about the tumbling act my Cream of Tartar had been doing. The guide was pleased that I finally listened to my doctor. My friend did not know I had experienced the exhaustion and she certainly had no knowledge about the incidents with the Cream of Tartar. Now, that's verification!

My favorite application of table tipping for personal growth is that of communication with my Higher Self, spiritual guides and teachers. Everyone has spirit guides, a Higher Self and teachers who can accelerate his spiritual growth through their communications with him. It is a joyous event to acquaint yourself with the warm, caring, evolved, nurturing and healing other-dimensional friends that are concerned with your successful spiritual growth in this incarnation. Because of your connections with your spirit guides and teachers you will discover you are never alone. This will eliminate any loneliness you may have when you remember this and activate your telepathic bond with your spiritual helpers. You will begin to enjoy and allow their supportive involvement in your everyday life. You will be able to gain an expansive view of each of your lessons. You will know when you have finished with a lesson. Believe it or not, you often rework repetitively, through ignorance or habit, the same lesson that you have already accomplished. You will enjoy knowing about spirit's vantage point when you have a problem and they have suggestions. Through these types of direct communications you can get through many of your spiritual lessons with ease and even a certain amount of speed. Also, You will gain a deeper and clearer understanding of this life's karmas through discussions with your Higher Self.

When you are working through a difficult time in your life, it may seem unfair but, you will no doubt discover that your meditations are not as effective as usual. You may not be able to recall your dreams. You can feel blocked and alone. You feel vulnerable to all the negativity that surrounds you. Take a deep peaceful breath, relax! This usually happens when you are at the doorway of a wonderful and exciting spiritual breakthrough. It is at these times that table tipping is a comforting and powerfully effective tool because it may be the only way you can directly work spiritually through the blockages with speed and ease. You will be delighted to discover that these are the cycles in your life when you are going through spiritual initiations. Your spirit guides will be able to explain to you some of the steps you can take to facilitate this important cycle in your spiritual growth. They will shower you with love and supporting energy giving you spiritual rewards empowering you with their cooperation.

With proper use of the table and its powerful group energy circle principle, it becomes a means of communication that allows for you to travel through many dimensions and levels to "touch" the vibration of and to "speak" with the spiritual hierarchy, Ascended Masters, masters, The Brotherhood, intergalactic beings, lords of elementals and many different types of angels and heavenly hosts. Thus far, I have found that the table, due to its ability to raise the individual sitter's vibrations, is unlimited in its capacities to connect you with any dimension.

The first memorably effective connecting experience I had with my Higher Self was achieved through table tipping. I discovered that my Higher Self is an energy that embodies symbols which inherently explain what I am as a whole being. I learned that my Higher Self is not an individual or a personalized energy but that it is a massive spiritual essence filled with unconditional love and an unlimited acceptance of what I am. If I allow the flow of its energy to blend within my personal energy, it constantly heals me with the power of its unlimited love frequency. Another fascinating aspect to consider in your spiritual quest for knowing the Self (Self will always refer to the Higher Self.), is your communication with your other soul parts. You may need to assimilate some of the soul energy you have left in some past experience either in this or another life. You will be assisted in that process by your Higher Self.

You can find out about your twin-soul energy and other members of your spiritual family group who are souls that have worked with you since your individual beginnings. You may discover that there are persons who are around you in this incarnation that may be working through similar lessons and purposes in this lifetime because they are active members of your spiritual family.

An additional tipping exploration possibility to ponder is the chance to exchange information with persons who are presently incarnate but are "out-of-body" due to the fact they are physically asleep at the time you are tipping the table or are consciously traveling while their physical body is resting in meditation. This type of situation gives you a unique chance to research the out-of-body experience. At specific times some students have agreed to work this process through with great success. It is a verification that you are indeed out-of-body when you consciously send a message to others who are table tipping at the same time you are out-of-body and there is agreement among the sitters about the details of the message given by the traveling soul.

You can work with your dream experiences through the table. There is full cooperation from your Higher Self, spirit guides and teachers to discuss their individual role in your dreams. Dream study will allow you to realize that you talk with spirit and deceased loved ones quite often during the sleep state even though you may not have conscious recall of the event. You will discover that you have been studying in special spirit classes and if you cannot recall these studies consciously the table will help you understand the principles with which you have been working. You will find that you may have been soul traveling to another location to negotiate special spiritual work such as teaching, sharing knowledge or healing on many levels.

Because you will be able to "talk" with your Higher Self, spiritual guides and teachers, you will be able to research past lives, gain access to your karmic records or have conversations concerning lessons in the relationships and situations in this lifetime. You can explore your personal akashic records.

You will achieve a new level of inner peace through understanding many situations from a spiritual perspective that was not previously readily available to you.

Through your communications you will understand that physical death is a step, like graduation, progressing your spiritual self to a new experience within a different dimensional level of being. You can feel the realness of your past lives and your spiritual experiences between lives in the spiritual realms. Experiencing this feeling while being physically alive, creates a calm that only can be described by feeling it yourself. You may reawaken deep feelings about your almost forgotten familiarity with your own immortality. You can release any fear you may have had about death and the death experience. Perhaps this special calm will help you work through other fears you may have as well. Part II of this text will explain in further detail numerous exploratory purposes for table tipping.

The expanded vibrations you have encountered through the energy circle of your table tipping experiences will expand and empower you as an energy unit. You will be able to apply the energy of your newly reached higher vibration in many spiritual ways. You will have many more inspirations throughout your day. You can expand your creativity through some of the spiritual connections you have made through the table. You can have better dream recall. You may have vivid spiritual dreams, possibly lucid dreams and soul travel experiences when you sleep.

I was greatly inspired to rely upon the value of the spiritual purposes for table tipping by a person I had occasion to publicly view several years ago. There are many spiritual table tippers, but there was one in Southern California who was a very special loving and dedicated lady. Because of her spirituality she wished to be anonymous. She used this tool for healing and receiving God's messages. The first time I saw her, she shared with the excited audience that she had been tipping since she was a very small child having learned how from her mother. She told us that she tipped daily in the early morning for messages from spirit using the table to spell out, letter by letter, each word of their messages. She had devoutly and patiently compiled these loving healing concepts of wisdom into a beautiful text that she distributed for free at her demonstrations. Up until the mid 1980's She often publicly demonstrated table tipping doing healings and giving spiritual blessings and truths presented by her guides and Jesus.

One of the many exciting events she related happened to her on January 27, 1967. She was tipping in the early morning doing her daily routine, when she received a letter-by-letter message from a spirit named Ed White, one of the three Apollo 1 astronauts who lost their lives in the disastrous fire just hours before. This dear, humble lady was unaware of the accident at the launch site and dutifully received the message as to what had gone wrong inside the space capsule that fateful morning. Ed's spirit informed her about a specific valve type component which had failed. Armed with the accurate technical name of that part and the name of the engineer who would understand the problem she notified the authorities of this authentic information. She humbly denied herself major recognition by declining to be presented in a television program concerning this wonderfully evidential event. Her experience with the astronaut's spirit and hundreds of my own encounters with spirit through the table leave no space for doubts in my mind that there is life after death and that table tipping is a reliable and credible as a source for celestial and truthful information.

There are several paths to enlightenment and many tools you could choose to use along the way. But, due to my personal experiences and observations of hundreds of others who have experienced table tipping in classes and seminars, I am convinced that this tool is the most direct and practical. As a process it stands alone in its ability to assist the spiritual seeker to develop their inner knowingness with great strength and reliably progressed speed. This tool's ability to help you search through questions of personal development is profound. I have witnessed detachments and the releasing of blockages through healings on all levels that occurred during the somewhat short time of one table tipping session that could have taken weeks or even months of meditational work and/or counseling to be accomplished with such a comparable spiritual depth.

There is no question that once you start table tipping regularly you will discover many beautiful spiritual reasons of your own for participating in such a rewarding experience.

"BEING IN THE PHYSICAL BODY YOU ARE IN THE ILLUSION THAT YOU ARE ALONE, BUT YOUR SOUL IS IN THE CONSTANT AWARENESS OF THE COMPANIONSHIP OF SPIRITUAL FRIENDS. THUS, YOU ARE SEEMINGLY SEPARATE BUT NEVER ALONE."

CHRISTOPHER

CHAPTER THREE

The Type Of Table To Use.

THE TYPE OF TABLE chosen for tipping should be constructed of all natural materials. Wood allows for the appropriate blend of energies between spirit and the physical persons seated at the table. The best structure would be dovetailed and glued but it is likely you will have to settle for some metal screws being part of the construction of the table. I personally do not recommend metal, plastic or other synthetic material tables as I believe they effect the quality of energy received, especially if you are a novice in the esoteric sciences.

There is an infinite variety of shapes, sizes and styles of tables from which to select your spiritual table. However, you must consider the sitter's comfort. Height and shape can effect how long you may want to sit and work with the table. I prefer rounded shapes because they allow freedom of placement of the sitters and reinforce the circle of energy concept. Besides the obvious physical benefits of being round in shape there are many valid emotional, mental and spiritual effects that a circle provides in a spiritually oriented process. The circle shape of a round table reminds me of the American Indian medicine wheel that is used to perform ceremonies that are centered upon; the primordial force of life that brings forth the light, the will of the Great Spirit and the spirituality within, and lastly the respect of the earth and all that is in existence as a brotherhood sharing the life force of the Great

Spirit. Its circular shape also brings forward images of the sacred intimacy of the brotherhood and discipleship of King Arthur and his men. I encourage you to use a round table because it can reinforce these beautiful principles.

An additional consideration when choosing a table is the placement of its legs. When the table starts movement, its legs and feet can hurt your own feet if they are placed wrong in reference to your seated position. I prefer the pedestal type table since it enables people to have adequate leg and foot space.

If you are unable to find a pedestal table, you can use a four-legged wooden card table. I have participated in some effectively informative sittings using a friend's antique wooden card table. In a pinch, I have used a piano bench, a large old-fashioned kitchen table and a parsons table. Rectangular and square tables can work, but inevitably someone is uncomfortable sitting at a corner of such a table.

When considering size, it is best that the table not be too heavy or large. When a heavy table begins moving, tipping, swaying, walking or whatever, the weight can damage the surface of the floor. Also, if the table thrusts in your direction its weight can physically hurt if it should strike your body. There have been times I have had bruises on my knees and legs from a light weight table bumping into me. I do not want to consider the results of a heavy table in such a circumstance! It is helpful if the table is lightweight or portable enough to take with you to a friend's house to tip. The table that we used on our yacht was small (but efficiently productive) because I needed to be space and safety conscious when storing it aboard. The power of the energy circle around a table is effected by the consciousness of the persons sitting around it, not by how many persons are present for a session or the size of the table.

The durability of the table's composition is necessary to consider for it must be able to withstand movement without deteriorating. One must realize that tables were not purposely constructed for walking, tipping and spinning, - so beware of old or poorly constructed tables. I have experienced a table literally breaking apart while in action. We were able to escape injury and fortunately, had another table handy to complete the session. Lucky for us the experience was only unnerving.

Sometimes, You may find the appropriate table located in an antique shop or used furniture store. This may create a vibrational problem. All physical things have the capacity to pick up and accumulate the vibrations from their surroundings and from the persons who previously owned them. The vibration of the table itself will attract a like vibration when tipping. Because you are intending to connect with the higher realms it is essential to clear or cleanse thoroughly a pre-owned table of all possible negative vibration. I will discuss the method to do this in detail in chapter 4.

I was fortunate to locate and purchase a fine table several years ago from a local catalog outlet store closeout sale. This table is 18" in diameter and 22" tall. It is solid oak with two small metal parts, a pedestal and three legs. It functions perfectly with as many as eight to ten sitters. I also have a beautiful solid birch Shaker style table (handmade by a friend) for tipping with a larger class size group. This table is 28" tall and 33" in diameter. It was designed so the top is removable for easy traveling in the car. Because of the Birch wood and the small amount of metal involved in its structure, this table vibrationally attunes to the refined energies of the higher realms with a powerful ease. Wood amplifies the softness of a vibration creating a higher spiritual energy attracting a like energy. Different woods attract with a different amount of softness, almost as if you would say that the wood effects the volume of your energy circle vibration.

You will discover that a table the size that is efficient for tipping can cost anywhere from $50 to over $1000. The more simplistic the table (no inlay work, no carvings added to the surfaces, no decorative finishes, etc.) the less interference with spiritual energy. The expense of the table does not warrant spiritual effectiveness. All the table needs to be is simple and wooden. An arson case I worked on once was settled by the incredibly accurate details given to me through a small pine wood table bargain priced at $5.95 that I was fortunate to find several years ago at a department store liquidation sale.

One evening at a large rambling ranch house, the only table that was available to tip with was round and constructed of metal and glass. Even though we performed the protection ritual several times we could not connect with the higher Light beings that our group was used to reaching on a regular basis with a wooden table. The glass did not seem to be a problem, but Christopher told us that the vibration of the heavy cast alloy metal was holding us within its dense vibratory range. We were not content with our information or the sources we reached so we moved our session to another sitter's apartment and used a large wooden kitchen table. Once we were there, we immediately were connecting with very refined energies upon starting our session. Thus, we were the same group energy, but we were using a wooden table and different location and were able to reach the desired spiritual dimensions with ease.

In another instance my friend and I spontaneously tried a to perform a table session with a plastic resin table. It performed but we felt divided from the sensation of feeling our guides and their love. It felt like our session had moved into a dimensional level of a cold mental process devoid of the warmth and feeling of energy movement and exchange. We quickly quit using that table and drove to my house to pick up one of my wooden tables to continue the session. Then, we were able to see, hear and feel directly each message because the energy flowed freely between us and the other dimensions.

Once you have selected and designated a certain table for spiritual table tipping use, *respect it*. You should not use it as an end table nor for any functional purpose other than tipping and receiving spiritual information. You can cover it with a piece of natural cloth, I prefer white silk, and place it in an undisturbed, quiet area of the house clear of daily traffic. I store two of my tables in the guest bedroom closet that is in a closed off part of the house. Another is stored in my meditation and creative work room. Remember, all physical objects pick up energy from their surroundings and the people around them. Be responsible! Protect your table from any negative influence areas, situations and people that might be in or visiting your surroundings. You will want to store your table in the most positive energy area of your house. If your table is accidentally exposed to negativity, you will need to redo the original process of cleansing and dedication to the Light of God that you performed when you first obtained it.

When you have chosen your table and have it at home, your next step is to cleanse and prepare it for tipping. Since you are directing this table towards spiritual table tipping you will want to dedicate it to the Light of God. You are now ready for the information in the next chapter about how to properly prepare your table for spiritual tipping.

"BEINGS OF THE DARK NEED LIGHT TO EXIST. THEREFORE, BE A BEAUTIFUL, BALANCED AND PEACEFUL ENTITY OF LIGHT DEVOID OF PETTY FEARS AND JUDGEMENT, FOR THOSE ARE THE OPENINGS IN YOUR ENERGY FIELD THAT ATTRACTS THEIR DARKNESS."

CHRISTOPHER

CHAPTER FOUR

Protection - An Essential For Spiritual Table Tipping

"DANGER! THIS TOOL MAY BE hazardous to your well-being." That is the label that should be attached to table tipping. Being a physical tool, similar to the pendulum that is used as a connecting link between the third dimension of form with the fourth and other invisible dimensions, you must have spiritual intent and use appropriate protective precautions when using it.

An excellent piece of advice is to *never use it by yourself, never consider it a game and never use it in a party-like atmosphere. Always follow protective procedures carefully.* If you are depressed, overly emotional, have been drinking alcohol or taking drugs, you should not work with the table. The energy surrounding you at these times will only attract "astral spirits" or negative energies. These spirits will not be able to help you in any way and are never desirable for you to attract to the table for any purpose.

Because the table is a physical tool, the closest dimension to connect with contains the astral planes. The lower astral planes are where negative thought entities and earthbound entities are found. Negative thought entities are literally other-dimensional monsters created from negative

33

thoughts, depressions, fears, anxieties, hate, anger, rage and envy issued by us here on the physical plane. Earthbound entities are those spirits whose physical bodies are dead but are unaware or unbelieving they are dead and because of this they are in a state of confusion. They are not reconciled with God to go on into the spiritual dimensions for their spiritual growth. There is no purpose to communicate with either of these types of entities. *Indeed one needs to employ certain protections to be free of them*. There is no question that a person who is emotionally and/or mentally disturbed attracts these negative entities and should not use the table as manifold harm can come of this. Since the person is vulnerable and probably not in control, he or she will allow the guidance of a "friend" from the other side to control him or her. Always remember a spirit that is truly of the "Light" (One who is reconciled with God and itself.) will never want to control your life for any reason. If this type of control ever occurs, you must immediately question at what level your informant is placed.

Through special techniques or procedures, the denser physical quality of table tipping can be transformed into an inner knowingness experience shared and verified by the group present. The result being spiritual table tipping - a vibration raising experience that leads to a development of a personal trust in the inner process of the clair senses so that each person can receive for themselves accurately without the table tipping process through practicing this trust while doing spiritual table tipping.

Always be positive in attitude and direction when using the table. In the spiritual dimensions like energy attracts like energy. If you are a spiritual person and practice spirituality in all aspects of your life, you are a lot less likely to attract negative energy.

The direction or intent of your approach and questions will set both the mood of the session and who is attracted to participate on the spiritual level. For example, if you want to know about a future event at work or about what person you should date or marry, or if you should buy a red or blue car, you create what I call a "fortune telling" atmosphere which attracts lower quality or less evolved entities to answer your questions. Ironically, these entities can be less evolved than yourself. Remember, just because they are dead does not make them wise. My attitude is that when we travel down the road of life, while we are in the physical body, it is as if we are traveling in a car while spirit has access to a helicopter. Nevertheless, that spirit must be evolved enough to be aware of its capacity.

When you first work with the table it is wonderful to operate it with someone who is experienced but that may not be possible. Use the same common sense in your new spirit friend relationships as you would with a new physical friend relationship. Do not assume that all information given is directly appropriate at first. In a short time, you will receive some terrific verifications and you will be able to discern which spirits are resonating with a more appropriate frequency for you.

Now let us discuss the physical preparations you need to make in order to get a proper start. First, consider the table itself. Whether it is new or used, it will have been possibly exposed to negative energy. It must be cleansed. Make a solution of one half cider vinegar and one half salt (sea salt is preferable) and apply it with a cloth to all the surfaces of the table. As you are doing this, picture in your mind that you are cleaning out and clearing away any negative energy in that table. With prayerful thought say aloud or think, "I cleanse thee of all possible energies that have come into thee and pray that thee are clean of any vibration that would be not of the frequency of the Light of God." If you believe in Jesus Christ, then you can say "I do this cleansing in the name of the holy powerful Energy of Jesus Christ." This process is a psychological, emotional and spiritual representation of your intentions for this table.

Once this process is complete, you can rewipe the table with a water moistened natural cloth to remove any salt residue.

Before each table tipping session you will once again wipe the surfaces of the table with a vinegar moistened cloth or paper towel to reinforce the intention of that original cleansing in case the table may have absorbed some negative energy while it was stored.

Whenever you are preparing to operate the table, be sure that the physical location that you have chosen for the tipping session is appropriate. You can table tip at any time of day but the room should be bright or artificially lighted. Make sure the area you have chosen is quiet, free of confusion, and away from all interruptions. Stay away from traffic areas in the house because other persons passing by during a session will affect the energy around the table. I have tipped in large and small rooms with great results. Tipping on our yacht in San Diego was a good example of a small atmosphere in which we had wonderful experiences. We used the ship's compass as reference to ensure we were working with the North-South energy flow. We tipped in the main salon and sometimes I felt that because we were on water, we had clearer and more powerful connections with spirit. On some occasions, we tipped with great results at sea while underway to the port of Avalon at Santa Catalina Island.

I have discovered that my spirit guides enjoy the fragrance of sandalwood incense so I sometimes burn it before and during the tipping session. There are times I enjoy burning a white candle with the intention that I desire to engage only in White Light conversations. Vanilla is an effective essence to use to clear the ethers of negative energies. Under certain negative conditions I prefer to burn a high quality vanilla scented candle. The burning of American Indian sweetgrass or sage cleanses the etheric atmosphere and summons positive spiritual support.

If you meditate regularly you will notice that it is

easier to reach the energies of the Light and maintain their presence around you during your table sessions.

When you have the room, the table and the persons with you in this experience ready, you are set to begin your spiritual protection procedures. Be sure that your fellow sitters are in mental and emotional balance and have not been "drinking" or taking drugs.

Have the persons gather around the table, seated in a circle. They must sit with their feet flat on the floor, without crossing their ankles or knees because the crossing of personal energies affects reception. Have everyone place their hands palm up in their lap in a comfortable position with their backs comfortably straight and their eyes closed. A state of internal peace is needed to do the grounding, balancing and centering processes.

The following technique is a combination of ideas learned from teachings given to me and from reading two wonderful books. One book entitled THE PSYCHIC HEALING BOOK,[2] by Amy Wallace and Bill Henkin, tells not only of a grounding process but also of necessary information about energies and spirit. The other text is COMPANIONS IN SPIRIT,[3] by Jack Grant and Laeh Garfield. Their book explains grounding and explores the subject of spirit guides beautifully.

In order to comprehend this grounding process, you need to understand that you have an energy area around and within your physical body known as an aura. Even though the physical body is all that we can perceive with our physical eyes we are much more than a physical body. The physical body is like the tip of the iceberg of our life force existence unit because our true being extends several feet outward from it. There are several layers within the energy area that extends from the physical body. One of these layers extends a small distance from the physical body. This immediate layer reflects our life force and can be called the etheric body. The next layer of energy which surrounds and permeates both the etheric and physical bodies is the astral body. This body is comprised of two layers within itself which are the emotional and mental parts of ourselves. The third layer extending even further outward from the physical body is the spiritual body which is also comprised of several layers. All of the energy bodies surrounding and permeating the physical body contribute to our whole being and form what is known as the aura making us an individual energy unit. Figure 1 on page 40 illustrates the extension of the etheric body. Figure 2 on page 41 illustrates the extension and involvement of the astral body. Figure 3 on page 42 illustrates the extension of the spiritual body into the aura.

The aura with its layers of energy bodies has hundreds of vortices (spiral-like openings) which receive and send energies to and from the air space around our physical and energy bodies which is termed the ether. These vortices are called chakras which is a Sanskrit term for whirling wheels of energy. Each energy body layer is connected to all the chakras.

Figure 4 on page 43 illustrates a profile view of a chakra as I clairvoyantly perceive it. A chakra receives and sends energy from each of the layers of energy bodies in the aura as well as from external energy sources. It appears like a spinning vortex funnel that could be described like a miniature tornado when you look at the profile of a human body. There are smaller funnels within the original vortex. The placement of the chakra on the body will effect how many inner funnels are present. Each chakra placement has a different number of inner funnels. These inner funnels are like colorful petals in a living, moving energy flower. These smaller funnels create an in and out flow of energy to each of the bodies mentioned above - the physical, etheric, astral and spiritual. Figure 5 on page 44 illustrates what a chakra looks like to the clairvoyant eye when viewed from the front.

These chakras occur throughout our entire body but, there are seven primary and four secondary chakras that are directly involved in your spiritual growth process when doing table tipping. Figure 6 on page 45 illustrates the locations of these chakras. The first or root chakra is at the base of the spine, the second is two inches below the navel and the third is two inches above the navel in the solar plexus area. The fourth chakra is located at the heart center. The fifth is at the base of the neck and is known as the throat center. The sixth is the area between the eyebrows known as the brow center and the seventh is at the top of the head and known as the crown center. Keep this information in mind as you close your eyes and visualize each step of the protective grounding process.

Figures 1, 2 and 3 not only illustrate the extended energy of the different energy bodies but they also show which chakras are most directly involved with those particular bodies. This information is relevant when you are cleansing blockages from the chakras as presented in chapter 8 of this book, as well as, in your protective visualizations.

This procedure may seem long and involved or even ritualistic but I have found it to be powerfully protective. I will not proceed to operate the table without its step-by-step performance. Any time I have frivolously skipped any part of this or the advanced protective technique I have not been satisfied with the quality of the information received from the session.

Seated in the position previously described allow yourself to relax and clear your mind of intruding thoughts. As a group you can pace yourselves and breathe in unison. Unified breathing amplifies positive spiritual results whenever there is a group in prayer, meditation or physical tool processes. That is why singing and praying together in a place of worship is so powerful. Next, concentrate on picturing, sensing or feeling the following process. It is important that each detail be followed as described to achieve complete grounding. Spend the time to do it. Imagine that you are growing roots - one from the arch chakra area of each foot and one from the first or the root chakra. I picture a strong tree-like root that travels through the floor and foundation of the building in which I am seated. I see the root grow deeply into the earth through rock and soil down to at least thirty feet. Notice that the earth has a peaceful calming energy. I picture this energy with a honey color. Feel the comfort of the calming earth energy as it is

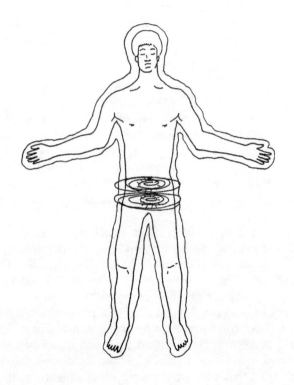

FIGURE 1: The **ETHERIC BODY** shown around the *physical body* with its primary chakra connections - the first and second chakras.

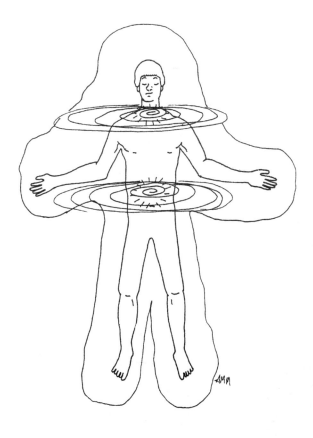

FIGURE 2: The **ASTRAL BODY** shown around the *physical body* with its primary chakra connections - the third and fifth chakras.

FIGURE 3: The **SPIRITUAL BODIES** shown around the *physical body* with its primary chakra connections - the fourth and the seventh chakras. If you imagine overlapping figures 1, 2 and 3 you can perceive a complete picture of the energy bodies around the physical body.

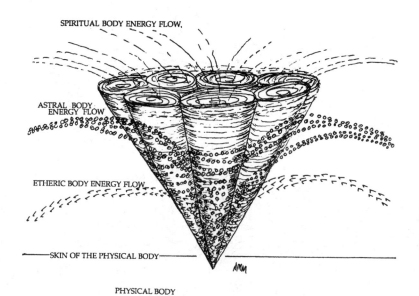

SPIRITUAL BODY ENERGY FLOW.

ASTRAL BODY.
ENERGY FLOW

ETHERIC BODY ENERGY FLOW

SKIN OF THE PHYSICAL BODY

PHYSICAL BODY

FIGURE 4: **AN INDIVIDUAL CHAKRA.** The structure of a chakra viewed from the side. Because the chakra is made up of flowing active energy it is difficult to illustrate it exactly as clairvoyantly perceived. The chakra is a spiraling vortex that funnels into the physical body through the other body layers surrounding it. This vortex is in bright clear colors when unimpeded by energy blockages. There are vortices within this vortex giving the chakra a flower-like appearance. For the sake of illustration and since all the individual energy bodies send and receive energy through a chakra the *spiritual bodies* are rendered in *dash-like* energy flow, the *astral body (mental and emotional bodies)* in *circles* of energy flow and the etheric *body* in an *"L"-shaped* life force energy flow all blending into the physical body through an ever active vortex.

INDIVIDUAL SPIRALING ENERGY VORTEX

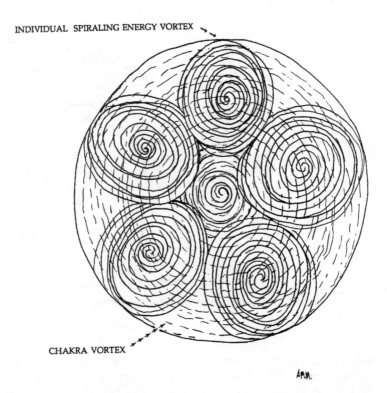

CHAKRA VORTEX

ARM.

FIGURE 5: THE VORTEX OF AN INDIVIDUAL CHAKRA as
seen from a direct frontal vantage point shows the smaller vortices
within the original vortex which composes the energy pattern of the
chakra. The number of smaller vortices within each chakra depends
upon its location in the energy body system.

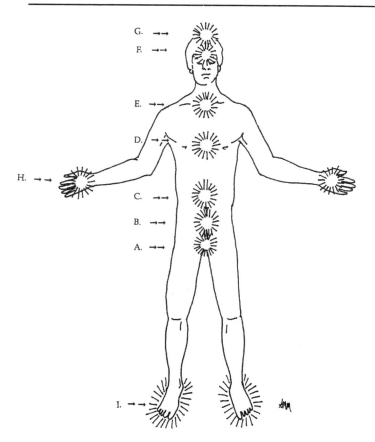

FIGURE 6: THE CHAKRA PLACEMENTS THAT ARE DIRECTLY INVOLVED IN THE TABLE TIPPING EXPERIENCE. First the seven major body chakras: *A.The root chakra* placed at the base of the spine. *B.The spleen chakra* placed a few inches below the navel. *C.The solar plexus chakra* placed a few inches above the navel. *D.The heart chakra* placed at the heart center. *E.The throat chakra* placed at the base of the neck. *F.The brow chakra* placed at the forehead area. *G.The crown chakra* placed at the top of the head. Then these specific minor chakras of the hands and the feet, *H.The palm chakra* placed at the sensitive area of the center of the palm of each hand. *I.The arch chakra* placed on the sole of each foot at the center of the arch area.

attracted to your roots. While you relax and breathe in this calm state of mind, imagine that as you inhale, you are continuing to bring more of this peaceful energy up into your roots with each breath. Continue sensing the energy rising up your roots to the arches of your feet. Once it arrives at the arches of your feet absorb the calming energy and begin to fill your body slowly as if it were an empty container welcoming this wonderful peace. While the energy is in your feet sense it soothing each muscle, tendon, nerve, blood vessel, bone and calming the skin itself until you feel you have released all tension. This visualization protects the etheric and physical body energy while table tipping.

Say to yourself, "I am relaxed, letting go, releasing all tension in my feet." Taking time, proceed to your ankles, calves, knees, and thighs. Sense the same letting go as you bathe each area of your body with this honey colored energy. Repeat the same phrase to yourself referring to each area while focusing on it as you go through the rest of your body. When you have coaxed the energy up to the pelvic area remember that you have previously visualized another root growing from the root chakra to bring in more of this peaceful flow thereby increasing the quantity available to fill the torso area of the body. Allow this energy to fill the abdomen.

Say to yourself, "This peaceful energy flows around each and every one of my organs, soothing it with calm, healthful energy, relaxing it and allowing it to perform in a healthy, natural manner." When the energy fills the solar plexus area envision it strengthening and balancing the astral energy body by sending it outward into your aura through this chakra.

Relax all the tendons, nerves, bones (especially the spinal column, vertebrae and nerves), blood vessels, skin and muscles continuing to send the calming energy up into your chest. As you breathe the energy into your heart area feel and see it strengthen and balance your spiritual body layers by flowing the energy in and out of this chakra.

46

Consider each organ and take time to release any tightness that is within it. When you reach the shoulder area concentrate particularly on relaxing those muscles for often there is much stress there. See the color of the energy bathing your shoulders with peace. Move down both arms, relaxing the muscles, tendons, nerves, bones, blood vessels and skin. When the energy comes into your hands imagine it forming a fountain coming up out of the palm chakras flowing out, over and into your aura wrapping a blanket of calming peace all around your body and under your feet.

Now consider your shoulders again bringing that honey colored energy into your neck and relaxing all the bones, tendons, nerves, muscles, blood vessels and skin over the area. All during this visualization you are talking to yourself about relaxing and letting go - releasing all tension.

At last, breathe this flowing peaceful color into your head area relaxing the jaw and letting it go slack. Relax the cheeks. Next concentrate on the eyeballs, the eyelids and eyebrows. Take time to ease each muscle in the eye area because much of the body's tension rests there. Sense the energy relaxing and releasing all tension until you have filled the entire head. Next, allow the peaceful energy to fountain out of the crown of your head flowing into the upper aura and enveloping you in a complete peaceful auric egg.

Now envision a huge white cloud over your head filled with a powerful collective of the vital life force of God energy. See the cloud open and shower out a broad stream of white light energy that envelops your **peaceful** auric egg. This beam then flows directly down through the egg pouring energy into your crown chakra. Mix this sparkling white life force with the golden honey earth energy stirring it in a clockwise motion. Feel it charging you with healing energy and clearing out all negativity. Know that it is cleansing and invigorating your whole being as you inhale it. Slowly bring it in filling your head to your neck and continuing down through to your shoulders. **Fully incorporate the power of its healing energy!** (If there are any current physical problems allow an extra amount of healing white light energy to bathe and soothe the problem areas.)

Continue sending the white energy downward through the arms to the hands and shower it out of the palm chakras into the aura declaring it to be a powerfully protective force that neutralizes all negativity. From your shoulders, bring the white energy into your chest, again mixing it with the earth energy. Continue to sense the white life force energy flowing into the abdomen and throughout the pelvic area.

At this time, concentrate on the root leaving your first chakra and going into Mother Earth. Since the white light has been cleansing and clearing, realize that you can release any negative energy down this root. Now, you must bless the released energy with love transmuting it entirely to be harmless to Mother earth or anyone else.

As you continue to inhale, direct the flow of this invigorating energy into your thighs, knees, calves, ankles and the feet cleansing and releasing all upsets, disturbances, negative emotions, thought patterns or physical body cell memories from past lives caught in those regions of your body. Release them down the roots that are extending out of the arches of each foot into Mother Earth. Once again bless the released energy with love and transmute it to harmlessness.

Take a deep relaxing breath realizing that you are now fully at peace and protected inside and out. Reaffirm that you are within a completely perfect auric egg full of earth's harmonizing peace and God's life force energy of healing and protection. Tell yourself you are in a perfect state of strength and balance.

Imagine that in front of your body is a white line - much like a center line on a highway at night. Focus on that line and with your imaginary psychic hands grab it and hold it upright centering it in front of you. At this time say, "I am balanced and centered and that centering is strengthened with the power of the protective force of God."

Next, visualize a strong, wide, white beam of

light streaming down from the God force energy cloud above you going straight through the table deep into the ground. With your eyes still closed picture yourself, the other sitters and the table itself filled with a blinding white light in a large all white area. See this white energy clear away all negativity from all the surrounding ethers. I often picture a white cloud on which there are only ourselves and the table. Visualize this white light area as a sphere in space and surround this sphere with mirrors facing outward much like the reflecting planes of a mirrored ball that you may have seen in a ballroom above the dance floor. The purpose of the mirrors is to protect the energy within the sphere and to reflect back any undesirable energy attracted to the light. This sphere can be open at the top for Light energies to enter for communication.

With the visualizations completed, all of you can say the Lord's prayer together or any other invocational prayer that you feel comfortable with to attract the God Force and follow it up (as I do) with the beautiful old prayer, "The Light of God surrounds me. The love of God enfolds me. The presence of God watches over me. The power of God protects me. I am of the Light of God and only those of the Light of God can come near me." You now have completed your protection process and are ready to proceed with your table tipping experience.

(The protection and grounding meditation presented in this chapter as well as an alternative energizing, grounding and balancing technique to prepare the more experienced table tipper for connecting with the higher more refined spiritual realms is available on audio cassette tape. Please refer to the end of the book for more information.)

NOTES

2. Bill Henkin and Amy Wallace, THE PSYCHIC HEALING BOOK: (Berkeley, California: Wingbow Press, 1978) distributed by Bookpeople. Refer to information on pps. 42, 68-70.
3. Leah Maggie Garfield and Jack Grant, COMPANIONS IN SPIRIT: (Berkeley, California: Celestial Arts, 1984.) Refer to Chapter 3, Grounding and Meditation.

"ALL THAT IS FELT AND EXPERIENCED IN A PHYSICAL INCARNATION I S FOOD FOR THE SOUL'S GROWTH. AS A SOUL EVOLVES, THE FEELINGS OF PAIN OR PLEASURE ARE LESS INTENSE FOR THEY ARE EXPERIENCED WITH DETACHMENT FROM WITHIN THE GODSELF PLACEMENT OF INNER PEACE."

CHRISTOPHER

CHAPTER FIVE

Table Tipping Techniques

WHEN THE PROTECTION WORK is completed, the sitters may place their hands lightly on the surface of the table. You are now ready to create a spiritually strengthened energy circle. The energy circle is best connected if all of your hands are close together with your thumbs touching and with your little fingers touching your neighbors' little fingers. At times, you will need to place most of the palm of the hand lightly on the table allowing the palm chakra to be in contact with the table's surface. Breathe in and out in close unison so that you are breathing as a group. Visualize the white light energy you brought into your being during the protection process and send it pulsating outward from your palm chakras into the table. See it traveling to your right from palm chakra to palm chakra creating a circle of pulsating white light including the table and all of the sitters' hands. Expand the circle outward horizontally extending it to the perimeter of your protective sphere.

Now concentrate on your own previously visualized white cloud of God Force energy that you used in your protection process. Focus on connecting it to the other sitters' clouds creating an energy circle ring of all of the sitters' individual protective white clouds.

Next visualize the white light pulsating from your arch chakras traveling down your root into Mother Earth and see it travel to your neighbor's arch chakra roots on your right continuing to connect all the sitters, reinforcing the circle of energy at this level.

Now relax, feel and visualize the pulsating power of these three white energy circles. Note that their power is from the same source, the universal All. See and feel this knowing or awareness of universal oneness as a magnetic energy bonding the three; the other dimensional / ether energy circle above you, the spiritualized physical body / table energy circle at your palm level and the denser physical body / neutralizing peaceful Mother Earth energy circle below your feet. Breathe in the universal awareness power and combine all three circles blending them into one large all encompassing energy circle that extends horizontally as wide as you can strongly image your sphere to be. Then see it extend above and below all of you as far as you can focus upon traveling it with a concentrated strength. Now sensing its almost electric-magnetic spiritualized power visualize yourself, the others and the table totally immersed in its harmony. Deeply feel your spiritual intent to connect with the most powerful of expanded Light beings, those that reflect the highest truths available to you and your group at this time, through the cosmic rhythm of the bonded universality of this energy circle.

Physically having most of your hand on the surface of the table satisfies the temporary need for sending extra energy to secure the spiritual energy circle connection with the table. As a result the table motion will begin more quickly.

Once the table is moving and the energy circle is complete, all the persons at the table will need just their fingers in contact with the table. They will not need their hands to touch each other as it is more comfortable this way when tipping for long periods of time.

There are some agreements to be made at this time between yourselves and spirit. Whoever owns the table is usually the operator. This person will have to designate a spiritual guide (the Table Guide see chap. 7) who will be the guardian entity and the ambassador who collects the other needed spirits to the table tipping session. If another person seated at the table is chosen to be the operator due to their past experience at tipping, it will be with the permission of this Table Guide because it still will have to continue to be spiritually responsible for the table's energy.

The operator is responsible for the context and the sequence of the questioning. This simply keeps order in the situation. Believe me once you begin tipping you will understand how important it is to ask the questions clearly and without assumptions. Every question needs to be answered before another question is asked. The operator is the one who rechecks the answers received and determines the accuracy of how well the other sitters understand spirit's answers.

All present, both spirit and the sitters, must agree upon the movement patterns the table performs for an answer. The operator indicates aloud that one tip of the table is **No** and that two tips are **Yes**. Three tips for **Maybe** may also be acceptable. If a numeric answer is needed, **tell spirit to lift one leg per count** until the number is reached. The table will tap in rhythm as the count goes beyond one. It is best if the operator counts aloud with each tip for accuracy. Spirit is to stop the table's movement when the appropriate number is reached. If the number contains several digits ask for spirit to work with you on each number one at a time. For example, if the number is a historical year and spirit agrees this is so, ask if the first number is a one, a two, etc. until the appropriate number is given. Then work if necessary through to the second number, the third and lastly the possible fourth. With this technique you can determine exact dates as well as numbers of people or the numbers of years involved when certain incidents occurred.

When spelling a name or a place, spirit can **lift one table leg** as the operator starts with calling out the letter "a" and proceeds through the alphabet, letter by letter, until the correct letter is reached. At that point, the table will **remain with one leg up in a hesitated suspension,** thereby identifying, the correct letter. The operator can then restate the letter aloud to spirit asking for a **Yes** or **No** tip to verify if the agreed upon letter is the correct one. Taking the time to work through words with the letters of the alphabet, you can arrive at actual names of persons and spirit, as well as names of physical locations, schools, towns, ships, countries and other planetary locations. Remember, there are some individuals who use the alphabet technique to receive accurately (letter by letter to spell each word) all messages from spirit. If you are having difficulty receiving knowledge telepathically this is an effective manner to understand spirit.

Once the operator is chosen, it is important that all of the sitters cooperate with his or her energy by concentrating on a single purpose. The sitters must be open minded and without expectation in order to receive the answer to the question at hand. When the question is presented, it is a human tendency to think about your own next question. This lack of mental focus negatively effects the energy for the answer to the question presently being considered by spirit.

How to ask questions and **what to ask** are the most significant factors in table tipping. Improperly stated questions produce incorrect answers and erase the purpose for asking in the first place. So, to formulate questions to spirit, one must remember spirit is absolutely literal and respects all the spiritual laws especially those concerning free will and privacy.

When stating the question, you may intend to say one thing, but by the way the question is worded say another. For example, a lady was praying daily due to her poor financial circumstance, "Please God, let me make money!" As time passed, she was effective in her prayerful pleas. She was offered a position with the Federal Mint printing money. Beware as you may indeed receive the exact answer to your poorly stated plea. Be clear and literal about what you are asking.

The spiritual law of free will, which is in effect for almost all souls on all dimensions be they spiritual or physical, effects the manner in which you state queries. If you ask, "Should I do something?" or "Will I do something?", you give away your power of free will to another. A spirit who is of an evolved state of being or of the "Light of God" will not participate in controlling your life. Therefore a proper way to pose a question is, "Is it in my best interest to ------?". Proposing the question in this way allows spirit to note that you have decided to possibly progress in a certain direction, but that you are open to opinions as to how such a direction will work out from their vantage point. They will work on this idea with all of your best interests in mind, physically, mentally, emotionally and spiritually. Thus, when you have received an answer you will need to recheck each aspect. For example, the answer could be **No**, but it may mean **No** only in one aspect. For example, it may not be in your best interest physically at this time to make a trip, but it could be beneficial to your emotional or spiritual well-being. You could then find out when it would be in your whole best interest to make the trip.

The spiritual law of privacy effects questions posed about something or someone which is not your purpose to know. There are occasions in which you are asking about someone else's private business. A spiritual guide for a person not present at the table may not come to the table to share information without the permission of the absentee. The only time a guide for someone else volunteers to come on the table is when it is important that the sitters receive a message for the immediate well-being of that person. It is also possible that you are asking for answers which would deter you from learning lessons through a situation, because then you would know the outcome in advance. Knowing an outcome may take away a spontaneous opportunity to learn something very necessary for your growth. Please remember these spiritual laws when formulating your questions and responding to the answers given.

Begin your question format by asking for one of the sitter's guides to come to the table. Direct this request for a specific person seated at the table. You may even want to ask for a certain guide associated with the sitter. (The individual guides and their positions are explained in chap. 7 Part II.)

As the table begins its first movements, be careful not to allow it to touch your knees or any other part of your body. Your only contact should be with your hands or fingers. Keep your hands in touch with the table and go with its movement, but do not effect it with movement or pressure of your own. I mention pressure because often I have had people rest the weight of their arms, upper back or other body areas on their hands as they put their hands on the table. For effective tipping one cannot put weight or pressure on the table. Actually, your hands should lightly touch the table with your arms free to be ready to move with the table if for some purpose it needs to "walk". The table should not come into physical contact with any other part of your body but your hands until you have ascertained who the energy is that is creating the movement.

As soon as the movement is initiated and you have stated the signal directions for **Yes** or **No**, then ask, "Do you come in the Light of God?" If you believe in Jesus Christ, you may ask "Do you come in the Light of Jesus Christ of biblical times?" *If you feel comfortable that this question is answered with the proper Yes movement and with no hesitation then proceed.* **Always be assured that the entity moving the table is a Light being of God.** Recheck this fact as often as possible, especially if the sitters have not developed clairvoyance or any other form of soul sensitivity so that they can sense with a definite awareness the vibrational quality of the communicating presence.

Beings can transfer off the table easily. There are several reasons for them to do so. You might have asked for information not presently known to the individual spirit present. That entity will then leave to obtain help for answers. During the few moments of hesitation which occurs when it has left the table another entity from the astral dimensions can move the table and answer the question inaccurately. This means you have to be very aware of any change in the styles of movement or the "feel"of the motion, *so please take note of any hesitation in movements of the table itself.* Many times incorrect information can be received from an astral entity who sneaks in while a spirit guide is on the search for answers.

Entities from the astral dimension will take energy from you if you let them. That is why one should not let the table rest on a knee or any other part of the body unless the sitters are certain that the entity is a Light being of God. If such contact happens by accident, then it is a good precaution to take a sea salt shower or bath to wash away physically, emotionally, mentally and spiritually any negativity you may have received and to restore your natural energy balance. Once in the shower, moisten yourself all over with water and then sprinkle sea salt over your wet skin. Allow the salt to dry for a few seconds and then rinse it off while you mentally cleanse your whole being of negativity. This technique also works well any time you encounter negativity in your daily life whether from persons, places or situations with which you have been in contact.

Often, when an astral energy is present, there is pressure in the solar plexus that causes you to experience the sensation of nausea. Sometimes you will experience a physical sensation of pulling if the entity withdraws energy from you. Either of these sensations or any other physically discomforting sensation is good reason to take your hands off the table. You will then need to reprotect yourself, the other sitters, the table and the surrounding atmosphere before restarting the process. Also, redo the energy circle visualization. **IF REPROTECTION DOES NOT CURE THE SITUATION, DO NOT TABLE TIP AT THIS TIME.** It may be that there is presently no way to clear the atmosphere due to other dimensional negative conditions you cannot fully understand or past life spiritual unknowns about the sitters that will not allow the energy to flow properly without changing your present seating order around the table.

When a physical person at the table is a strong and willful being, his or her energy can also effect how the others feel and the table's movement. It is not always a spirit responsible for the effects that are being sensed. There are some individuals (whether or not they are table tipping) who pull energy from others. Many times they are unaware that they are doing it. Once they learn about this tendency a strong willed person can overcome it. There is an explanation for the energy drain these individuals can create. Often a drain occurs due to their need to control that which is outside of themselves to feel secure. Such a person is vibrationally off balance. This creates a natural vibrational need for an energy balance which results in a pulling of spiritual energy from others. The best solution to this insecurity is to understand that the only being or situation you can control is you and your own free will.

Physical discomforts can also occur due to a special balancing or healing that is happening between spirit and yourself or between spirit and another sitter. If spirit insists it is of the Light of God but there is still physical discomfort for someone present at the table, have that person remove his or her hands from the table while the other sitters obtain information from spirit to determine the cause of the discomfort.

Spirit will allow you to experience a physical sense of discomfort when there is a blockage in one of your chakras. The discomfort symbolizes that you have something to work through to clear that chakra. It is a common occurrence when you are first table tipping because the guides will take the opportunity of table tipping to help you grow along your spiritual path by balancing your energy unit. For example, during one session I had pressure in my throat. It felt as if I was about to get laryngitis and I had great difficulty actually speaking. The guide that was present was working with me to help me to grow through an understanding of my past lives.

I asked if she intended to have me experience this discomfort. She said **Yes**. She let me see, in a vision, a life when I had chosen to be born into a politically active European family. In that life, I was a strong-willed female who disapproved of the manner in which my father manipulated the people. I became outspoken about the rights of the people without thought of the consequences to my family and myself. When the people rose up in turmoil against my family, I was imprisoned and after suffering a great deal of indignities I died a lonely and unpleasant death.

Because of how I felt about those events at that time, I brought into this present life the stored physical cell memory of those painful experiences and with it a blockage in the throat chakra. I realized it is easy to say, "I forgive", while living without the active sense of the pain I endured in that lifetime. I knew I needed to re-experience it to cleanse myself. I meditated on that lifetime several times recreating the emotions endured during imprisonment. In order to forgive the others and myself and to release the blockages I activated the reality of the pain and once again sensed the situation as I had actually perceived it then. Interestingly enough, before I did this cleansing, I had experienced many sore throats and colds that usually gave me laryngitis. After facing up to that lifetime and releasing the blockages, I have had very few sore throats and rarely a case of laryngitis.

Another way to stop the physical discomfort at a session is to tell the spiritual being to stop such action immediately. Because of our free will and the fact that our physical bodies are a very strong and dense energy, the spirit must respect our request in this situation. As an example, one gentleman spirit who came to the table was a deceased relative of a lady sitter at the table. In order to give me verifiable evidence that he was who he said he was, he gave me chest pains so that I would know for sure that he had experienced a heart attack while driving, which caused the accident that killed his physical body. As soon as I started to experience these uncomfortable sensations, I telepathically demanded he stop this manner of communication and speak to me (as I could hear him) or let me see (in vision) what he wanted to tell the lady at the table. The pain stopped as rapidly as it overtook me in the first place.

As a result of this incident, I learned many lessons. One was that due to my own openness I often experience pain in my own body which belongs to others. Now that I am aware of this fact, I take mental note of it and tell myself the discomfort is not mine and I do not choose to endure it. With blessings of love I send the discomfort away by transmuting it to harmlessness. Another lesson I learned was that I am in control of my being. No other being, including spirit, can make me its victim unless I allow it through ignorance or wrong thinking on my part.

There are times that having the table touch you or lean on you will be a desirable and beautiful experience. When it is being done by a "Being of Light" you receive a loving healing or energy exchange. This being's love energy is sent directly through the ethers and the table to you through the power of the energy circle. Sometimes the table leans on you when spirit wants to give a warm spiritual hug which is a comforting reward that resonates deeply into your whole being.

When you are experiencing your first table tipping session with new persons, a certain amount of time may pass before the table actually begins movement. We have experienced a wait of up to thirty minutes before any movement occurred. On the other hand, there are sittings that the table starts movement almost immediately after the first question is posed. Be aware that during the time it takes for the table to start moving there is much going on in the other dimensions to prepare for the movement.

The spiritual beings around the table work diligently to balance the cycling of the frequencies between the energy bodies of the sitters for better communication. Spirit guides and teachers need to interconnect their own frequencies - especially if they are from different levels of spiritual existence because they have to interact to obtain information for you. All of this energy and dimensional alignment activity creates various frequency changes that go on all around your body and at all levels of your being while you patiently wait for the start of movement. To me, the exchange of energies is more beautiful to see clairvoyantly than a Fourth of July fireworks display. There are electrically bright beams of colored and white lights beyond physical description which create spiraling designs and symbols all around the people and the table often filling the entire room with delightful visual beauty.

When the table begins movement, there are instances when it may tremble and shake. At other times it feels as if the table is breathing. Usually, within a few minutes after the sitting begins, everyone present notices the energy exchanges both physically and emotionally. There can be tickling sensations in the hands and the arms. Often there is a noticeable feeling of heat going up and down the spine. The heat can be felt in the areas of the body where the chakras are located. The energy can be experienced as if it were electrical causing the hair to stand on end on the arms and sometimes at the back of the neck. Cooling breezes may pass by or touch you and at times, you may feel a chill-like sensation coming over your body. The physical experiences can be as varied as the types of sitters and the individual spirits will allow. An awareness of special emotions can occur, which create almost overwhelming feelings of bliss or the warm sensation of being hugged all over. The point is, once again, awareness. Be open to each sensation so that you can fully receive and interact with the loving energy that comes through the energy circle of the table to communicate with you.

The feeling of warmth is most often felt with healings whether they be spiritual, emotional, mental or physical. The almost "hot" feeling that can go up and down your spine is due to the raising of your Kundalini energy. Kundalini is a Hindu term for the central energy line within our being. It can be thought of as the bioelectrical core or center of our life force energy. Kundalini energy is often called the serpent as it has been associated with the fiery energy that slowly rises from a coiled position at the root chakra and moves upward along the spine as the connecting line for the energy openings of all of the chakras.

There is much speculation as to whether one should consciously work with the development or activation of one's own Kundalini energy. Once it is awakened and ascends up the spine, Kundalini opens the person's awarenesses on all levels. **Be careful not to work at raising this energy in case you are not balanced enough on all levels to be prepared for its powerful energy surges.** *It is claimed that through ignorance one can do serious physical, mental, and emotional harm to oneself through working with Kundalini without proper experienced guidance.*

Spiritual energies around the table can perceive each other and each physical person present by the appearances of their auras. An Aura which can be photographed by Kirlian photography is like an ever moving energy "fingerprint" of our attitudes and directions. Once the aura is identified, spirit works with the energy to our best advantage. It is my personal belief that the colors and symbols of the aura are outward evidence of our intentions and clues as to how spiritually evolved we are. There is no denying what it shows. Any spirit who knows us recognizes us by our aura and understands our problems and needs by the condition of our aura. When spirit works with you, it works with your aura itself. All healing begins in the auric body and works its way from the spiritual layers through to the mental, emotional layers and physical body in that order. If your Kundalini is being worked with by your spiritual guides and teachers, it is to your betterment spiritually. Nevertheless, I have **never asked** the guides to work with my energy body unit in either the aura or the Kundalini energy areas because it is unnecessary to do so.

The guides have always known when I was ready and when it was appropriate to help or heal in these areas of concern. Then they suggest how I can work with them to improve the balance of my energy body unit.

When the spirits do choose to work with your energies, the result is that they usually raise your frequencies. Sometimes frequency changes can have strange physical side effects. Your heart may beat quickly and at other times you may feel dizzy and a little out of balance for a moment. Whenever you finish a table tipping session, always take note of how you feel physically; immediately after the session, later on that day and even the next day. You will find there are times you feel charged and energized and at other times you will feel drained and tired. Date and record these feelings and sensations and examine your records to determine if and how you are being effected by your physical partners or the spiritual entities. If you discover you are tired after tipping then in the very next session ask your guides why that is happening. Ask them what action should be taken to abate this problem.

The energy of the persons seated within the energy circle affects the starting of the table's movement. An atmosphere of unconditional love, free of judgement, enhances the energy connections needed for movement.

The problem of no movement can be due to the type of information you plan to request. For example, what you want to know can be very personal in nature and spirit may determine that it is not in your best interest to share or discuss this knowledge in the presence of others. Spirit is always considerate and discreet with its primary focus being your best interest. Other causes for lack of movement are; atmospheric electrical conditions, the presence of an astral entity being blocked by the Table Guide creating energy blockage and a lack of clarity in the question you have asked.

I have been asked how many people can table tip

together at one sitting. Uneven numbers seem to work best, but it will work well with just two people. If you are doing a sitting with two people, it is best to be seated in North and South positions. Both physical and spiritual energies of the earth flow in the North to South pathways. Your own energies function best when you are in flow with these energies. Animals choose sleep positions according to the North-South flow of their geographical area because they are sensitive to the earth's energy currents. It has been proven in my experiences that it is the best of energy practices for the table's operator to be seated in the Northern position.

Should another person enter the room while you are tipping and wish to join you, it is necessary to redo the protective procedure and the energy circle empowering process. The person may have brought with them negative energies from the experiences of their day. Remember that **any negativity** changes the vibration in the ethers surrounding the table. You must be actively alert at all times to maintain a positive energy atmosphere through positive attitudes and actions.

When you request that a specific spirit guide come to the table and the table responds by moving, the next important consideration is politeness between spirit and yourself. Be as respectful with spirit as you would with a dear friend. They have done considerable work to balance the different frequency levels in order to communicate with you. Because their frequencies are faster and lighter it can be an unpleasant experience for them to be "on" the table with you; however, you will soon discover that your guides are so anxious to communicate with you that they will lovingly endure any discomfort in order to make the direct communication. One of my guides explained to me that when I have not worked with balancing my energy through prayer or meditation the ether around me is thick and stifling for the guide to experience. An unbalanced energy state can make it uncomfortable for the guide to remain in close contact with me.

Once spirit has moved the table, ask the question, "May I please speak with my (whichever category you choose) guide?" The next step is to ask further questions in proper sequence. It is very necessary to ask first if the guide has any messages it wishes to share, before posing questions. Ask, "Do you have any messages for me?"

When spirit comes to the table it is dedicated to a special purpose and etiquette requires you to respect this intent. It is the same as when a dear friend stops by your house to visit, you know he came for a reason. You courteously inquire about the reason for his visit and listen to his response before bringing up your personal concerns. Any entity that presents itself in the table tipping session is there with the primary intent of communicating a message and it is your privilege to receive it.

A message from spirit is usually very open-ended with just a few specific items of data or it may be broad in spectrum, for only on special occasions are they totally detailed in content. When you do receive a specific message, it is because this guide has been trying to share the information for some time due to its importance to your total well-being.

Your next question to the guide would be, "How many messages have you for me?" Use the table's counting technique for a count. Then ask if the first message (since there could be more than one) is a spiritual one. If the table tips a **No** then ask, "Does it concern my relationships with the people in my life?" If the response is **No**, then continue on with these questions until you receive a **Yes**. "Does it concern my work place?" "Is the message about my health?" "Is it about my emotional well-being?" "Is it about my mental well-being?" "Is its purpose about my getting to know you better?" "Is it about my progress on my life's path?" "Is it about your love for me?"

Many times the guide wants you to know they are

present around you all the time, loving and supporting you in your efforts to learn through life's experiences. Their messages of love can be emotionally touching and deeply healing. The table itself may move towards you and lean on your body allowing the spirit to give you a spiritual love hug. You will feel incredible support and sense a feeling of deep love beyond which is normal to experience on our physical earth. It is an expression of unconditional love beyond verbal description.

Messages from the guides can be difficult to understand when you are new at table tipping. You need to work with and focus upon your telepathy during this time. If a thought pops into your head, no doubt it is part of an intended message from the guide. Be sure to ask the guide by verbalizing the thought if it has any connection with his message. Thoughts which form pictures in your mind are often clues. And remember, if all else fails, you and the guide can use the alphabet technique with the table movements to spell out part of or all of the message.

During the time that the operator of the table is presenting the questions that were previously discussed, all the sitters need to be open and aware, listening on all levels of their being. Hopefully, they are seeing in their minds a color, a symbol, words or images that would be clues to receiving answers to the questions posed. If all the sitters are concentrating on perceiving the message, each person will soon pick up clues in one way or another. Each time something comes into your mind tell the operator what has been received, whether it be a symbol, image, thought, word or color so the operator can then proceed to ask spirit if indeed it is part of the answer to the question at hand.

Once you have received the message state to the guide, "Your message is - (here repeat exactly and clearly what you believe the message to be in its entirety)." *You now need to*

---

*receive a **Yes** movement from the table to show that the guide agrees that you understood the message as accurately as possible.*

If the table tips **No**, you need to check each part of the statement you believe to be the message in order to uncover the inaccurate or misunderstood part of the message. When there is a meeting of the minds ask, "Have I received all of your message clearly?" and wait for the response movement of the table.

Then ask, "Have we made any mistakes in our understanding of the message?" There may be a hesitation before the table moves because it takes time for spirit to check telepathically what is in your mind as an understanding of the answer. If the table movement is affirmative and there is more than one message from the guide you can proceed to the next one.

When you have received and understood all of this specific guide's messages, you may pose questions to this guide. *Be very aware that the guides are not anxious to consider your questions at first if they have messages.* It is not selfishness on their part. It is simply more efficient for them to present important information first. Often the messages they give will answer many of the questions you had in mind in a broader and more expansive manner.

An instance in which the standard method of questioning the guides could be different is when you have a spiritual quest in mind. Then you may have several written questions about which you have pondered or meditated on during the day in the hopes that spirit will be prepared with lots of information. When you are studying esoteric concepts, such as asking about your soul's progress or about blockages which directly affect your spiritual progression, it is a good idea to prepare questions ahead of time. You might want to unveil past life information. You might need an overview of your aura and chakras to find out where you have blockages and ask for an understanding as to how they manifest themselves in your life at this time. Spirit will offer suggestions for working through these blockages and produce a more efficient and balanced "You" in the process. It may come as a surprise that your soul chose for you to encounter certain problems in life just to clear a blockage as simple as the fear of rejection or the lack of self-confidence. It is good to review some of your problems in this life with the guides in order to unveil these fears. You will then be armed with the understanding to conquer them.

During the table tipping session there will be times that the table just keeps moving. Continuous movement can be confusing because there is a sense that spirit is constantly sending an affirmative answer. Sometimes this is the result of asking too many questions too fast, thereby confusing spirit. Sometimes, the questioner is asking a question while another sitter is thinking about a different question. Spirit is telepathic and if there is a diversity of thoughts at the table during the same time period it confuses the answers. There are other times, however, that all that movement is simply showing off spirit's excitement that you are receiving the information they have wanted you to understand for some time. Whatever the reason, it is best to stop constant continuous movement, by placing your hand gently on the center of the table, when you have received your answer so that the energy is cleared and spirit is concentrating on the question to be posed next.

There will be many differences in the type of movement the table performs. Some guides spin the table first as a way to identify themselves. Others may begin with a certain signature, such as, a slow tip to the left, a fast tip forward and then "to and fro" before actually tipping the answer to your question. Be sensitive to the feel of the movement for much can be expressed that way. There are certain hesitations before tipping a **Yes** that give you the hint you do not understand the concept clearly or that there is more to the answer than you have understood at this time. A hesitant **No** can also mean you are headed in the right direction of thought generally, but not directly on target.

There are other instances when the table may stop for a second. The implication is that you have asked a question improperly. Perhaps you phrased it in a manner that could not be answered with a **Yes** or **No**. In your eagerness you may have slipped more than one question into your query: "Is it in my best interest to believe I understand my lesson at this time *and* am I working with it?" This question is obviously two in one and cannot be answered adequately with a **Yes** or a **No**. It fascinates me, as an operator of the table, how many times people ask questions in this manner creating confusion in spirit as to which part of the question the sitters want answered. Always compose simple, direct and one part questions.

If you have asked a question of spirit and it does not know the answer, the table will stop. Spirit has three ways of handling this situation. One is to wait until you figure out there is a problem with the question you have asked. The second way, is to leave the dimensional area of table tipping in order to consult with another spirit who is knowledgeable about your area of quest. The third way is to leave the area to research spiritual records for the data needed. In all cases, what you witness is no table movement. When the spirit is present ask, "Do you know the answer to this question at this time?" Of course if it does not, it will tell you **No**. Then you may request that it leave to discover the answer or that it connect you with a spirit that does have the knowledge to answer the question. If you receive no movement response to your inquiry, then you know that this spirit has already left the table space to retrieve an answer or to find someone who can answer.

Noticing the table has changed its movement pattern, whether it be subtle or obvious, is important for effective and accurate table tipping. There are many times while spirit is away from the table to seek out data for you that an astral entity can slip on and continue to answer your questions, having great fun creating misunderstandings and even changing the energy of the table tipping experience. When this happens the negative energy atmosphere caused by an astral entity presence may cause your spirit guides to step back and not participate in the rest of the session until you notice the difference and redo the protection process. *Be aware at all times concerning the feel of the table and you can feel the energy difference.* When you do question the "energy feel", immediately ask with insistence, "Do you come in the Light of God?" If the answer is No *or the least bit hesitant* say, "Get off of our table in the name of God (or Jesus Christ), we will speak only with entities or energies of the Light of God who speak the truth of God." Then you must redo the protective and energy circle processes. Remember, that because you are in physical form you have great power over spirit due to your free will and when you demand that they, the astrals, leave your space, they will do so.

Whenever you do table tipping you will want to take notes or tape record the experience. If you are tape recording be sure to say aloud that the table answered Yes or No to the questions posed. I know from experience that the sound of the table moving does not tell me if the table's answer was Yes or No. Keeping careful records in a table tipping notebook or journal saves time and organizes what you have learned.You will have references to answers that may not have had full meaning to you at the time, due to your level of awareness or learning. They will become more meaningful in the future as you grow in spiritual understanding. You will also see the patterns that portray the strong points and qualities of your different guides and teachers. You may discover that certain guides like to predict either earthly events or possible personal situations. There will be times that the sitters are different yet the same message will be verified. This gives you confidence and confirmation. Finally, you can assess the accuracy of certain guides in events that occur according to their predictions. I have some students who keep newspaper clippings of predicted events that occurred as foretold in their table tipping journals.

When first working with a new-to-you Spirit Guide always proceed with caution and reserved suspicion if it claims to be someone well-known historically or spiritually. Also remember that your guide's guidance is formulated from the various possible successful directions and choices you planned for this life before your birth while you were in spirit.

There are times when a sitter present might wish to ask a question that may be of a private nature that they are embarrassed to present in front of others. If that is the case, the sitter should notify the operator that they have a private question to present. All the other sitters must remain quiet and open-minded while the person thinks the question, thereby sending the question telepathically to spirit, and the table will proceed to move for an answer. It is of great benefit to the questioner if any of the sitters receive a general or a symbolic answer to his or her question. Reactions like these will provide verification that the questioner understands spirit's answer. After all, one of the primary purposes of the table is its ability to be a social tool, providing the benefit of objectivity through the presence of others. If you want to work out several private concerns, it is best to research them through meditation and then have them verified through the use of the table.

With most of the basic techniques for table tipping discussed, you are ready for the adventure of a general understanding about some of the spiritual energies themselves and the non-physical dimensions in which they reside.

*"IT IS BEST TO REMEMBER THAT ALL BEINGS,
FROM ANGELS TO ANTS OR EARTH TO THE
UNIVERSE, DESERVE UNCONDITIONAL LOVE
AND RESPECT FOR THEY ALL ARE UNIQUE
EXPRESSIONS OF GOD ENERGY."*

CHRISTOPHER

CHAPTER SIX

Table Tipping Communication And The Spiritual Dimensions

BECAUSE TABLE TIPPING IS an inter-dimensional experience, we need to discuss spiritual states of being and the layers of spiritual placement. Spiritual energy is present everywhere and all levels or dimensions of its vibration pervade our third dimension. There are many differences in the vibrational states of spiritual being. The table allows you to be in the physical, third dimensional world while simultaneously being in touch with the invisible fourth and other dimensional worlds which contain all the different vibrational states of spiritual energy. The table is a physical bridge to those spiritual dimensions of energy that are Divine.

The term dimension refers to measuring in one direction, such as length, breadth and thickness. When discussing esoteric matters dimension can relate to level or degree of vibrational placement. The idea of dimensions and spiritual levels or planes is a concept about which entire books are written. It is not a simple concept. Be aware that there are layers of vibration within each dimension and that there are dimensions within dimensions.

When the subject of dimensionality is researched through spiritual means the data given is often incomprehensible and perhaps difficult to express in words. In this chapter, I am presenting the information that spirit has given to me in table tipping sessions. I am also including some of my personal understanding of the dimensions obtained from meditational, dream and spiritual travel experiences that have been verified through the table. I have chosen to present the information as simply as possible in order to give you the basics for your use in table tipping. The chart on page 98, portrays a general and simplified layout of the spiritual dimensions. You can utilize this chart to determine which dimension is of interest to you for your specific quest.

Please remember that within this chapter I am categorizing an infinite energy existence into ten basic placements that I call dimensions for the sake of simplicity. This does not mean that there are only ten dimensions. When dimensional existence is discussed with spirit, there can be varied ways to categorize God Force energy existence which would create many more dimensions or placements of energy vibration to be considered. However, for the purposes of table tipping, spirit suggested that I present the ten dimension format.

Presently, I am actively researching the subject of dimensions by consciously experiencing fascinating journeys within the spiritual realms. I am writing another exciting and spiritually informative book about these travels and what it has been like for me to balance being a multidimensional individual in a physical body since childhood. Within this text and its sequel you will be able to discover some of the thought-provoking truths that wise Light beings share with me along this intriguing pathway of exploration.

First dimension is the inertia for movement forward which travels in one line of action either forward, backward or to the side, but it is a singular action from start to finish.

Second dimension occurs when two first dimensional lines connect creating the two directions of length and width. The law of attraction flows within this dimension and creates the connection of those lines.

Third dimension is the addition of density to an object. A square (which is two dimensional) now becomes a cube. The cube has length, width and thickness. The third dimension creates form and form creates the need for time and space. When a form occupies an area no other form can be in the same space. Time must exist in order to indicate how long a form takes up a certain amount of space so another form can later take up the same space. An example being that when you occupy a chair no one else can comfortably sit in the same chair until you are finished sitting there.

Fourth dimension is the area of the invisible subtle matter that does not fit into the pattern that governs solid third dimensional matter. Our electricity, microwaves, X-rays, television and radio transmissions and radiations of light and sound waves are in this dimension.

The fourth dimension is also the placement of psychic capacities such as, clairvoyance, clairaudience, prophetic vision and long distance vision and therefore is the first dimension of normal spiritual entity activity. There have been reported instances when a spiritual entity interacts with and communicates through fourth dimensional energy tools such as through the telephone, radio or television. The fourth dimension contains the first level of spiritual telepathy (communication between spirit and an incarnated person) and all mental telepathy (communication between mind and mind that occurs between living or incarnated persons). It is the first plane of connecting with the deeper facet of Universal love.

Within the fourth dimension is the mental/emotional plane which exists within the etheric energy field that surrounds the earth known as the earth's aura. The earth's mental/emotional plane contains all of human thought or the human consciousness as well as human emotion. You need to be aware of the existence and the power of this plane when you receive predictive or informational material. If your sources are from the earth's mental/emotional plane you will connect with thought forms that are only the concepts that are within the majority of the incarnate and discarnate human minds on and around the earth. When answers to your quests are inaccurate, you may discover that this has been your source. Always check to determine if you are communicating with an actual spiritual entity that would resource the akashic records. Carelessness about evaluating the origin of your communications can result in inaccurate information or predictions and may be the source of some of the predicted "doomsday" information that is presently so prevalent.

This is also the plane that contains human creative and inventive concepts allowing for several persons to create or invent identical or very similar projects at the same time even though the persons involved are totally disassociated. When a person is inspired spiritually, such as in deep meditation or spiritual dreams, and he ponders it a great deal, it is automatically transferred to the earth's mental/emotional plane. Once the inspiration is within this plane it is then available for all humans to think about enabling them to actually manifest the concept into physical form. Many times inspiration is given to you by spirit just so you will think about it which accomplishes spirit's mission to seed the concept into the earth's mental/emotional plane entering it into human consciousness. So do not become frustrated when you are given so many beautiful inspirations that you do not have the time to materialize them. Realize you do not have to do them all. You have already done a wonderful service for spirit just to bring the idea into this plane. Relax and choose carefully which one fulfills you and release the others.

Fifth dimension is the plane of mental or intellectual spiritual energy where design and organization comes into being. From this plane the plan of a design comes into three dimensional form. For example it is in this plane that allows for specific blueprints of a fixed design of frequency of vibration. That is why quartz crystals and snowflakes are always six-sided and why a specific type of oak tree sprouts only a specific design of oak leaf and a particular shape of acorn. The organizational thoughts from which matter follows the laws of individual design function in this placement in orderly independence without coming into conflict with each other. This is the plane of the Universal creative plan and the first level of the Ultimate Mind. This dimension is a fascinating source for knowledge about new forms or species that will come into being as the Universal All is evolving.

When I reached a certain level of meditational experience, I traveled through a fascinating corridor into a "Light" much like the Light described by those who have had a near-death experience. When I am within the presence of this Light I feel as if I have reached the Source. I know I have touched the experience of unconditional acceptance, nonjudgement and the most perfected love I can expand my being to experience at my present spiritual vibration. When I experienced this Light I felt such ecstasy that I was convinced I had reached God. Then as I grew in awareness, developing an openness emotionally, mentally and spiritually, I traveled through this Light and further into more expanded and utopic areas of spirit.

Whenever I reach a newer level of experience for me, within a dimension, I am unable to physically describe this new experience. I must return to that level many times to expand my vibration allowing me to develop my comprehension and perception of that placement of spirit. I gain a deeper understanding of spirit and my spiritual self through these spiritual dimension experiences. I feel I must know myself, wholly, to know God. As I work with knowing who I am on inner levels, I expand myself to experience more of God and Its levels of both inner and outer dimensional life force expression. Since I am ever evolving, I cannot honestly say I have experienced the highest of dimensions. Spiritual wholeness and perfection is always present and available but we can be limited by our vibration or consciousness as to what part of it we can perceive or comprehend.

There are other dimensions that to my knowledge include the sixth through the tenth. When I discuss the dimensions within a dimension I like to use the term reality. The levels of realities that the table tipper can reach exist between and include the third through tenth dimensions. They are the levels available to the table tipper for sources of information. It is important to have an awareness of their existence so that you can contact the proper dimension and the specific reality you need within it which will work best in your quest for knowledge.

Within each reality is a special awareness. Beings within a certain dimensional reality may be limited in knowledge and awareness to that dimension alone. But, at any level of reality, an entity will have access to reality levels below it as they will be of a slower frequency. Thus usually an entity or energy is limited to its own frequency of reality and those of a slower frequency.

All that exists is energy vibrating within certain waves of activity which can be thought of as a frequency. We humans can sense differences in the speed of frequencies. For example, sound can be heard as different tones according to the frequency of the sound wave vibration of each note. There are sounds that the human ear cannot hear physically even though they exist. The silent dog whistle is a wonderful case in point. Visually humans usually perceive only the slower waves of light activity. I believe there are variations of hues of known colors that exist but we do not physically see. We can perceive water when the molecules within it are at their slowest frequency and we see it as ice. When the molecules move at a faster frequency we see it as water. At its fastest rate of molecular activity, water is almost invisible to us as steam.

There are waves of energies that we need tools to help us perceive such as radio or television waves. When waves of energy are resonating faster than our normal sensory perception can perceive they exist in the fourth dimension.

In the third dimension we express ourselves in the physical body composed of dense matter and we can perceive the reality of physical form. We relate to all that can be perceived in this way as our reality. In the past man's attitude has been that only what he can perceive with the physical body senses is, in fact, reality. But as man evolves he learns of other realities. Science has brought about the understanding of the "new" although philosophers and metaphysical thinkers knew of other realities in ages past.

You are now aware that there is more to you than just your physical body. There are unseen layers that make up the mental, emotional and spiritual bodies. These bodies extend from the third through to the fourth and other dimensions. It is through these energy body extensions into other dimensions that you are able to communicate with spirit while you are within a physical body.

As you study about dimensions you will realize that they all coexist in the same area that surrounds you in the third dimensional earth and universe. Spiritual frequencies are just faster cycling. They are not up or down, they are everywhere. Through your table tipping experiences the statement "God is everywhere" will develop into a deeper level of personal experience and awareness.

In the third dimensional world of form the first reality is that of minerals. Mineral awareness exists in rock, stones, crystals and the soil of the earth itself. There is a hierarchy of spiritual energies which is responsible for the life force that exists in minerals. Even though we consider this life force to be limited in capacity it is viably present - growing and learning in the expression of creation. The spiritual energies working with this reality could be considered Lords of this life force energy. They have a responsibility to help it express its minerality and progress along in its evolution. Some schools of thinking consider these spiritual Lords as Devas. This reality may not necessarily be aware of other realities within its dimension but its spiritual hierarchy would have awareness of other third dimensional realities.

The second reality of the third dimension is that of plant awareness. The life force energy of plants is more evolved than that of minerals and has its own hierarchy of spiritual helpers. You may have heard of them as fairies, gnomes, elves or earth elementals - all of which could be considered the spirit guides of plants. There are angelic entities that are overseers of these spiritual helpers of plants. Some of these would be the Terra and Flora Angels.

You can communicate with the fairy kingdom through the table. They will be joyous. They love to help in your understanding about the care of plants. They will share with you regarding the earth's well-being. They will help you see that the earth is a living entity and that it is directly effected by your actions and thoughts. They will help you get in touch with earth energy to cooperate with healings of the earth. The "elementals" of earth, air, water, and fire can help you with your own physical energies by carrying the needed elemental energy into your aura. For example, if you are a person who needs to be around water in order to be in full power and balance but you are living in the desert, the next time you are around a body of water ask for assistance from the water sprites. They will help you absorb the water element energy while you are around the water that you will need in the future. They will maintain the presence of this water-based balancing energy in your aura while you are in the desert for a long periods of time if you arrange for them to continue to support you in this process.

The third reality of the third dimension is the animal reality. Animals have spiritual life force energy that usually performs as a group soul essence and some types, due to their level of evolution, have spiritual guides in other dimensions. Here again we have a hierarchy of spiritual helpers. Some levels of Cherubim angels often work with the reality of animals. Be aware that there are energies *between* these physical existences also. An evolved animal energy that is not incarnate at the time can be between realities in spirit. In other words, if your pet calico cat died and has not yet reincarnated it can be in a reality that is between animal and human realities.

Sometimes animal spirits come through on the table. They may have known you in this lifetime but now are in spirit. They might want you to know about their present spiritual condition and how they dealt with their crossover (physical death).

Once I was participating with a group of sitters in California and the table began a strange movement. It progressed around in a circle in a trot-like movement making a tra-lump, tra-lump sound with its legs on the floor. As it was going around we were all confused about what the energy could be. We asked the energy to spell out its name. With considerable effort it tried with no success. We were receiving mental pictures of a penny or a coin. We asked if its name was "Penny" and the table hesitated. Then it occurred to me, the ex-school teacher, that the name began with the sound of "p" as in penny. In response to that question the table moved excitedly for a **Yes**. Next we received pictures of friends or buddies. The word, pal, came to my mind. The table jumped with a joyous **Yes, Yes!** The energy was definitely reading my thoughts. At that point one of the sitters looked shocked. "My Lord!" She said. "Are you my horse Pal?" The table jumped instantly for a **Yes** movement. The sitter explained that she had sold her horse about one and half years ago to a young man in his early teens. The horse reported that it had gotten the colic and died.

Pal said he had completed his spiritual work of being a horse energy and he wanted to know from the sitter if he had been a good friend and an effective horse. He wanted to move on in his spiritual evolvement. She told him how wonderful he had been and as she did so, recalled how human-like he had been and how sad she had felt to part from him. Nevertheless, she had to move to the city because of her work and there was no time or place for him.

He told her that since he had made this connection with her through the table, he could now move on in spiritual placement immediately instead of having to wait until she was in spirit to help him. She was so moved by the experience that she called the home where the horse had been living. She confirmed that the horse had died of colic soon after she sold him.

It is important to remember that animals telepathically communicate with thought pictures. They are not as word-oriented as are we. Domesticated animals who live lives as pets evolve spiritually through their interactions with human kind. Since they share lives with humans, they can learn more about the emotional body through an association with human emotions such as love. Having experienced life as a pet they are usually telepathically adept.

Pets can have spirit guides that will come on the table to help you understand your pet and its spiritual lessons in this life. Often a pet you cherish has shared many past lives with you. When you ask the pet's guide about its problems you will gain an understanding of your own problems. All too often, a pet acts out a hidden worry or fear belonging to its owner. Due to the sensitive bond between the animal and the soul of the owner the pet supports its owner by absorbing any negative energy in the home and then transmutes it. But there are times when there is an overload and the pet becomes ill or lethargic. Thus when your pet is ill, it is very important to communicate with its guide for a spiritual understanding of the problem.

The fourth reality of the third dimension is the human awareness reality. This reality is the one you occupy. It is the first reality of life force expression which allows the self to be conscious of itself. This quality of having identity with awareness is an essential step to expanded spiritual evolution. The self learns it is its experience. The human soul senses its need for spiritual growth while it is incarnate in physical form. This consciousness added to the gift of free will is what differentiates the human soul from the previous levels or realities.

Having a physical body which consists of minerals gives us a deep connection with the mineral reality and the earth. Having the ability to procreate, we have our bond or connection with the plant reality. Then, because we can sense and feel emotion we have our bond with the animal reality. We are not above these realities - we are a part of them. However, with our spiritual and mental capacities it is our birth-right to participate, with awareness, in the fourth and other dimensions as well as the third.

The fourth dimension is the first level of reality that is truly the home of that which is subtle or invisible to us.

There is matter at this level - but it is refined and of a faster frequency. *In truth, what we consider matter is spirit expressing itself in a denser form of energy.* Remember that this is the plane in which our spiritual abilities resonate. If you send a message to a friend telepathically that message travels through this reality. Because this reality is all subtle vibration, there is a basic sense of universal oneness here.

The fourth and fifth dimensions are constantly interacting with the third dimension. The present level of the earth's evolution and humanity's spiritual growth creates a thin veil between the third and the fourth and the third and fifth dimensions. All of your manifestations start within the fourth or fifth dimensions. Your conscious awareness of these and other spiritual dimensions opens the way for a flow of direct interaction.

The fifth dimension has several levels of realities. Within it are many levels of astral reality. I have limited our study of the astral realm to four categories for a more simplistic view. Through conversations with the guides, I have come to understand that there are several layers or planes of beingness within each of the four realities that I will present to you. The astral realm is one of the most extensive and complex realms of existence. The guides say that an entire book could be written about its structure and contents.

Using my system of the four astral levels, I believe the lowest two astral realities contain energies that are in a dark state of being. I will call these the fourth and third astral realities.

At the fourth or the lowest level (which to me could be considered Hell) the energies are the slowest of spiritual frequencies and are very negative in intent. They are greatly disturbed and out of balance with God and all that is. These energies are malfunctioning and are unable to work with truth, wisdom or love. These realms include energies and entities from all previously mentioned realities that are between lifetimes *and* that are outside recognition of the plan of creation without any intention to turn to the Harmony and Love of God or to anyone at this time. It is my understanding that if an energy or entity does not wish to make the decision to actively participate with the All, then after a long period of testing in this reality, it loses its life force vibration to such an extent, due to a slowed frequency, that it loses its capacity to be. It is important to know that these entities are starving for life force energy.

The next level of astral reality or the third is the area of thought forms. Thought forms are manifestations of human thought that radiates form incarnate and discarnate beings. When a thought is presented with intense emotion it has great presence. Thoughts in this realm seem to have a life of their own and can exist for some time. The length of their existence is determined by the concentrated focus and emotional energy generated from the human or spiritual mind from which they originated. They can be clairvoyantly seen as monsters representing fears, hates, envies, angers, anxieties or negative emotions. They can also be ideas or designs that are beautiful and that are represented here as wonderful colors and forms.

Within this level there are colors more beautiful than can be perceived physically as well as shapes that are grotesque and hideously ugly. If we could perceive our thoughts as the forms they really are, we would be much more aware of the responsibility for our thinking habits.

The third area of astral reality is also home to our desire body. There is no question that the energy we project through our solar plexus which exhibits as our needs, desires and obsessions is powerful and truly affects the table. The energy of desire generates in our own ego and our own selfishness. It is very controlling and is sensed by others in our everyday life as well as in the table tipping experience.

It is possible to rise above this lower energy level when the needs and goals of life are directed towards the good of all - towards the universal good. It is possible to express yourself at a level above the desire body when situations are not considered solely from the vantage point of effect on self but how they affect mankind and spirit as a whole. Within the universally spiritual soul, there is an active recognition that we are all working together as one in a universal bond.

There are two higher levels of astral reality in the fifth dimension. The next level, the one I call the second, is the home of the earth bound entity; i.e., the soul that is not willing to go on with its spiritual plan at this time. This soul could be convinced that its earthly experiences (in its last physical incarnation) would be judged harshly if it met with God or with the Light. It may have an addiction to drugs, alcohol, food, sex or any other material thing which it just does not want to give up. These souls enjoy their addictions through coexistence with a living human and experience the times when that human engages in the entity's addiction. Think how often have you heard the statement, "He just isn't himself when he is drunk, he acts like another person." Well, indeed, in these cases he really is not himself when he is drunk as there is an astral entity with him experiencing the drunken state through him.

Often these astrals are the "ghosts" in homes and certain locations. They do not want to leave their earthly existence to go on into the spiritual realms because they believe they have some unfinished business. They are confused and need help. Sometimes, they are not even aware that they are physically dead. They are not of any informational value to you, the table tipper. Later in the book we will discuss some ways to help these energies when you and they are ready. It is possible that the third, second and maybe the first astral realities could be the Purgatory to which churches refer.

The next level, the first of the astral realities, is where a soul that has recently crossed over (due to a physical death) from the physical plane or third dimension resides. This realm is composed of the soul worlds. Many times a soul, when traveling here, will believe it is heaven or actually the spiritual realms. There are several bright light beings that work here, but it is not their home. Sometimes, when a person meditates they will reach this realm and believe they have traveled into the spiritual realms. This soul region is not the true home of the spiritual Self (the Higher Self) because the spiritual realms are beyond the frequency of this plane. The newly transformed soul, i.e. one that has passed through the veil of physical death, can rest here shortly if it so desires for many reasons. The soul may wish to view its physical family for a few hours or days before going into evaluation and the Light. It may need some time to rest and collect itself due to the nature of its physical body's death process. It could have chosen time to adjust to its spiritual existence and to go through some personal soul assessments.

The fifth dimension also contains some records of past lives - the personal Akashic records. This is not the highest source of recorded spiritual information but it is a start and a beneficial source to the soul when preparing for evaluation.

There is a place in this dimension for entities residing in a body-like form called a Light body. The true Light body is a form of a Light being and is sensed but is not always visible to us. It is usually living a life on other planets. This body contains a spirit more evolved than ours. The body itself is less dense because the cells are filled with light and are more refined than our physical bodies. Some of these beings are called Star beings or Starborns. Another group is often referred to as the "Space Brothers". They really enjoy communicating with you through the table as they are dedicated to helping the earth and its inhabitants. Their consciousness is based upon actively living Universal Love, so they come from a society whose ideals are based upon Christ consciousness i.e., living fully for and from the God energy within. Their dream is that one day our earthly society will reach an utopic level of existence. These beings actually seem to be in a dimensional placement between the fifth and including the sixth dimension.

Please refer to the illustration of the four major levels of the astral plane (page 89, Figure 7) to see the relationship of the astral levels to each other. You will then understand that there are only a few sources within this dimension that you would want to work with through table tipping.

The sixth dimension is a reality of an expanded awareness level of evolution. The energies and entities here have opened their awareness to a more experiential knowing of God and Its wisdom through actively experiencing the plan of creation. At this level of reality there is a constant conscious participation in the plan of God - a sense of just being and a definite participation in the perfected God love. This dimension would be the first reality of Light a spirit can achieve after physical death. It is most often where this spirit will reside during evaluations and decisions concerning its next choices for growth. It is the true spiritual reality that is above the soul worlds. In this reality there are ongoing classes available which teach about the existence in a human body, the soul, spirit forces, the Higher Self and the Divine layers of the Self. These classes are often visited by humans in dreams and meditation. There are Cherubs, Flora, Terra and several other types of angels residing here as well as many sacred souls.

During one sitting, a Cherub came on the table to communicate with a sitter who was an artist who sculpted and painted animals. The Cherub wanted her to know that it works with her to help her render the spirituality within the eyes of the animal subjects in her paintings. This Cherub said the purpose of its inspirational involvement with her art work was to let man understand that God expresses His love energy in animals too. The Cherub's wish was for man to love animals with respect for the God expression in their life force and to understand we are all in oneness with God. During several different sessions we discovered that a musician's creativity was often inspired by these angels.

The sixth dimension also contains the spiritual archive records, prophetic knowledge and information about

ONE: The higher soul worlds, the garden of peace, past life records incarnated "Light bodies"; i.e. Starbeings.

TWO: The earth bound entity not yet corrected with itself or God. The lower soul worlds.

THREE: Negative thought forms, fear and hate monsters created by negative emotions and selfish desires.

FOUR: A slow vibrational sea of those of extremely negative intent, out of balance with God's plan, functioning in non-truth.

FIGURE 7. THE FOUR ASTRAL REALITIES.

reincarnation. Music occurs at this level. It is not exactly earth-like music but it is recognizable as something like the performance of ethereal instruments. However it is far more refined than that heard in our plane of existence. It is enchanting and softly calming, similar to a choir of angelic voices and clear bell like harmonies.

The seventh dimension is that of expanded awarenesses which involve more of the White Light and Love essence of the God Source. At this reality reside those spirits humans have called Masters. Masters (sometimes referred to as "The Brotherhood" or "The Brotherhood of Light") are souls who have mastered their physical, mental and emotional bodies. Being spiritually balanced they are powerful because they have achieved a disciplined control over dense vibrations and matter, and are in no way a slave to it. They have power over natural laws and always work within spiritual laws.

These benevolent beings no longer have to return to the earth plane to learn or grow through earth experience lessons and have no earth level karma to complete. Masters work with souls who are in the third dimension because they work for the good of the Whole. Masters will help you towards spiritual enlightenment through the sharing of their expanded love and knowledge about the Universal truths.

Spirit guides reside in the seventh dimension also, for they too work with the physical earth plane. The purpose of their work is to help and support you while working through your lessons and karmas. In spiritual cooperation with you, they are gaining growth through your own efforts. You can "experience" a heavenly music at this level of reality. It envelopes you with a vibration and color that is not actually heard or seen but is instead experienced within your whole being. Here there are also Light Angels and angels that work with those trying to overcome the demands of the desire body. Your Guardian Angel can be on this level in order to vibrate closer to your energy while you are in the physical body.

The eighth dimension is the reality of the more

encompassing Light as well as the energies that are faster vibrating with an extensive expansion and involvement with a sense of perfection in God. This is the realm of wondrous bright Light beings, who work with God's plan in very significant ways. They work with the other planets of our solar system as well as this and other galaxies. The Illuminated Masters reside in this reality. They are working directly with the aspects often presented as the Seven Rays of God: Will, Love-Wisdom, Activity, Harmony, Concrete Knowledge, Devotion and Ceremonial Order. There are many names given to these Masters who are also known as Chohans of the Seven Rays. Some of the names you may recognize are: Master Morya, Master Kuthumi, Master Djwal Kul, Master Hilarion, Master Serapis Bey, Lord Maitreya and Master Comte de St Germain. These are the Illuminated Masters or the adepts that can present themselves in a body here on earth if they wish. Their manifested body is of refined matter and does not die. A clairvoyant often perceives these Chohans when they are not in their manifested bodies as spheres of brilliant white and golden white light sometimes displaying flecks of color.

There are also Group Minds in this dimension. They appear as a ring of medium-sized spheres of light and sometimes they are all in a metallic gold coloring. These energies always work with persons who have creative projects to produce that will affect mankind for the better. They are often represented by one entity who communicates the sum of their thoughts. The group mind energy is powerfully creative and has the capacity to resource all cosmic information - past, present or future - considered necessary for their benefactor.

At this dimension, there is another level of spiritual wisdom classes available. They are centered around information about the highest of truths, the most ancient of knowledge and the secret wisdoms. The classroom itself is a large etheric hall with volumes of knowledge from all worlds and the vibration of this hall itself has a very special effect on your being. Many human spiritual Selves travel there during dreams or meditation without conscious memory of the event.

There are several types of angels (including the Archangels) present in the eighth dimension. Here, celestial music is a vibration that permeates your being with peaceful bliss. It carries you through indescribable experiences of ecstasy. There have been times that the melody is organ-like and other times that it is just an experience of rhythm that sends waves through your heart and spirit like the united heartbeat of the universe. When you experience this universal rhythm it creates an integrated sense of balanced unity within the whole you. Sometimes you can physically sense waves or rushes of this energy during your waking life as it expands your whole energy unit as a result of having touched into this universal rhythm dimension.

The ninth dimension includes Seraphim Angels and Heavenly Hosts. Here are the wise, immortal beings that had no need to physically incarnate.

This is a realm of total light and balance. It is a realm of formless thought. Sometimes one symbol within your own being develops from touching this reality that is worth one hundred words or a multitude of concepts. Embracing this reality fills you with energy segments of inspiration and wondrous ideas that continue to feed into your being for hours and sometimes days. Once you have experienced this reality it is difficult to explain in earthly terms. It is a level of pure existence with total balance that has no needs or desires. It is a state of complete satisfaction. It is beingness which is peacefully comfortable for it is the pure expression of the All. It is the home of the spirit of truth and wisdom.

The tenth dimension is the purest and primal essence of God, the Source. To my knowing and comprehension it is a Mother/Father God essence for it is soft, gentle and totally accepting in the complete knowledge of what you are, like a Mother. But it is also the strong, protecting and guiding energy of a Father. It is the Father, The Son, and the Holy Spirit. The Holy Spirit as the communicating bond between the soul, the

Higher Self and God is often present during a table tipping experience that is totally centered upon knowledge about God and the evolutionary plan to return to Its Wholeness and Perfection. The Holy Spirit is often perceived as a beautiful blue and gold flame or a sparkling gold energy which exists in a spiraling vortex that is in constant motion.

The tenth dimension is the home of the Christ energy- the Christ consciousness - the total awareness that all is God. This level is almost impossible to explain in our language as it is truly home, the fulfillment of inner yearning. This dimension is beyond satisfaction, ecstasy or bliss. It is the home of nothing - and yet all that is simultaneously existing. There is an indifference at this level that is uniquely Divine. There is no desire for any kind of activity - however, when you embrace it, you experience that *you are action, you are all, you are nothing, you are beingness to perfection.*

The eighth, ninth, and tenth dimensions are sources filled with spiritual nourishment. When you touch these realms you will experience what I consider an initiation preparation. Once you have reached these dimensions through the table tipping experience you will be able to achieve them more easily in meditation because your auric frequency has already touched their energy vibration. The more you relate to these beautifully Divine frequencies the more your aura changes and adapts to and with Its perfection.

After repeated exposure to these frequencies you are forever changed spiritually. There is no going back nor is there ever a desire to return to an existence without an awareness of this energy in your being. The experience creates in you a wonderfully elevating personal and spiritual growth which is accomplished through sensing Divine Love. Best of all, it blends you with your Higher Self in a manner which allows you to be in this union with your Higher Self to the fullest extent while in a physical body. That blending when it is perfected completes our mission in physical form. It allows us the ability to be a Master.

During one of your beginning experiences with table tipping a deceased relative may approach you at the table. I often wonder if this happens due to the comfort and familiarity one feels with a family member creating greater openness to receiving information. It might also be due to the soul-bonding that is present (due to lives together) which makes these inter-dimensional connections easier to achieve. In either case, spirit knows that familiarity allows you to trust the information received and to be comforted by it. Initial table tipping experiences are often given by family, friends, even pets, that are in spirit and have been known by you in this life. Communication from such familiar beings validate the table tipping process as true, accurate and to be trusted.

Whenever a relative in spirit comes on the table it is best to verify that they are indeed who they say they are. Sometimes the data they telepathically give to another sitter who never knew them will be just what is needed to satisfy you. When I first table tipped my deceased mother came on the table. Although I was very excited and pleased she was there, I wanted to verify her information with my father who is living. She was excited to do just that and proceeded to give details of her first date with Dad. She described the circumstances of her mother's disapproval. She gave the particulars of the date including the time of the year and a detailed description of the new car my father drove. Dad later verified the information and was very pleased to discover that mother was happy on the spiritual plane.

I was thrilled. But I was concerned. If this happens to you - you should also be concerned. Because, if a relative in spirit spends time with you are they being held back from their spiritual progress by being tied to you? I asked mother if she was working in spirit. She told me she was studying to be a spirit guide for a little girl. In a short period of earth time she would be taking on that job. I wanted to be sure that if she spent time with me she would, in no way, hinder her spiritual growth. However, during her time of spiritual guide study, she was capable of working with me without retarding her growth. During months of communications with me through meditation and the table she taught me about auric color. I now understand the symbolic meanings of the colors I see in people's auras. It is now a tool I can use to help others.

I have always tried to maintain communication with a deceased relative within spiritual limits. I do not encourage such communication to you, but I am aware that relatives may communicate with you just so that you can believe in your future table tipping experiences. Also, there are instances where relatives have unfinished karma with you and need to complete that process in order to progress spiritually. This can be accomplished through the table. Many times it is a simple, "Do you understand why I acted that way? Do you forgive me?". Karma can easily be resolved through the dimensions if unconditional love is present. Finally, there are instances of a relative unknown to you in this lifetime who works with you to help you along your spiritual path. It can be a grandparent who died before you were born.

Table tipping can be used to assist souls who are in the process of evaluation, allowing them to settle things with you personally in order to move on in their spiritual work. Often, there is a necessity for forgiveness, to clear up misunderstandings and to be released from guilt. All of these can "lock" a soul in place until it has cleared up the lessons or the karma through table communications. Without this chance their soul would have to wait until you also are in spirit.

You are now aware of the many levels of spiritual energy that are available to you for information through table tipping. The types of questions you ask can designate what level will respond to you. If you ask fortune-telling questions, such as, "Should I marry George?" you will very likely be talking with the one of the astral realities. Remember, wanting answers to fulfill your wishes creates pressure from the desire body and will keep the quality of your answers at that level.

Historically most of the great spiritual minds tell

us to be desireless. Needing certain persons to be in your life or having fixed and definite ideas about a certain job, a friend or a relationship actually diminishes your capacity to be open to all that is available. Remember when you ask from the desire body level (not the spiritual plane level) your answers will be inaccurate because you are not placing your questions from spiritual intent. Ask, "What lesson am I to learn from this? Are there more lessons than one? Is there karma to complete?"

You will find out with accuracy what you want to know if you approach spirit with universal loving intention and remain within the spiritual laws of free will and privacy. Spirit will share with you what you need to learn and sometimes discuss your options hinting, in the process, which approach is best to use to learn the lesson as completely as possible. This is guidance that honors your free will.

There is no limit to the numbers of or the quality of the dimensions and levels of realities that can be contacted through the table. The quality of the dimension contacted is affected by three factors. First, you must have a spiritual intention for contact. Second, you need to practice your spirituality and apply the wisdom given. Third, you will discover that regular meditation times will enhance your vibration to a more pleasant spiritual level. Remember that in spiritual energy concerns, "Like attracts like."

Through the table you should be able to contact spirit guides, the corrected dead, saints, angels of all orders, Lords of Devas and elementals, heavenly hosts, your Higher Self, Masters, Ascended Masters, Immortal Wise ones, Deities from other planetary systems as well as from our own solar system, the Space Brothers and other Lightbodies, Archangels, the Holy Spirit, Christ, Jesus, The Divine Energies, mineral, plant and animal energies and the spirits involved with them, and more.

You are only limited by your beliefs, fears, personal emotional and mental restrictions, your awareness level and your personal spiritual vibration. Letting go of opinions and judgments frees you to expand and open your awareness to the adventure of experiencing advanced spiritual dimensions that have always been there but may be new to you. Touching the vibrational level of these dimensions opens your awareness to wisdoms that may, at first, seem unreal to you. Your mental security zone boundaries will be broken down by concepts that can feel foreign or almost unacceptable to you as they unfold. This can make you feel uncomfortable and strangely out of balance. When this happens remember that you only need to accept that which is livable or comfortable for you at the time. I have always remained open minded to the information received, but there were some instances when the concepts were so diverse to my previous beliefs that it took as long as a year for me to have personal validation and to understand and assimilate the information.

You will discover that, due to your table tipping experiences, you will re-evaluate you beliefs more often than you have previously done. As a result, you will be more open than ever before to discarding limiting old belief systems to create the void for new, more practical and useful ones. This whole process makes you feel light, free and more joyful.

DIMENSIONS AND REALITIES OF PHYSICAL AND SPIRITUAL EXISTENCE

TENTH DIMENSION *GOD (MOTHER-FATHER)*
FATHER-SON-HOLY SPIRIT

NINTH DIMENSION *SERAPHIM ANGELS,*
HEAVENLY HOSTS,
ETERNALS, WISE IMMORTALS,
SPIRIT OF TRUTH AND WISDOM

EIGHTH DIMENSION *THE ILLUMINATED ONES,*
ARCHANGELS, GROUP MINDS,
CHOHANS OF THE SEVEN RAYS OF
GOD AND HIGHER CHERUBIM ANGELS

SEVENTH DIMENSION *THE BROTHERHOOD OF LIGHT,*
LIGHT AND GUARDIAN ANGELS,
SPIRIT GUIDES AND SACRED ONES

SIXTH DIMENSION *CHERUBS, TERRA AND FLORAL ANGELS,*
SPIRITUAL ARCHIVE RECORDS,
THE CORRECTED DEAD AND ANGELS

FIFTH DIMENSION *THE FOUR LEVELS OF ASTRAL*
REALITIES,
LIGHT BODIED STAR BEINGS,
THE REINCARNATION RECORDS
THE SPIRITUAL BLUEPRINT OF FORM

FOURTH DIMENSION *INVISIBLE SUBTLE MATTER,*
SPIRITUAL AND MENTAL GIFTS

THIRD DIMENSION *SPIRIT EXPRESSING ITSELF IN FORM*
AS: HUMAN, ANIMAL, PLANT AND
MINERAL REALITIES OF ENERGY

SECOND DIMENSION *THE LAW OF ATTRACTION*
EXPRESSED IN TWO DIRECTIONS

FIRST DIMENSION *THE INITIAL MOVEMENT IN ONE*
DIRECTION

PART TWO

THE ROLE OF THE TABLE IN YOUR SPIRITUAL GROWTH.

EOLVING SPIRITUALLY AND OPENING YOUR SIXTH SENSE.

"THE SO-CALLED UNSEEN SPIRITS THAT ARE ALWAYS WITH YOU RESONATE CLOSELY TO YOUR VIBRATIONS AND PURPOSE IN THE GAME OF LIFE, THEREFORE RECOGNIZE THEM AS SUPURLATIVE INTERACTING TEAMMATES." CHRISTOPHER

─────── ⊦⟨𝕀⟩⊦⟨𝕀⟩⊦⟨𝕀⟩⊦ ───────

CHAPTER SEVEN

Meeting And Communicating With Spirit.

A. SPIRIT GUIDES

DUE TO THE SPECIAL relationships that I have had with spirit guides for most of my life they are a subject close to my heart. The first memory I have of understanding that I was "seeing" a spiritual guide was when I was five and in the first grade. Since I considered this glowing being a Guardian Angel, I was not aware of the real depth of our relationship. My Catholic upbringing made me feel it was inappropriate to ask questions of him so I thought of him as a protective, guiding and silent partner.

When I was six, I attended a spiritual retreat at school during which the priest spent much time discussing the attributes of helping spirits, saints and Guardian Angels. I was delighted. The priest opened the doorway for perceptual conversation between my angel and me.

The first verbal communication I received from him was to tell me that his name was Christopher while he imaged himself superimposed over a picture of St. Christopher the protector that I had at the time to reinforce my understanding. I clearly remember hearing him say, "God loves You" and "God is everywhere." This message came through me with a comforting feeling of God being all around and in me, the air and in every living thing. It seemed from then on that

Chris and I had a friendship difficult to match in human form.

For the next year I silently enjoyed his guidance and instructions. When I was seven years old I told my mother about Christopher. She was very open, but I knew at first she tested his information. Later on she would often ask me for his insights in several family situations. This was wonderful until one day I shared with a friend about "seeing" Christopher. She let me know immediately that she thought I was strange and withdrew from associating with me ending our friendship. This made me feel very alone and different. In time, with the help of my mother and Christopher, I was able to understand that I was not abnormal. But because of possible misunderstandings, mother and I agreed to basically keep Christopher's existence a secret. After that I did not tell anyone else about my angel or the other angels that I saw around people.

As I grew older, especially while I was in high school, it was wonderful to know what to study and when "surprise" tests would be given. This helped me to be an excellent student. Interestingly enough I continued to think of Chris as a Guardian Angel until about fifteen years ago when I heard about the concept of spirit guides. Then when I discovered table tipping, discussions with Chris were totally different when I learned from him that he was and is my Chief spiritual guide. He told me that he allowed me to see him as a Guardian Angel because that was within my comfort zone of understanding. I was curious to know if the angels I had seen around other persons, were indeed Guardian Angels. He told me that most of them were spirit guides.

There were many times in my life when I was not interested in seeing Chris or in relating to him. Sometimes, even I denied he was there. I can honestly confess that during my college years I noticed him very little. Because of my studies in psychology I decided that seeing or hearing such things as angels certainly was not normal or healthy activity. Several years into my married life I realized that many messages of protection and special information were being given to me and each time the knowledge was accurate and very helpful. I decided to open up and listen. I apologized to Christopher for being thoughtless and ignoring him and then I became concerned about the wasted time I could have shared with him. Chris understood, admitting that most spirit guides go unrecognized throughout all their work. He said that human recognition of their existence is advantageous to the spiritual progress of both the guide and the guided and that cooperation speeds it all along.

Since I have been actively engaged in learning about my relationship with Christopher through the table, inspirational or channeled writing and meditation I have discovered that he is my twin-soul. That means he is another part of my Higher Self. He has decided to be with me spiritually throughout the duration of this physical lifetime. He will be present at and go through the physical death experience with me. I understand a guide can choose to be present but does not have to endure the actual experience. Apparently, Christopher's help will take me through the transition with no loss of consciousness and little if any adjustment to the spiritual realm. This is tough duty for a guide because it is a dense and smothering experience for him. Once I am over to the other side we will both be comfortable and aware. He and I have shared so many past lives that we have played out most of the relationship roles one can experience in human form. Many of these interactions were family relationships or as mates. Our last life together ended in Germany in the middle 1800s.

One of the most fulfilling purposes for table tipping is meeting and creating a rapport with your spirit guides. They are excited to have you come to a realization about their existence and to directly work with you. If you have not seen, heard, felt or sensed in any way that spirit guides are with you, you will create an opening up of these senses through the table tipping experience.

Because of your table communications, you will improve your awareness through the information you receive from the guides about themselves. Once you open up your heart and mind to their energy you create a bond which lessens any obstacles that are between the dimensions. You may be able to see, hear or know what they are thinking even when you are not using the table. You will discover that working with the guides through the table will acquaint you with the role they play in your life. You will be amazed as to how much they interact with you. Your table conversations will foster an appreciation of the perseverance and creativity with which they work things through in your life.

You will discover there are many guides working with you. Each one has a special vibration and a certain manner in which they approach and move the table. If you remember the feel and type of that specific movement it will become an identifying signature for that guide. Then, if the guide unexpectedly comes on the table you will know who it is by the movement the table performs. My sister-in-law's chief guide was a circus clown in a past life with her. He performs an adorable little spin-like dance action with the table whenever he comes on the table. I have a guide who tips to the left, then right and then to and fro.

If you are attentive you will notice an energy change in the table as well as a difference in movement with each spirit. These sensations seem to be a key to each spirit's personality and vibration. Guides who know you well and are close to you in vibration will have a stronger thrust in their movement of the table. The higher, more refined dimensional energies have a soft, levitating and lofty movement.

Later in this chapter we will discuss some of the functions of these guides, their basic classifications and their purpose in that placement in relationship to you and your present incarnation. Communicating with these guides will enhance your spiritual growth through knowledge about yourself - the whole you - and what you have chosen to do in this life. You will open the gates to past life information and understand how those experiences apply to the lessons and karmas in this incarnation. Table tipping makes it fun to get to know your guides for you will directly experience their personalities, love and best of all, their sense of humor.

Let us explore just what spirit guides are. They are personalized God-Force energy without a physical body. How you perceive them may change from time to time, because they are pure light energy and not subject to physical laws. I have seen Christopher as a sparkling blue white light, a blonde curly haired male child, a man who is well-dressed as a European looking professional man of the middle 1800s and as a blonde haired youthful angelic looking male. I understand that the appearance he forms is the result of my subconscious mind receiving symbols from his energy as part of his message. All of the variety of appearances can be confusing if you are not aware that the guide is capable of such energy manipulation. Having an awareness that they are light energy, you can familiarize yourself with their basic essence, either by auric colors or energy sensations, so you will always recognize them.

The guides are spiritual entities because they are a spiritual energy that have self-awareness of being an individual soul or Higher Self vibration. Thus, there are beings separate from your own being who are present around you etherically for the purpose of loving support. However, there are energies that are actually other parts of your own being that are around you. I sometimes think that past life personalities of yourself are mistakenly thought of as a spirit guide by some people.

Guides are Light-beings because they have taken the effort to evaluate their spiritual progress and are aware of their evolutionary placement on the path to spiritual perfection. They know what lessons they are working through in spirit.

Due to the fact they are not physical, they do not have the same emotional feelings we do, nor do they need a sense of time or space, since those realities are only necessary for the third dimension. There are many guides who have no sense of time at all. They do not relate to the idea of years, days, hours or minutes. When you ask questions that involve time the only accurate answers will come from guides who have recently incarnated and still have a memory of earth time. Of course, there may be a special circumstance of a guide who for some reason is watchful of earth time. Remember this fact when discussing time with spirit and when asking questions which include general terms such as, *soon* or *later.* Whenever you are dealing with a question involving a sense of timing be sure that the spirit you are questioning has an awareness of what you mean by time.

Guides are aware of the spiritual laws and abide by them. They will never invade your privacy because that is spiritual law. They do not sit on your shoulder to watch and evaluate your every movement because they never judge you. Also remember *the guides will never make decisions for you* because that would violate the spiritual law of free will.

Guides are souls/Higher Selves that are in the spiritual realm. *That does not mean they are all-wise and all-knowing.* They are not the God Source Itself. They are a part of God as are you. They are his helpers and your assistants from the spiritual dimensions. From their vantage point which is free of the physical body and the denser layers of the emotional body, they can see and know much information because they are in a dimension where the past, present and future exist together. They have the ability to gather data and wisdom from knowledgeable souls, energies and consciousnesses. Nevertheless, these guides are limited to their levels of awareness and experience within the spiritual realm.

Your guides may be working through some lessons and karmas with you. That is why it is important to recognize that there are several guides working with you. They may be on different levels and have diverse talents. Many have access to the Akashic Records which are, the spiritual record of all that has happened to you and what is to be in the future.

Expressing themselves in spiritual bodies the guides possess the higher emotions of unconditional love, tolerance and compassion, plus the virtues of understanding, patience, forgiveness and individual strength. I have never experienced a guide being angry or at wits end with me and I certainly have given them cause to feel that way many times. I treasure their positive attitudes, inspirations and their joyous sense of humor. They are able to empathize with my emotions for most of them have memory of the physical body experience from their own past lives.

Some guides know you better than you know yourself. The sharing of many past lives with you has given them insight into your full personality. Some truths which are hidden from you by the veil of the consciousness of your physical body can be seen by the guides, so they are aware of all your talents and qualities.

Remember that the manner in which guides identify you is by the auric energy you radiate in and around you. This is the reason spirit is not concerned with names. They recognize and identify each other by the completely unique auric energy which surrounds every being. There are times a guide really does not care about having a name. When you truly want a name for your guide explain that it is important to us in the physical body to identify each other by name and that we are more comfortable with that process. The guide will lovingly respond with the information.

Since guides perceive your auric field there is no hiding from them. If you have not responded to their help by acting on the information given you through the table they will know it. There are times you may sense their frustration with this fact but due to their warm, all-accepting love the guides are kind enough to repeat their information several times at many different sittings. They are aware of your weaknesses and strengths and that knowledge gives them patience. When you feel that your guides expect a great deal from you, realize that they know your abilities, strengths and weaknesses from a macro level of existence and take pride in their expectations.

Your spiritual friends know your plans for the whole span of this physical life. They will encourage and support you by coordinating events and people to help you through this plan. They are the ones who place key people who are supportive of your goals into your life when you are prepared for them.

One of the most frustrating experiences for a guide is when you do not focus on any certain goal and are constantly changing your mind about your needs. During such times they cannot help you because they are unable to read your needs.

Sometimes, they have to stand by helplessly while you do nothing and are in what I call neutral gear without going anywhere. Once a decision is made the guides can work out the appropriate means to have the Universe support you and assist you in achieving your goals. You can remain in neutral gear your whole life and make very few choices to work out your lessons and your guides will still love and support you.

I was informed by the guides that there were several recent past lives in which I coasted in neutral gear. I lived life unaware that I had any control over what happened to me. I perceived myself as a victim of life and avoided the responsibility of lessons. The table tipping experience makes you aware of your choices in life and gives you an understanding that you, on a higher level, chose your present situation, no matter how unpleasant, to use as a learning tool.

Each of us has many spirit guides working with us at all times. Certain ones remain with us throughout most of our physical life. There are others who work with us temporarily. This gives them the chance to work out some small lesson or karma and then move on. Some guides we simply outgrow and others outgrow us.

The spiritual energies choosing to be spirit guides study diligently for this job and practice to be effective as spirit guides. Some of those in your group may be working with you as an apprentice guide who learns while helping those experienced guides assigned to you.

The energies that are your guides received your stamp of approval before your birth into this incarnation or during an out-of-body experience. Their working relationship with you is mutually agreed upon and bonded in love. These energies almost always have had past lives with you or have worked with you in spirit. They are not strangers but intimate caring spirits that have interacted with you often in your span of existence.

Your guides are usually of a higher vibration than you in order to have the assurance of being helpful. When you work with your spiritual growth by applying yourself to your lessons, karmas and meditate regularly, you create an open and clear channel between yourself and the guides. You heighten your frequencies and expand your consciousness in this manner.

Guides attune to your frequency as best they can, but your cooperation through spiritual growth releases many barriers to that connection. In spirit, like attracts like, so all the work you do to raise your consciousness, whether it is through study, prayer, meditation or every day work with awareness of self, pays off beautifully.

There are spiritual helpers on all levels that are pleased to communicate with you. The higher you reach into the spiritual dimensions the wiser and more universally pure are the truths you receive.

When talking to the guides through the table remember that they love you and often just want to communicate their love. They will often praise you and sometimes even present you with an etheric reward that is placed in your aura. I have seen them put etheric crystals or flowers in the aura to be viewed permanently by all in spirit.

Always allow time for their gifts and expressions of love for they are experiences you will always treasure. Allow the table to come close to you or even rest upon you when the guides wish to give you loving energies. The touching of the table on your knee or body allows a direct channel of this love energy into your physical being. Believe me, it is a wonderfully healing sensation.

It is important to know as many of your guides as you can for they all have specific qualities and capabilities to assist you. The following list of types of guides will help you decide to whom to direct what questions. This is not a complete list of all the guides that you may find available for you, but it includes the general classifications. In the list are: the Chief Guide, Karmic Guide, Psychic Guide, Timing Guide, Creative Guide, Joy Guide, Blueprint Guide, Health Guide, Table Guide, Galactic Guide, Master Guide, Relationship Guide, Crystal

Guide, Pendulum Guide, Universal Guide and a Gatekeeper. There may be many others working with you such as an Economic Guide, a Nature Guide, elementals or lords of elementals, Political Guides, Healing (doctor-type) Guides and several types of Universal Guides. You have to explore and ask how many guides are working with you as you communicate with the ones you meet through the table tipping experience.

As you learn that you have each of these guides and more, it is important to keep records of your information. Since the guides are not always conscious of names, once you receive a name, write it down and do not forget it. It is a good idea to date the information you receive to help you with understanding how long you have had a certain guide. You will notice more easily if there are any changes among those who are working with you in a specific area.

Receiving the name of a guide does not have to be a difficult process. Now that you know how to use the alphabet procedure use that method to receive the name. Another identification technique is to ask the guide to telepathically put the name in your mind. Whatever comes to mind, ask aloud if that is the guide's name and you will receive the **Yes** or **No** movement. All the sitters can tune in to the discovery of a name, it is such fun when others "hear" the same name.

The next section of this chapter is devoted to identifying each guide's role in the various levels of your present incarnation. I have presented suggested questions that are appropriate for each guide previously listed. These questions are designed to help you to get to know the guide and to directly receive their individual guidance.

Through the use of these questions you will learn about yourself and your life through the perspective of the guides' loving perceptions. Most of the questions are formed for a **Yes** or **No** response which is the easiest way to use the table to gather information. However there are questions included within each list that will give you the experience of using your spiritual-psychic senses in order to gain information. Each time a question like this is asked, everyone in the group of sitters will have to clear their mind and open up to "tuning in" to; thoughts known instantaneously (intuitive thinking), images and symbols seen within their mind (Clairvoyance), aromas lingering in their sense of smell (Clairscentience), tastes in the mouth(Clairsavorance), physical sensations in the body, emotional feelings (Clairsentience) and words heard within and outside the body (Clairaudience). When this is the means used to determine an answer you are using spiritual telepathy. I will use the code (T) when the question is best answered by this means. Practicing this method to receive from spirit is easiest while you are within the power of the table's energy circle. After you have practiced spiritual telepathy through your table experiences there is the wonderful result of increased awareness of the guides within yourself to be sensed on your own all the time.

If the group's ability to receive through spiritual telepathy is not working well then you can use the alphabet technique, presented in chapter 5, to receive letter-by-letter each word of your guide's message. (A) is the code for using this method. When it is suggested that you use the number technique from chapter 5, the code is (N). Another code I will use within the questions listed is (PFQ) for the instances where I give some possible followup questions to the one presented in the numbered list.

THE CHIEF GUIDE

The Chief Guide is the guide most familiar with your energies. Usually this guide has known you in several past lives and is your loving best friend throughout most of this physical incarnation. The Chief Guide, or any of your guides, androgynous energy depending upon your past experiences with it or how it is working out its evolution.

One of your first requests, in a table session, should be for your Chief Guide to come to the table. You can initiate the table's movement by asking, "Will my Chief Guide please come on the table?" Immediately after the first movement of the table it is of utmost importance to ask, **"DO YOU COME IN THE LIGHT OF GOD?"**

If the table's first movement for the sitting is your Chief Guide, it is a good idea to ask, "Are we protected at this time?" This allows you to know from the guide's perspective if you have completed the protection process well enough so that only Light-beings are present. If the table says **No**, reprotect yourselves and the table before you continue.

I will now list some of the questions you may wish to ask of a Chief Guide. Remember to form questions that can be answered with a **Yes** or **No**.

1. Do you wish to be recognized as a male energy?
2. Do you wished to be recognized as a female energy?
3. Are you an androgynous energy?
4. Will you help us with a name by which you wish to be identified? (A or T)
5. Have we worked together in spirit?
6. Are we connected through past physical incarnations?
7. How many incarnations have we had together? (N or T)
8. Were we in any relationships together in past lives?
9. Were we members of the same family?
10. Were we mates?
11. Were we friends?
12. Were we enemies?
13. Were we rivals?
14. Do you have an understanding of earth time?

14. Do you have an understanding of earth time?
15. Can you give me the most recent date in earth historical time when we were both physically incarnated at the same time? (N or T)
16. Can you give me a date in earth historical time when we physically knew each other last? (N or T)
17. Did we have a past life together in the 19th century?
18. Can you help me to determine the geographical locations where some of our lives took place?
19. (You can ask specific locations at this point.) Ex., Was our most recent past life together in England?
20. Is there a specific reason why you have chosen to be my Chief Guide?
21. Is that reason connected with karma? (PFQ)
    A. Is that reason connected with love?
    B. Is that reason connected with our spiritual family relationship?
    C. Are there other reasons?
    D. What are they? (A or T)
22. Have I ever been your spirit guide?
23. To your knowledge have I ever been a spirit guide?
24. Do you have the capacity to travel through many dimensions? (Here you can use the material from the spiritual dimensions chart on page 98 in chapter 6 and ask specifically about each dimension.)
25. Have we shared existences together on another planet within this solar system? (PFQ)
    A. Was that planet Saturn?
    B. Why did I spend time there? (A or T)
26. Do you have a specific symbol that is your signature?
27. Could you please send a picture of this symbol into our minds? (A or T)
28. Are there any subtle physical signal sensations you can let me feel now to know of your presence around me?
29. Will you please let me experience that signal now. (T)

30. Can you allow me to sense this physical signal even when I am not using the table?

31. Is there a special feeling I can experience for a signal to let me know a **Yes**? (PFQ)
    A. Please send it now. (T)

32. Is there a special signal for a **No**? (You can repeat the PFQ, A. from question 30 here.)

33. DO YOU HAVE A MESSAGE FOR ME? (This is the most important question you will ask and once you know this guide and it should be your first question when opening your sessions with your Chief Guide. A or T)

34. Do we have lessons to work through together at this time? (PFQ)
    A. Will you help me to understand what these lessons are?
    B. How many lessons are there? (N)
    C. Help me to know the details of the most important lesson now. (A or T)

35. Am I presently working on a personal soul lesson?

36. Do you have any advice about how to work through this lesson? (A or T)

In summary, there are some significant thoughts to be considering when communicating with the Chief Guide. Many times, the name and gender shared with you by this guide help you to recognize it as you knew it in your most recent past life together. You may discover that you have studied together or shared some spiritual experiences together that are relevant to the now of this life. Knowing and understanding past life relationships helps you comprehend the reasons for your present connection.

I have discovered that the reason some persons "see and hear" their guides so easily is that they themselves have been a spirit guide in the recent past. Having performed this spiritual task in the past themselves makes them naturally aware of their spirit friends.

Another fascinating concept to explore is to ask for an understanding of a symbol that a guide will present as its personal signature. Christopher's symbol is a red rose. Knowing about this symbol is important. Your guide could be trying to alert you physically to a certain symbol in your everyday life and now you will recognize it. I live in a dry region where it can be difficult to raise beautiful roses which are my favorite flower. I have planted several rose bushes but there is one bush that thrives. It constantly blooms large fragrant blossoms all over the bush. One day I noticed fairies around it. I asked Christopher about the bush. He said he had assigned fairies to it giving it a special energy to survive the extremes of the desert climate so I could always have red roses from him. There are many times red roses come into my life. I know that Christopher creates these instances to demonstrate his supportive loving bond with me.

I have another guide that assists me in information gathering and inspirational writing whose symbol is a hummingbird. There are several of them in my yard but there is one that is a remarkable metallic golden tan with a black head. This bird only appears when I meditate and do inspirational writing. It perches outside my window in full view of where I am sitting remaining still during the time I receive information. There are occasions that these spirit guide symbols occur for validation. Whenever they happen I always feel the warmth of love and joy.

Gaining access to the special signals which are your physical sensations is as wonderful a tool to use in your every day life as the signature symbol. When this process is at work you can have a direct sense of your guide's assistance anywhere and anytime without the table. Some of the physical signals given may be a sudden rush of goose bumps or a warm feeling around your shoulders which is the normal sensation of a spiritual hug. I have one guide who delicately tickles the bottom of my left foot to let me know that he sends a sign of approval. I have another guide who creates a softly noticeable blue light in my field of vision as a sign of support. Ask your Chief Guide to let you experience a subtle physical signal if it wishes to use one with you.

Usually after your first table tipping experience you will be acquainted with your Chief Guide. Thereafter, it is appropriate to begin the session by asking for the Chief Guide and then asking if it has any messages for you. When you do this you allow the guide to express first what it considers important knowledge for you in your present life situation.

When you are new to table tipping it can be difficult to understand the message because you have not posed a question that can be answered with a **Yes** or **No**. Remember, you can have the guide use the table to spell out the message letter-by-letter. However, it is best to work with the concept of messages when you are a little more experienced at receiving psychically through the table. When you do feel ready, use the suggestions in chapter 5 concerning understanding messages from your guides.

There are endless questions you can pose to your Chief Guide. As you open the doors to spiritual thoughts many questions come to mind. Since your Chief Guide is the coordinator of all your spiritual guide activity, it will introduce you to your other guides and teachers and bring them to the table. Your Chief Guide knows how many guides and teachers are working with you at this time and the relationships you have with them. It knows what spiritual lessons you are working through at this time. You could ask how many lessons you came in to complete during this incarnation. It is the Chief Guide who coordinates the activities of your other guides according to your needs.

Christopher helped me to refine my meditation techniques. He was wonderful because there were many times I was frustrated with meditation. He always had the perfect suggestions for appropriate solutions to my energy problems at the time. He told me about directionality in meditation and was very specific about where I should sit due to the energies in my house. He knew I was unaware of the energy conditions that caused problems in my balance.

When formulating questions just remember that other than your Higher Self your Chief Guide is the one who usually knows the answer to your questions. If he does not know he will find the answer elsewhere or bring to the table a being who has the needed knowledge.

When you have finished communicating with your Chief Guide be sure to give him your love and appreciation for his answers and support. Ask him to bring to the table another guide of your choice. Just state which one is needed. Or if you prefer, you can dismiss your Chief Guide and request that your Table Guide come to the table to do the job of calling in other guides.

In order to help you with the decision of what guide to request, let us proceed with what the other guides' functions are.

THE KARMIC GUIDE
The Karmic Guide is involved with just that - your karma in this lifetime. Karma has a natural spiritual flow and will come into your life to be worked through regardless of your conscious involvement. However, having a conscious awareness of a karma helps you make choices about how to process it most efficiently and effectively.

The concept of karma in a modern sense means spiritual balance, thus whatever energy is or was exerted, a like energy is returned. It is the law of balance in cause and effect. In the Old Testament it meant an eye for an eye. In the New Testament Jesus taught about love and forgiveness - "Who shall cast the first stone." Karma is neither good nor bad, it simply exists for us to have opportunities to develop our awarenesses within a structure of balance. When you are in balance you will not be likely to create new karma. I believe that if we act from a spiritual level of love and let go of ego that we have the ability to step beyond the need for karma as a teacher. I feel that the human moral need to classify everything as either good or bad creates karma and if we let go of judgment in our lives we can release ourselves from karma.

Being impersonal can raise one above karma. Taking situations personally clouds your forgiveness and pulls you out of the unconditional level of love. It can make you forget you have choices and allow you to violate your own free will through your attachments to personal feelings. Thus detachment is a major step towards freedom from karma. Detachment from a pattern of habit, a person or an object frees us to change and enables us to more deeply enjoy what is in our lives. Detachment means you love enough to honor completely you own and another's free will. Detachment does not include interfering or worrying, it embraces surrender.

Since you have lived other lives and are working through lessons, there are always special souls you have interacted with that return to interact with you again. It is as if we are all actors on the stage called Life. We perform with other actors who are most often the same actors because we are familiar with them and perform the best with them. In some lives, our role is to be the taker and they, the giver. In other lives the roles are reversed. Some roles we act out are uncomfortable. There is little doubt that a soul has to love you deeply if it is presently playing a villain role in your life. Due to the acting out of its part you are able to learn lessons and balance energies by playing out your part.

Remember that karma is an opportunity for growth. When something is karmic it is not easily reversible unless you have reached a level of expressing spiritual unconditional love. Through spiritual love you are able to release yourself from karma due to your forgiveness of yourself and all others which dissolves karma through the grace of unconditional love.

Usually karma must be played out. However, remember you are not a victim of the process of karma because you have free will and can act accordingly.

One sitter was experiencing frustrating weekends at her home due to the noisy neighbors who partied every Saturday and Sunday. Her irritation went on for over a month. She had discussed with the neighbors that the noise kept her awake. They were polite and agreeable when facing her but continued the racket each weekend.

She decided to ask her guides if it was in her best interest to call the police and press charges against them in order to have some peace. Her Karmic Guide immediately came on the table. He told her to be patient and understanding for she was in karma with the people and that the parties would stop in one more week. He informed her that if she complained to the authorities she would not complete her karma.

Just as the guide had predicted the parties and noise stopped and the sitter had completed her karma effectively. She did not press charges against these people. In fact, they moved away soon after the incident.

You must be aware that there are different types of karmas. Karma involves balancing of energy in ways of thinking and feeling as well as in personal and relationship interactions. Where you are born and live is karmic for the country and the city where you live each has its own karma to balance. There can be a racial karma such as being born into a certain race in order to experience prejudice or racial limitations and to achieve a balance within them.

There are three basic categories of karma you might want to address with your guides or Higher Self: personal, situational and relationship. Situational karma is allowing a certain set of circumstances to occur in life in order to learn how to balance energies, such as, through an illness or financial difficulties. Personal karma includes the personal manner or habit that effects your performance in a situation. Control, patience, tolerance, unconditional love - all fit into this area of karma. Relationship karma deals with your interactions with people. These people have been chosen by you, usually before you were born, because they were the best and most familiar soul for you to learn lessons through.

The Karmic Guide like all the others will need to be explored first to establish its name, gender and some recognition of the personality involved. You will want to know if you had relationships in past lives or in spirit.

You could ask how many karmas you came into this life to work through, but at times this can be discouraging.

Some of the questions you may wish to ask of this guide are:
1. Am I presently involved in any karmas?
2. How many karmas am I working through at present? (N or T)
3. Is one of them a relationship karma?
4. Does this relationship karma pertain to my family relationships?
5. Does it pertain to my mate?
6. Does it pertain to a friend?
7. Is it a work place friendship that is involved?
8. Is it a personal friendship that is involved?
9. Do you have any advice for me as to how to work out this karma to my best interest? (A or T)

10. Am I near the completion of this karma?
11. Do I have karma on the physical body level?
12. Do I have karma on a mental level?
13. Do I have karma on an emotional level?
14. Am I presently working through a situational karma?
15. Is this situational karma in my work place?
16. Is it in my home?
17. Is there any specific happening that I should know about that will allow me to work through this karma? (PFQ)
     A. Are you willing to share information with me about that happening?
     B. Does sharing information with me have a negative effect on my learning process in this karma?
     C. If not then please help me to understand the details of that happening. (A or T)
18. Does this situational karma effect me on all levels of my being?
19. Does it effect me on a mental level?
20. Does it effect me on a physical body level?
21. Does it effect me on a spiritual level?
22. Does it effect me on an emotional level?
23. Is this situational karma a pattern I have been working with in many lives? (PFQ)
     A. Do you have a sense of earth time?
     B. When did this pattern begin? (N or T)
     C. What were the circumstances of that lifetime that brought about this karma? (A or T)
     D. Are there details you can share with me that will give me a deeper understanding of myself in relationship to this karmic pattern? (A or T)
24. Am I involved in a negative karma at this time? (This is to determine if you are indebted to create a balance.) (PFQ)
     A. Can you give me insights about handling this

karma?
   B. Please give them now. (A or T)
25.   Am I involved in a positive karma at this time? (This
      is to determine if you are on the receiving side of the
      balancing. You can repeat the previous PFQ)
26.   Do you have any advice that can help me to grace or
      release myself from karma through unconditional
      spiritual love? (A or T)

   When you find out if you have a karma at any of
the three basic levels you may be able to understand the
reasons for some of your present conditions. Be specific when
asking about the level of karma. Physical body unbalanced
conditions or complaints can be the result of karma on a
physical level. You can discover the reasons for a mental
condition or an attitude, by asking if a karma is on a mental
level. You will understand feelings such as fear and anger by
asking if it is an emotional level karma.
   You can find out if a karma is a negative karma, -
meaning you owe an energy debt or if a karma is a positive
karma - meaning that you are the receiver of the energy. In
this instance the terms positive and negative have no reference
to good or bad. Positive karma is when the energy flows
towards you and negative karma is when the energy flows from
you. Positive and negative karmas create a constant flow of
energy movement. However, if you maintain a state of
unconditional love a personal neutrality happens. You become
"in sync" with the universal flow of energy which is a higher
vibration than the earthly karmic flow. At this level of
vibrational flow you will notice a deep sense of unison with the
All which allows you to grace karma.
   I learned that I had a personal pattern in karma
which is situational, because I have been working with self-
confidence through many lifetimes. I find there are many
situations presented in this life as opportunities for me to clear

that karma. Through my discussions with my Karmic Guide I now know that the problem is a blockage that has affected me on all levels of my well-being (physical, emotional and mental) and slowed my spiritual growth for several lifetimes.

You may discover that a karma is long-term and will occur throughout most of this physical life. For example, your marriage can be karmic due to the fact that you and your marriage partner have a constant balancing and teaching interaction with each other. I see that as a fun, positive and supportive situational as well as relationship karma.

PSYCHIC GUIDE

Now you know how to become acquainted with each new guide that comes to the table. Once that is accomplished you can move on to the questions pertinent to each guide. The Psychic Guide is involved with your spiritual-psychic growth. Almost always it has studied with you in the psychic areas of your past lives.

My Psychic Guides have changed several times due to my growth and new requirements for effective spiritual progress. You may ascertain that there are several of them employing energies to assist you in this facet of your being. There are two Gypsies that like to participate with me while I do psychic readings. One is male and the other is a motherly female. They have known me in several past lives when I was Gypsy during the fourteenth through sixteenth centuries.

There is a mysterious green-eyed female guide who likes to work for me doing the research to locate deceased relatives and friends of students and clients who request such information. She is my strongest supporter in the crossing over of souls, which we will discuss later on in this book. This guide has shared several past life temple experiences with me. She expends great amounts of effort to support me in my psychic growth by pointing out the blockages I have had and explaining how to clear them. I feel her supporting love energy with me always.

Another Psychic Guide I have I perceive as a huge black man in a vivid red loin cloth and shirt decorated with beautiful Macaw feathers. He is a warrior and a strong leader. His role is to be my psychic protector. He keeps me safe by reminding me of my own strength. He warns me not to collect or demonstrate fear whenever I am near less than Light forces or actual Dark energies because of my work. His strength gives me courage and security when I am in an area that I sense has unsavory spiritual energies or powerfully negative people. He is a universal level Psychic Guide because he can be assigned by me in special instances to protect others.

Some of the questions that are appropriately within a Psychic Guide's area of expertise are the following;

1. Can you help me to know some of the psychic abilities I achieved in my past lives? (This guide does not have to have lived with you when you mastered these abilities. It can read this information from your aura or your soul records.)
2. Do I have the ability of clairsentience?
3. Do I have the ability of clairvoyance? Clairaudience? Psychokinesis? Channeling Healing energy? Mediumship?
4. Do I have the abilities to be a physical medium?
5. Do I have the ability to be a mental medium?
6. Do I have the ability to be a spiritual medium?
7. Do I have the ability to channel?
8. Is it in my best interest to be a voice channel?
9. Is it in my best interest to be a conscious channel?
10. Is it in my best interest to do trance channeling?
11. Is it in my best interest to channel in the form of inspired writing?
12. Is the channeling I can do for personal use only?
13. Is my channeling for public use?
14. Is it in my best interest to own a table and use it for

spiritual growth?

15. Am I prepared or ready to work with the table at this time?

16. Do I have the ability to interpret dreams for others?

17. Do I have the ability to receive predictive dreams?

18. Do I have the ability to lucid dream?

19. Have I learned any psychic skills in a past life I shared with you?

20. Do you have a sense of historical earth time? (PFQ)
(If this guide does not understand earth time or history, ask it to get the help of a spirit who does, such as your Chief Guide.)

21. Would you tell me historically when I practiced these talents? (PFQ)
A. What time in history did I practice these talents? (T or N)
B. What talents did I practice at that time? (A or T)

22. Do you have a sense of the geography of the earth?
(If this guide does not know earth geography then repeat the process you used for question 20.)

23. Can you tell me where I studied to learn how to develop these psychic abilities? (A or T.)

24. Have I ever misused any of my psychic talents in past lives?

25. Can you help me to understand in what way and why that happened?

26. Was it due to my lower ego expression?

27. Did I have a need to control others?

28. Are there other reasons why? (A or T)

29. Have I grown enough spiritually to use these abilities effectively and positively in this lifetime?

30. Have I ever been persecuted for practicing my psychic abilities? (If the answer is **Yes** proceed to the next question.)

31. When did that persecution occur? (N or T)

32. Did I ever suffer a death for using my psychic-

spiritual abilities?
33. How many times? (N or T)
34. Do I have blockages that prevent my awareness of my full psychic ability due to the fears stored in my body's cell memories from these persecutions? (PFQ)
A. Can you tell me where these blockages are located? (A or T)
B. Will you give guidance as to how I can release these blockages?
C. Please give that information now. (A or T)
35. Is it in my best interest to be using these talents in this lifetime?
36. If so, which one of the psychic skills is it in my best interest to use? (You will have to go through the list of skills mentioned before one-by-one getting the answer for each ability. PFQ)
A. Will you give guidance as to how to best use this skill?
B. Please give me that guidance now. (A or T)
37. Is it in my best interest to develop any new spiritual-psychic abilities in this lifetime? (PFQ)
A. What ability is in my best interest to develop? (A or T)
B. Have you any guidance on how to best develop that ability?
C. Please give that advice now. (A or T)
38. Do I have more than one psychic guide at this time?
A. If so, how many? (T or N)
B. Why do I have more than one psychic guide? (A or T)
39. Is it in my best interest to use my psychic talents to work for the good of others in this lifetime?
40. Which talents would they be? (Again go through the list one by one. Example: Is it the ability to channel healing energy to others? Then determine on what level you have the ability to heal; spiritual, mental, emotional, physical. Ask about each level

when identifying the talent.)

When you inquire about the different types of mediumship you will need an understanding of the different levels of being a medium. A medium is a person who connects one plane or dimension of existence with another. For example, if you find out that you are a physical medium, it means you can use physical tools to communicate with spirit such as a pendulum, the cards (Tarot or regular playing cards), a crystal ball or the table. A mental medium is one who has the telepathic capacity to connect mentally with persons who are physically incarnate and other dimensional existences such as other planetary beings that could be between the fourth and fifth dimensions. If you discover that you are a spiritual medium it means you have the ability to connect with spirit on all planes or dimensions no matter how evolved they may be. You are also capable of channeling the information received.

It is very helpful to determine if you are a voice channel or one who receives through writing. You may be a channel for music or visual arts, such as painting or drawing. Next, you will want to question if the channeled material you receive is for personal use only or is it to be shared with others in a public manner.

When you ask about dream abilities, you may discover that you have the talent to go into the dream state with a conscious quest, have a dream and wake up with your answers. You can determine if you have the ability to have predictive dreams (the receiving of precognitive information about yourself or others) or prophetic dreams (the receiving of precognitive information about world events and happenings). Your Psychic Guide will help you understand how you can personally develop your dream abilities and conscious recall.

The Psychic Guide is willing to help you with

understanding how to awaken past life psychic talents. It will give you personalized instruction and directions as to how to manifest psychic talents that may be new to you in this particular life. This guide's goal is to help you to comfortably relate to the other dimensions on an inner level so you can grow spiritually with an independent awareness. Be open to its unique guidance about your spiritual-psychic abilities.

TIMING GUIDE

This spiritual entity should have a sense of time including an ability to acknowledge earth time. A Timing Guide is directly involved with the cycles in your life and with the proper timing to activate or detach from things in your life. This guide will lend its knowing to the everyday problems that are concerned with the elements of earth time as well as that of spiritual timing.

This spiritual friend will help you become aware of the specific timing of spiritual meetings that may include your spiritual Self during your meditation or sleep. These ethereal gatherings can alert you to new growth levels and possible initiations that you are going through as well as to the preparations you can make to be consciously aware of the processes of your spiritual growth. (I believe that initiations are personal spiritual energy events that help to ground into your whole being the new vibrational levels of personal growth achievements you have accomplished.) I have been consciously aware of a few I have had. During such a ceremony spirit establishes within your aura the higher vibrational level that you have achieved, creating a stability to that level and establishing it in your aura in a rather permanent manner. The initiations I have witnessed are very ceremonial and have beautifully raised my whole being to my newly earned growth level with a strong degree of permanency. Spiritual growth levels strengthened by initiation ceremonies tend to reinforce your personal strength enabling you to stay on your spiritual growth path with fewer energy setbacks.

Often your Timing guide can let you know if you are a Spring or a Fall energy person. This means that during one of these equinoxes you spiritually vibrate with a special attunement that can activate an alignment power of conscious awareness during your meditations and dreams through which you can be made aware of your spiritual assignments for the year. It is at your special equinox that you are blessed with the gifts of spirit. Often a full earth year will be required for your being to absorb, balance and bring these gifts into practical use.

Throughout all of our lives we grow within nine year cycles. You might ask in what year in the nine year cycle you are presently expressing yourself. The first year is one of personal growth, independence and new starts. The second year is for receptivity, patience and includes emphasis on partnerships and cooperation with others. The third year is a time for expansion of mind and self, creativity and bringing about fruition. The fourth year is centered on organization, applying yourself practically and laying out the groundwork for physical projects. The fifth year is for planning and taking action in areas of change that have a long term effect. It is a time of power and magnetism. The sixth year is focused on the home and family, responsibilities; it is a time of beautifying yourself and your atmosphere. The seventh year is for self-introspection; it is to be a quiet time of rest and not a time to take on new projects or concerns. The eighth year is for balancing out responsibilities and organizing your strengths; it is a time of power money, emotional balancing and successes in the physical plane. The ninth year is a time of endings, cleansing, detaching and letting go. It is also a time of travel and universality.

Some of the questions you can ask of this guide are:
1. Have you recently incarnated here on earth?
2. Are you aware of the manner in which earth time is measured such as by the clock or by the calendar?

(You are fortunate if the answer is **Yes** to this question because it means this guide is capable of helping you with all time cycles; spiritual, mundane and personal time-related questions.)

3. Is it in my best interest to start my project (Please describe your intended project clearly.) at this time?

4. Am I ready at this time for new levels of spiritual awareness?

5. Am I ready for any new spiritual assignments? (PFQ)
   A. Is it in my best interest to consciously know about these assignments?
   B. Will you give information as to what they may be?
   C. Please give that information now? (A or T)

6. Am I beginning any new spiritual lessons at this time? (PFQ)
   A. Is it in my best interest to know about these lessons?
   B. Will you help me to understand what they are?
   C. Please give me that information now. (A or T)

7. Are there any spiritual meetings I will attend soon?

8. Is it in my best interest to know when these meetings will be held in order to be prepared? (PFQ)
   A. When, in earth time, will the next meeting occur? (T or N)
   B. Is it in my best interest to be more actively and consciously involved ?

9. Is there any preparation I can do to enable me to be conscious of my attendance during one of these meetings? (PFQ)
   A. Will you help me to understand what that preparation is?
   B. Please tell me now what I can do to be prepared? (A or T)

10. What time of day is it best for me, on a personal energy vibration level to meditate? (N or T)

11. Am I personally affected in any manner by the phases

of the moon? (PFQ)

A. Is it in my best interest to know which phases effect me and how? (A or T)

B. Please give me that information now. (A or T)

12. Does the timing of any of the sun's activities such as solar flares, sun spots, eclipses or seasonal placement affect my personal energies? (PFQ)

A. Can you help me to understand which one ?

B. Please give me the details about the effect of sun activity upon me now. (A or T)

13. Do any of these solar or lunar activities affect my spiritually telepathic receptivity?

14. Help me to understand in what way now. (A or T)

15. Do these activities affect my mental telepathy with other incarnate people?

16. Are you willing to answer mundane timing questions? (If the answer is **Yes** then proceed to the next questions.)

17. From your vantage point of timing, is it in my best interest to make any career changes at this time?

18. Is it in my best interest to move at this time?

19. Is it in my best interest to sell my car at this time?

20. If it is not the time to sell my car can you help me to understand about a better time to consider such a sale? (A or T)

Always make sure that the guide answers **Yes** to the question of whether it wishes to deal with mundane affairs before asking about the material life concerns. *Just remember that this guide's purpose is only to assist you with timing, not to make the decision that you should sell your car, or move, etc..*

CREATIVE GUIDE

This guide supports you in all areas of your creativity. It is a very inspirational helper that sometimes demonstrates incredible ingenuity in the means it uses to activate your capacities. Mine devises ingenious ways to communicate to me through the different people I encounter within one day. This enables me to consciously receive, piece by piece, spirit's creative idea. I have grown accustomed to the fascinating fun of gathering hidden clues from within the conversations people have with me throughout the day.

If you are currently involved in any of the arts: performing, visual, musical, literary, etc., this guide is very active in your scheme of events even though you are not aware of its participation. If you are active in any of these fields of creativity professionally this guide is usually experienced in the area of your specialty. Sometimes there are guides who are historically famous personalities inspiring the artists of today. You may have a recognized expert from the past who is your support and guidance for inventive endeavors.

If you are exceptionally talented in this life, your creative guide may have assistants working with it because of your special needs. Even though you may think you are not creative, you still have a creative guide stimulating you to do things in your own way - expressing yourself uniquely in whatever you do. This guide will help you to feel and express creativity as a spiritual flow of energy.

Through this guide you can research past-life creative talents. You can open your awareness to the role of creativity in your spiritual progress in this life.

Some of the questions you can ask this guide are:
1.   Have I had specific creative talents in past lives? (PFQ) A. Is it in my best interest to know what these talents were?
B. (If the answer is **Yes**) Please help me to know what those talents were now. (A or T)
2.   Was there a specific talent that I used as my means to earn a living in a past life?(PFQ)

A. What was that talent? (A or T)

3.   Was I ever historically famous in the arts? (If the answer is **Yes**, ask the following six questions.)

4.   Was my recognition in the visual arts?

5.   Was my recognition in the performing arts?

6.   Was my recognition in the musical arts?

7.   Was my recognition in the communication arts?

8.   Was my recognition in the scientific or medical vocations?

9.   Was my recognition in the philosophical field?

10. Is it in my best interest to be using any of my past life acquired talents in a professional manner in this lifetime? (If the answer is **Yes**, ask which talent it is by asking about different talents one at a time. You may also want to repeat this process if the answer to question 11. is **Yes**.)

11. Is it in my best interest to be using any of those past life talents as a hobby for my own pleasure in this lifetime?

12. Are there any creative projects that I came in to fulfill in this lifetime? (If the answer is **Yes**, follow up with specific questions to determine the details of the project.)

13. Is there a creative project that could have a profound effect on my spiritual progress in this lifetime? (PFQ)

     A. Is it in my best interest to know what that project is at this time?

     B. (If the answer is **Yes**) Please give me details about that project at this time. (A or T)

14. Is it in my best interest to be using any of my creative potentials for the good of humanity as a whole in this lifetime? (PFQ)

A. (To determine which talent it may be call out each talent in question form such as ; Is it my ability to sing?)

B. What is your advice about this talent and its use? (A or T)

JOY GUIDE

This guide is loving, humorous and sincere in its efforts to bring happiness and joy into your life. Joy Guides usually are very energetic with their table movements. You will know their job is to make you laugh and have fun by their antics on the table. This guide may be the one who has put a repetitious tune in your head. Mine is "Waltzing Matilda". It was a real awakening that this particular tune was coming from my Joy Guide. I know that throughout my life this particular tune comes into my mind often and it is always accompanied by a joyous feeling of personal inspiration.

These guides tend to make you notice rainbows, bird songs and the laughter of little children. They make sure those things and hundreds of other naturally happy events come into your life, especially when you are in rapport with their supportive efforts.

Their greatest frustration is that even though they have helped us by bringing into our lives little and big joys, we often are so focused on the negative aspects of our lives that we rarely allow ourselves to recognize and live joy.

Ask this guide for the physical signals it can give to let you know that it is present. A physical signal my Joy guide gives me is a bright white spark in my field of vision. I notice its flash in my eye when this guide is up to something to create a laugh or a silent giggle on my part. Determining the techniques which your Joy Guide uses to bring happiness into your life will help you recognize its work and fully enjoy its efforts.

Questions for this guide could be:

1. Do you have a special signal you could choose to use to let me know of your presence? (If **Yes** proceed to 2.)
2. Will you let me experience that signal now?
3. Please send that signal now. (A or T)
4. Have you brought any specific situations or persons into my life to create joy? (PFQ)
   A. What persons have you brought to create joy? (A or T)
   B. What situations have you brought to create joy? (A or T)
5. What are some of the concepts I need to be aware of at this time to attract joy to my life? (A or T)
4. What joys did you bring to me today that I did not recognize? (A or T.)
5. Am I aware of most of the happy events that happen to and around me within a day of my life?
6. Do you have any suggestions that will help me sense the joys of life? (A or T)
7. I know that enthusiasm is the natural spiritually flowing emotion, can you help me to understand what blockages I have that restricts my enthusiasm for life?
8. Do I have repressed anger that restricts me from feeling joy? (If the answer is **Yes**, use PFQ)
   A. Will you will assist me to understand the details of the nature of this restriction?
   B. Please send the details now. (A or T)
9. Do I have repressed grief that restricts me from feeling joy? (If the answer is **Yes**, use PFQ)
   A. Will you assist me to understand the details of the nature of the restriction?
   B. Please send the details now. (A or T)
10. Do I have fears that restrict me from feeling joy? (If the answer is affirmative, proceed with the next question.)
11. What fear restricts me at this time? (A or T)

12. Will you send to me a peaceful joyous energy through the table now, so that I can experience it and be healed enough to initiate my own spiritual flow of joy? (If affirmative use T.)

13. Do you have any guidance as to how I can develop my self awareness to the growth level necessary to allow me to always perceive ways to joyously approach any situation? (If **Yes** then use PFQ)
A. Please send that advice now? (T)

14. Are there past life patterns that are preventing me from feeling joy? (If the answer is **Yes** move on to the next question.)

15. Will you help me to discover what these patterns are? (If the answer is **Yes** move on to the next question.)

16. Please send to us an understanding of that lifetime and the situation that caused the restricting pattern. (A or T)

17. Please advise me as to how I can best release this emotional restriction. (A or T and proceed to the next questions.)

18. Is it in my best interest to release this restriction through a meditational technique?

19. Will you assist me at this time to understand what that technique includes? (If the answer is **Yes** use (PFQ) A. Is it a visualization technique?
B. Please tell me about the technique now. (A or T)

20. Is it in my best interest to release this restriction through bodywork such as therapeutic massage? (If the answer is **Yes** you can ask about specific types of body work such as Rolfing.)

21. Is it in my best interest to release this restriction through energy work? (If the answer is **Yes** then you can ask about specific types of energy work techniques such as Reiki.)

22. Would it be helpful to use crystals, minerals or stones in my work of releasing these restrictions?

23. Is it in my best interest to release this restriction

through chanting? (If the answer is **Yes** then ask the guide to help you know your personalized words to chant and the exact musical tones to use for your vibration, A or T.)

Through this guide I have discovered that I had many restrictions stored in the cell memory of my physical body from past lives. When I released them, with this guide's guidance, I was freed to enjoy the now.

Researching your emotions with the help of this cheerful guide will assist you to understand your emotional self which will help you express emotions in a healthy way. Freeing up and understanding your emotional self will release you from repressed angers and fears which will lead you to a natural peace and joy.

Through this guide you will touch into the memory of your real Self who is filled with joy. Each time you experience this joy of the Self, you will be able to feel and express it easier in your daily life.

BLUEPRINT GUIDE

This particular guide knows your plan or projected path for this life. I do not feel it is possible for a person to be off path. Sometimes a person's free will can change the pattern of the original soul plan. I think many of us, all too often, procrastinate by holding on to what we know and not moving forward into change. There are times we will actually suffer pain and endure great stress because a situation is familiar or comfortable to our emotional body. It is the emotional body which clings to the old routines even though they may be boring, unproductive and even painful. This guide then, is one you can ask these types of questions:

1. Am I actively participating with my original soul plan?
2. Has my personal being altered my original soul plan in any way? (If the answer is **Yes** then proceed to

question 3.)

3. Can you help me to understand what changes were made? (A or T)

4. Can you help me to understand why the changes were made? (PFQ)

   A. Did any part of my being sense a need to change the plan due to my personal self deciding I could accomplish more in this life than I had originally planned?

   B. Did the plan of a family member effect my plan?

   C. Did my whole self, (soul, Higher Self & Divine Self) feel the need to adjust my original plan?

   D. Is it in my best interest to understand at this time what was changed? (If **Yes** pursue the subject more.)

5. Is it in my best interest to make any changes in my present soul plan? (Sometimes because you have opened your awarenesses you can write a plan that is more direct and less difficult. Remember a part of your own being wrote the original plan - thus you, in agreement with that part of your being, can rewrite your plan if you are unhappy with it at this time.)

6. If it is possible to rewrite my soul plan, can you help me to understand how to do just that?

7. Will you advise me now about the specifics of that possibility? (A or T)

8. If I were to rewrite the plan can you give me specific details about why it is in my best interest to do so? (A or T)

9. Am I presently following my planned spiritual program?

10. Is the present type of occupation I am doing coordinating with my spiritual path?

11. Am I currently working through most of the projects that I chose to involve myself with in this life?

12. Is there a project, I need to be aware of, that is on my path that I have not started? (If the answer is **Yes** you will need to ask what that project is A or T.)

(PFQ)

A. Is it in my best interest to know what that project is at this time?

B. (If A is answered **Yes** ask B) What is the project? (A or T)

13. With reference to my life span in this incarnation am I up to date with my spiritual plan?

14. Is my current relationship with _____ in coordination with my planned spiritual path? (If the answer is **Yes** or **No** you can use PFQ)

A. Is it in my best interest that you give me more details about why?

B. (If the Answer is **Yes** then ask B) Please tell me why at this time. (A or T)

15. Do you have suggestions about any new persons or situations on my path that I need to be aware of at this time? (A or T)

HEALTH GUIDE

This guide does not replace your earth plane doctor; always ask him about your physical, mental and emotional problems. Nevertheless, your Health Guide has a special awareness of your well-being on all levels: spiritually, mentally, emotionally and physically. This guide sees your whole energy picture by observing your aura. It is available to answer your questions about your physical body: its weaknesses, strengths and physical probabilities that can be related to your present spiritual, mental and emotional self as well as your past life energy cell memories.

It can help you to identify allergies. All you have to do is ask about specific foods or airborne pollens, etc., one at a time. An example is, "Am I allergic to wheat?" My little niece was very sick so we asked her Health Guide for help. The guide told us that she was allergic to rice at the time. Her mother was amazed. But she said the information was surely correct, because in retrospect she realized the baby became ill right after she began eating rice cereal. Once the baby was taken off the rice cereal she was fine.

The Health Guide concerns itself with your attitudes and emotions since that is most often where your physical problems originate. Heed this guide's advice about your emotional and mental habits because you can prevent illnesses and accidents with its information. **WHENEVER YOU ARE EXPERIENCING A PHYSICAL HEALTH PROBLEM CONSULT YOUR MEDICAL DOCTOR** and this guide as to the real cause. Always question separately about a spiritual, mental or emotional reason for the condition.

Some typical questions to present to this guide are:

1. Do I presently have any allergies?
2. Am I allergic to any foods?
3. To what foods am I reacting? (A or T then verify what you receive. Such as, "Did I understand correctly that I am allergic to wheat?")
4. Am I allergic to anything in the air ?
    (If the Answer is **Yes** to questions 4, 5 or 6 use PFQ)
    A. Is it in my best interest to know what is the allergen?
    B. What is the allergen? (A or T)
5. Am I allergic to anything in my home?
6. Am I allergic to anything at work?
7. Do I have any emotional problems at this time that are affecting me physically?
8. Are these emotional problems based in fear? (If this is so - have the guide help you to identify this fear. PFQ)
    A. Is it in my best interest to know at this time what fear is causing my problem?
    B. Please tell me about this fear now. (A or T)
    C. Can you help me to identify its source?
    D. Is the source from past lives?
    E. Please give me some details that will render a

deeper understanding about this fear now. (A or T)

9. Are these emotional problems based in repressed anger? (If the answer is **Yes** apply the suggested PFQ for question 8 replacing the concept of fear with the concept anger.)

10. Are these emotional problems based in repressed grief? (If the answer is **Yes** apply the suggested PFQ for question 8 replacing the concept of fear with the concept of grief.)

11. Do I have any mental attitudes that are affecting me physically? (Always follow up **Yes** answers to questions 11 - 14 with direct questions to understand the specific details for understanding the causes.)

12. Are these mental attitudes based in fear?

13. Are these mental attitudes based in repressed anger?

14. Are these mental attitudes based in repressed grief?

15. Do I presently have any physical conditions that are carried over from a past life? (If the answer is **Yes**, PFQ)
    A. What is that condition? (A or T)
    B. Is it in my best interest to know the details of that particular past life?
    C. (If the answer to B is **Yes**, then ask C.) Please give me the details from that past life that will help me towards a better understanding of my present physical problem now. (A or T)

16. Is there a process that I can do to release myself from this condition?

17. Can you help me to understand this process?

18. Will you now tell me about a step-by-step method to perform this process? (If **Yes** then use PFQ.)
    A. Please give me the details of how to perform the process now. (A or T.)

19. Am I currently learning a lesson through a physical problem?

20. Are you willing to share with me what that lesson is?
     (If **Yes** then use PFQ.)
     A. Please share that information now. (A or T)
21. When I have learned this lesson will you advise me
     as to how to release the need for the physical
     problem in order for me to heal the condition?
     (If **Yes** then use PFQ.)
     A. Do you have any suggestions as to how to release
     the problem?
     B. (If the answer to A is **Yes**, then ask B.)
     Please give your suggestions now. (A or T)
22. Do you have any dietary suggestions for my whole
     well-being? (If the answer is **Yes**, use PFQ.)
     A. Are there specific foods I have been eating that
     are not beneficial for my well-being at this time?
     B. Is there a specific food that would be in my best
     interest to begin eating at this time?
     C. Please give your suggestions about my present
     diet now. (A or T)
23. Do you have any suggestions concerning my personal
     sleep patterns that may be of help to my well-
     being? (If affirmative use PFQ.)
     A. I am open and ready to receive your suggestions
     now. (A or T)
24. Do you have any suggestions about any of my present
     habit patterns that could be helpful to my well-
     being? (If the answer is **Yes** use the PFQ from
     question 23.)
25. Are there any physical body problems or defects that
     I have inherited from my ancestral gene pool that
     are not necessary for me to endure now for a lesson?
26. If the answer to 25. is **Yes** ask 26. Can you help me to
     identify what the problem or problems are? (If the
     answer is **Yes** use the PFQ)
     A. Please send that information now. (A or T)
27. Can you help me with how to release these problems
     from my physical body cells so that they will be

healthy? (If the answer is Yes use PFQ.)

A. Please tell me how now. (A or T)

28. Do I have any physical ailments that are karmic? (If the answer is **Yes**, proceed to the next questions.)

29. Can you help me to consciously understand why I spiritually have chosen a karmic ailment? (If the answer is **Yes** use PFQ.)

A. Please send the information you have to help me understand now. (A or T)

30 Can you help me to understand exactly what that ailment is ? (If the answer is **Yes**, use PFQ.)

A. Please send that information now. (A or T)

31. Is it in my best interest to clear up this karma and release this ailment at this time? (If answer is **Yes**, use PFQ.)

A. Are you willing to share with me how to do that?

B. (If the answer is **Yes** use B.) I am now open to your suggestions, please send them. (A or T)

32. Is it possible to balance this karma any other way?

33. Is it possible to grace this karma with love?

34. Is it possible to grace this karma with forgiveness?

35 Is there another suggestion of how to grace this karma?

36. Do you have advice about how to grace this karma?

37. I am open, please give me that advice now. (A or T)

TABLE GUIDE

This guide is necessary when you have your own table or when you are the operator of the table. The first question to ask of this guide is, "Is it in my best interest to own a table and use it as a spiritual tool?"

This guide's job is similar to that of a diplomat. It must be able to network and connect with all the varieties of spiritual energies you wish to communicate with through the table. It needs to know the rules for your table work because if it thoroughly understands all the techniques, it can teach each new entity approaching the table how to proceed with the energy exchanges necessary for communication with you. This saves a great deal of time and the possible frustration to all those involved.

The Table Guide must be alert and strong as it is a protector of the table, you and the other sitters. One of this guide's primary jobs is to keep the table within the white Light as best it can. You may continually check with this guide to find out if you are protected when you are using the table. You can give it the duty, with your permission, to interrupt communications at any time if it senses there is an astral or non-Light being on or near the table. Another aspect of this guide's job is to inform you if the energies of the physical location are inappropriate for table tipping.

Since this guide collects the energies for your communications it is important that it be multi-dimensional and have the special capacity to travel into many dimensions. Your Table Guide is the best entity to employ to start the movement of the table for each session. It is the guide who can close down the table as you and it give full appreciation to all the spiritual energies who worked with you during the sitting.

Once you have met this guide and established your working relationship, it will usually be present and working at every table gathering unless you request that it not participate for some reason. If this guide's energy seems ineffective in any way when you are tipping do not hesitate to ask for a replacement spirit for this guide's position. It is beneficial if you acquaint yourself with this guide's distinctive energy essence and its personalized style of moving the table for a quicker identification and an enhanced awareness of its presence. This awareness creates an effective relationship between you and this guide giving it much more efficiency in its job.

Some of the questions you will want to ask this

guide are:

1. Are you capable of traveling through several dimensions to request entities of all levels to come to our table?

2. Is it possible for you to connect with the spiritual hierarchy such as Archangels and masters to work with us if needed?

3. Are you capable of calling in the highest vibration of helpful energies available when it is necessary to assist us in crossing over souls? (The answer should be affirmative to questions 1, 2, and 3. If it is not - immediately make the request for a different, more powerful spirit to be your Table Guide.)

4. Are we protected at this time?

5. Are we seated in the best positions for a productive and efficient energy flow of our spiritual energy circle? (If the answer is **No**, the use PFQ.)
   A. Is it in our best interest to change some of the sitter's positions?
   B. Please lean the table towards the person who needs to change placement now.
   C. Please lean the table towards the position they need to take now.

6. Are we located in the most positive energy area available here? (If the answer is **No**, use PFQ.)
   A. Please tell us where it is best for us according to the present flow of energy available? (A or T)

7. Will you please interrupt the table's movement if there is a negative or astral energy present?

8. Will you demonstrate for us your special personalized style of table movement that is your signal to us that you are present? (If **Yes** use PFQ.)
   A. Show us the signal movement now?
   B. Please enhance the power of your energy field, at this moment, so that we may in some way familiarize our sensitivity to your presence around

us and on the table now. (T)

9. Is it in our best interest to begin each table session by calling you to the table first?

10. Then will you be the initiator of the table's movement at the beginning of each session?

11. Do you understand our **Yes** and **No** table signals?

12. Will you explain to each new entity that comes to the table about the appropriate rules for tipping?

GALACTIC GUIDE

The Galactic Guide knows the record of your spiritual and diverse form incarnations on other planets in this solar system as well as in other solar systems or galaxies within the universe. Sometimes, the information received from this guide seems impossible to believe from your present reference point of reality. This guide can open many horizons for you about your whole Self if you allow them to happen.

A Galactic Guide - if you can see it - is usually very different from you in form or appearance. Sometimes, it is just an energy and other times it is a light formed with color hues that you cannot perceive here on earth. I have seen Galactic Guides which look huge and hairy only because they are formed with a soft, furry, fuzzy light. Some of them are small and crystalline while others are radiant lights that form a wondrous flower shaped energy. You must be very open-minded when sensing and questioning this guide.

Some of the questions you might ask of this guide are the following:

1. Have I ever incarnated on other planets, suns or stars in past lives?

2. Have I experienced more life-times on other planets than I have here on earth?

3. Have I incarnated on other planets in this particular solar system?

4. Was any of my other planetary incarnations in some other dimensional form than third-dimensional? (If

the answer is **Yes** ask, use question 5. as PFQ.)

5. Can you help me to remember the appearance and other details about my existence in this form? (If **Yes**, then use PFQ.)

   A. Please send an image and an understanding of that form now. (A or T)

6. What was my existence like in that incarnation in reference to culture or social routine? (A or T)

7. What lessons did I learn through that type of existence? (A or T.)

8. Why did I choose that special existence to learn through? (A or T)

9. Are there any special gifts or abilities I achieved in my other world incarnations? (If **Yes**, use PFQ.)

   A. Please send information about them at this time. (A or T)

10. Did I ever incarnate on the sun of this solar system? (If **Yes**, use PFQ.)

    A. Please help me to remember what that existence was like now. (A or T)

11. Have I incarnated on or in planets outside of this solar system but still within this galaxy?

12. Have I incarnated on planets outside of this galaxy?

13. Was any one of these existences in a three dimensional form? (If the answer is **Yes**, use PFQ.)

    A. Have I experienced several different types of third-dimensional forms?

    B. How many different third-dimensional forms have I experienced? (N)

    C. Can you help me to see how some of these forms appeared? (If **Yes**, ask D.)

    D. Please send an image of one of the forms to me now? (T)

    E. Please help me to understand the value of my existence within that form now. (A or T)

14. Did I ever express myself in a purely mental form?

(If the answer is **Yes**, use PFQ.)
A. What did I learn while in that form? (A or T)
B. Please let me sense what that existence was like now. (A or T)

15. Did I ever express myself on another planet or sun in a spiritual body form? (If **Yes**, repeat PFQ for 14.)
16. Did I ever express myself in a fourth or fifth dimensional Lightbody form? (If the answer is **Yes**, repeat PFQ from 14.)
17. Do I have any missions to perform in this lifetime that are connected with these past intergalactic lives? (If the answer is **Yes** use PFQ.)
A. Is it in my best interest to know at this time what they are? (If **Yes** use B.)
B. Please give me an understanding of what one of them may be now. (A or T)
18. Is there any spiritual duty that I am to perform in this incarnation in reference to these space lives? (If **Yes**, repeat the concepts of PFQ from 17.)
19. Are there any people that I know in this lifetime that have shared other planetary lives with me? (If **Yes** use PFQ.)
A. Is it in my best interest to know who they are?
B. (If the answer is **Yes**, then use B.) Please send an understanding of who they are, now. (A or T)
C. Can you give me insights into what our life together in that existence was like?
D. (If the answer is **Yes** then ask D.) Please give those insights now. (A or T)

Some sitters find out that they are representing souls from another planet. Performing as teachers, they share their experiences in this physical body with souls on that home planet so they can learn vicariously. The souls on the home planet may simply want an understanding of the limitations of the physical body and by experiencing them through a volunteer, they do not have to be on earth or live an earth life themselves. The volunteer often travels out-of-body at night to the home planet, while the physical body is sleeping and shares the day's experiences with souls wanting to learn about planet earth.

You may find out that you have specific extra-terrestrial missions to accomplish while you are here on earth. You may discover that you are at one with the Space Brothers, who are here on and around the earth for service. Through your communication explorations with your Galactic Guide you may gain an understanding of why you have felt differently from the rest of the earthlings.

Due to past life other-planetary experiences you may have sensitivities you need to understand in order to awaken their usefulness. One sitter was extra-sensitive to physical vibrations and sound. Through the information from her Galactic Guide, she discovered it was a talent she brought into this life to use for reading the vibrations of the planet to predict earthquakes. She was also able to sense unusual sound wave vibrations from the earth and the physical body to determine where to direct healing energies.

Sometimes, a soul has a different emotional attitude from most earthlings due to a purely mental type of existence on another planet in a recent past life. Many answers to so-called problems of imbalance in this life can be discovered in discussions with the Galactic Guide.

This guide can be one of the most fascinating energies to call to the table due to the new understandings you can gain from its vantage point of experience with you as a whole spiritual being. Always take the time to ask it about the past life experiences it has shared with you and why it has chosen to be a guide for you now. Through it you will learn about other civilizations, societies and excitingly different realities, about which you may have consciously forgotten, that a soul can exist within to learn and grow.

MASTER GUIDE

The Master Guide is the special spiritual teacher who instructed you while you were in spirit preparing to come into this incarnation. Often this entity has not incarnated for many centuries or may never have lived an actual earth life. You may have worked with this energy only in spirit. Since it performs the role of spiritual teacher it seems less personal and somewhat stern in comparison to your other guides. Sometimes you will still work with it in spirit while you are asleep and are out-of-body. In the out-of-body state you may attend classes with this special teacher who acts then like a coach or a patient mentor. Before this lifetime you studied your lessons in the etheric halls of learning and you are now here performing them. The situation is similar to having a music instructor teaching you the performance techniques and the musical score while critically observing you practice. Then it remains in spirit and sends you on to the stage of life to perform.

This master knows the basic principles of growth that you are working through in this lifetime. It knows how you planned the circumstances of your performance and what lessons are within them.

I respect this guide and consider it as important as my Chief Guide. Realize its serious qualities and stern focus make it an effective and loving coach.

Some of the suggested questions for this guide are:

1. Am I involved in any of the major lessons I chose to learn in this life at the present time?
2. Can you tell me how many? (N)
3 Is it in my best interest at this time to know more about each of them?
4. Will you help me to know more about one of them now? (If the answer is **Yes**, use PFQ.)
   A. Please give me the necessary information to understand one of them now. (A or T)

(If there is more than one, with the guide's
permission, ask to understand each one.)

5. Can you tell me the number of lessons I came into this
life to learn? (If the answer is **Yes**, use PFQ.)
A. How many lessons? (N)

6. How many of these lessons have I already learned?
(N)

7. Can you help me to understand what those lessons
were? (A or T. Form PFQ questions for a **Yes** or
No answer to clarify your perceptions.)

8. How many of these lessons have I yet to learn? (N)

9. Can you help me to understand what they are? (If you
receive a **Yes** answer use PFQ.)
A. Please send information that will help me to
clarify what they are now. (A or T)

10. Have you any suggestions to help me learn any one of
these lessons effectively? (If **Yes** use PFQ.)
A. Please send them now. (A or T)

11. Have you any suggestions for improvements in my
performance in my present situation? (If **Yes** repeat
PFQ from 10.)

12. Am I studying in any spiritual classes with you at
night during my sleep?

13. What am I studying in these classes? (A or T)

14. Is there anything I can do to gain a conscious awareness
and a better recall of my night studies?

15. Is it in my best interest at this time to have a conscious
memory of my night classes? (If **Yes** use PFQ.)
A. What are your suggestions to enhance my
conscious recall? (A or T)

16. Am I involved in any other type of night work while I
sleep that is for my spiritual growth?

17. Will you help me right now to understand what that
work might be? (A or T)

18. Have you a message for me at this time? (A or T)
All of these questions are important to ask of the

Master Guide because it will give you a different perspective than any other source. But you will discover that inquiring about the same material is tremendously important to ask of the Higher Self due to the depth at which it can handle such inquiries. Questions for the Higher Self will be presented in an enhanced format in Part E of this chapter.

RELATIONSHIP GUIDE

When you are involved with certain people in an intimate way, you can use this guide as a resource to get help or understanding about that relationship. This guide seems to involve itself more readily in your longer term relationships. It expends a great deal of effort to assist you to maintain a balance in relationships and often helps to create the situations necessary for completion of your relationship lessons.

Once you are acquainted with this guide some sample questions for a Relationship Guide are:

1. Are you working with me in a certain relationship at this time?
2. Is it in a family relationship?
3. Is it in a relationship with a friend?
4. Is it in a relationship with a mate?
5. Is it in a work-oriented relationship?
6. Have I any past life patterns which are also personal lessons that I am working out in that relationship at this time? (If **Yes** use PFQ.)
   A. How many past life patterns within relationships am I working on at this time? (N)
   B. Is it in my best interest to understand what those patterns are? (If **Yes**, ask C.)
   C. Please help me to understand one of them now. (A or T)
7. Am I experiencing any personality patterns within a relationship circumstance which I have not been able to complete in past lives with that person?
8. Have you any suggestions to help me work through this lesson? (If **Yes** use PFQ.)

A. Please give me some advice now. (A or T)
9.   Do I have karma with this person?
10.   How many past lives have I shared with this
      person? (N)
11.   Were these past lives with this person pleasant
      experiences?
12.   Were they unpleasant experiences?
13.   Was there an unpleasant experience due to my
      perceptions of this person? (If **Yes** use PFQ.)
      A. Please help me to understand more about this
      situation now? (A or T)
14.   Is there more information you can share with me to
      help me understand this person from a spiritual
      vantage point? (A or T)
15.   Have you any suggestions that will expand my
      awareness about the situation of our relationship?
      (A or T)
16.   Have you a message about my relationships in
      general? (A or T)
17.   Do you have services or guidances to offer that I have
      not yet explored? (If the answer is **Yes** use PFQ.)
      A. How many? (N)
      B. What services are they? (A or T)
18.   Can you explain your services in detail? (A or T.)

This guide can relay messages between two physical persons. You can send your love and understanding through this guide to a friend with whom you have had a misunderstanding with the request that this friend understands your true feelings on a conscious level before you physically meet or speak with him again. I have witnessed great success with this technique. It creates a mending of the relationship which results in clarity and a deeper level of caring.

There can be a great temptation to use this guide incorrectly concerning relationships. It is not the work of this guide to tell you with whom to spend your time. Neither is it this guide's job to persuade someone to like you. It is definitely not this guide's function to find a mate for you.

CRYSTAL GUIDE

This warm spiritual friend loves, knows and understands crystals, minerals and stones of all types. Sometimes, it is a Lord of Mineral frequencies and therefore is a spirit that is directly involved in the growth essence and spiritual evolution of minerals.

If you have any personal questions about certain stones the inquiring process is really fun. Once you have this guide on the table you can place a stone, about which you have questions, directly on the table's surface. This provides a process for the Crystal Guide to evaluate that particular stone's qualities in reference to your vibration. Through this technique you can discover if that particular stone is of any frequency value for you.

Some suggested questions to pose to this guide are;

1. Does this stone assist me in any way? (If **Yes** ask How? {A or T})
2. Does it help balance my spiritual frequencies?
3. Does it enhance my emotional body frequency?
4. Does it help my mental well-being?
5. Does it help my physical body in any way?
6. Is it in my best interest to wear this stone anywhere on my body?
7. Is it in my best interest to wear it on a certain area of my body?
8. Is it in my best interest to wear it on the right side of my body for a balancing of my energy?
9. Is it in my best interest to wear it on my left side for a balancing of my energy?
10. Is it in my best interest to wear it somewhere else on my body? (If **Yes**, ask Where? {A or T})
11. Does the energy of this stone help me to balance a

certain chakra area of my energy body? (If **Yes** ask, "Which chakra?" {A or T})

12. Is it in my best interest to meditate with this stone?

13. Is there a specific place it should be on my body when I meditate?

14. Will you please help me to understand where this is? (A or T)

15. Is there a specific stone or crystal that will enhance my ability to do soul travel with conscious recall?

16. Do I presently own this stone? (If **Yes** use PFQ)
    A. Please help me to identify which stone it is now. (You can place a stone on the center of the table and ask the guide if this is the stone, repeating the process with all the stones you own or use A or T.)

17. Is there a specific stone I could get to help me with soul travel? (If **Yes**, use PFQ.)
    A. Please tell me what that stone is now. (A or T)

18. Is there a specific stone or crystal to assist me to have better dream recall? (If **Yes** repeat the PFQ for 17.)

19. Is there a special stone that will activate spiritual dreams for me? (If **Yes** repeat the PFQ for 17.)

20. Is there a special stone that will strengthen the health of my physical body at this time? (If the answer is **Yes** repeat the PFQ for 17.)

21. Is there a special stone or mineral that will encourage my self-empowerment at this time? (If **Yes** repeat the PFQ for 17.)

22. Is there a special stone that will help me to overcome negativity at this time? (If **Yes** repeat the PFQ for 17.)

23. Is there a special stone that will help me to open my psychic-spiritual abilities at this time? (If **Yes** repeat the PFQ for 17.)

24. Do you have any advice for me about crystals or stones at this time? (A or T)

It is best to have a mineral book on hand to ask

about the stones by their proper names. Sometimes you will perceive a color of a stone but have no idea what it is. Such a book can be very helpful in speeding up the accuracy of the communication if you do not have a specific stone to place on the table.

There are, indeed, certain minerals which enhance dream recall or assist your energy to attain spiritual dreams. I discovered that one of my Amethyst crystals has such a power for it never fails to help me with spiritual dreams. When I have questions and need spiritual guidance, I sleep with it in my pillow case. Sometimes, it tunes me in so powerfully to the spiritual realms that all of the high vibration activity wakes me up again and again throughout my sleep period. At that point, I take it out of my pillowcase and put it on the night stand in order to get some deep rest.

My Crystal Guide has shared so much exciting information concerning minerals and stones that I could never have found it all in books. This guide gave me an interesting explanation about what happens when you lose a favorite crystal or stone. Because the stone is kept around or on you for a period of time, you finally absorb its essence. When that happens, the essence of the stone enters into your aura and works with you as a permanent assistant. The physical stone at that point is an empty shell devoid of its energy and presence, thus it is no longer working for you in its physical state. When this process is complete spirit makes sure you somehow lose the physical stone for it no longer is needed.

This guide has told me about the new crystals and minerals that will be found, when humanity is ready for them. It discloses the general location (such as the state or the country) in which they will be discovered.

Other communications have said that certain geographical locations where stones or crystals are found have specific vibrations unique to those placements which affect the stones differently. Quartz crystals due to where they have been mined or found have certain specific vibrational patterns. The origin of your stone or crystal effects its vibrational capacity as it coordinates with your specific energy.

My Crystal Guide has enhanced my enjoyment, understanding and use of minerals and that knowledge enacted has had direct impact upon the speed of my spiritual growth.

PENDULUM GUIDE

This guide will teach you how to use your pendulum effectively. It will show you specific techniques that will improve your accuracy with this tool. You can investigate basic methods of swing, such as the direction the pendulum uses for a **Yes** or **No**. This guide can move the table to demonstrate the actual specific movement the pendulum would make. Sometimes, a clockwise circle is the indication for **Yes** and a counter-clockwise circle for **No**. Sometimes, a **Yes** movement is away from you and then towards you. A **No** may be a side to side swing movement. It is important to understand this information for it creates clarity in your pendulum work.

There are vibrational changes you can detect with a pendulum and this guide can teach you all the delicate details. It will help you in the assembling of a pendulum by telling you the best materials to use to match your frequencies with those of the pendulum. Mine was a wooden button on a thread and it performs the best for me even though I had purchased a beautiful crystal pendulum that never proved to be accurate. With the use of the table to verify the responses of your pendulum you will be able to fine tune your ability to work with it as a tool.

You may discover that you have more than one Pendulum Guide. Sometimes, one may be oriented to material world matters such as where to find water or what area of your yard is the most fertile to plant your garden. Another guide will direct the pendulum to answer spiritual questions such as is it in your best interest spiritually, mentally, emotionally and physically to meditate in a certain physical location of your house or yard.

When you have developed a rapport and bond of understanding with this guide through the use of the table, you may be able to dowse for water, find missing items and persons with great efficiency. Another interesting use of the pendulum is to detect energies in the home which effect your moods, health and communications with spirit or physical people.

Here are some suggested questions for this guide:

1. Is it in my best interest to work with a pendulum as a tool?
2. Have you any suggestions about the materials of which my pendulum should be made? (A or T)
3. Do certain metals in a pendulum work better with my energy?
4. Does silver work well with my energy? (You may want to ask about several different metals one at a time.)
5. Does wood work best with my energies?
6. Is there a specific stone or crystal which works well with my energy ? (If **Yes** use A or T to determine the specific details of which type to use.)
7. Will you demonstrate the direction of pendulum movement that is a **Yes** with the table?
8. Will you please demonstrate that movement now?
9. Will you demonstrate the movement for **No** now?
10. If you have a movement for a **Maybe**, would you demonstrate it now please?
11. Do I have more than one pendulum guide at this time?
12. How many? (N)
13. (If the answer to question 11, is **Yes**. then ask 13.) Please explain why I have more than one pendulum guide? (A or T)
14. Is it in my best interest to believe I have the ability to dowse for water?

15. Will you share with me the best technique for me
     to use for water dowsing? (If **Yes** use PFQ.)
     A. Please give me that information now. (A or T)
16. Will you help me to learn the techniques necessary to
     find missing persons with my pendulum?
17. (If the answer is **Yes** ask 17.) Will you please tell me
     what procedure I am to follow to find a missing
     person? (A or T) (You should always repeat back to
     the guide what you understand to be its message for
     a **Yes** or **No** to get verification. You can repeat
     questions 16 and 17 replacing the concept of missing
     persons with missing items.)
18. Will you help me to learn how to use a map and the
     pendulum for absentee dowsing to discover the
     location of things or persons?
19. Will you help me to learn how to use the pendulum to
     locate energy flows or blockage of energy flows
     within the physical body?
20. (If the guide answers **Yes** to questions 18 or/and 19
     then use PFQ.)
     A. Tell me how to perform the necessary technique
     now. (A or T)

GATEKEEPER

The Gatekeeper is the spiritual protector of your
being. This loving guide protects you whenever you astral or
soul travel during your sleep or meditation. If you find that you
are returning to your body at night with a "thump" and you
wake up with your heart beating quickly due to the shock of
such a sudden return to your physical body it is this guide you
question for the reason why. It will gladly render its help to
prevent these shocks from happening again.

The Gatekeeper cooperates in keeping negative
spirits out of your air space when you are working with a
physical tool such as the table or the pendulum. If you wish to
be a channel you absolutely need a bonded rapport with this

guide. It is also a necessary friend if you are doing any inter-dimensional communication work such as automatic or inspirational writing.

You will want to discuss your out-of- body travels with this guide. There is a difference between astral projection and soul travel. When you astrally project, you are traveling with the astral body in the astral realms of the physical world. When you soul travel, you leave the astral body behind and you visit many of the more refined dimensions for spiritual learning or healing. Sometimes, you might remember taking classes or sitting at the knee of some wise figure in a beautiful garden. If you recognize that you do get out-of-body feel free to ask any questions of this guide concerning the protection of your body as a vehicle for *your soul only.*

Many times due to physical injuries, surgery, drinking alcohol in great amounts or the taking of drugs (even prescription drugs) we can weaken our aura. Whenever the aura is weakened, torn or damaged astral energies can attach themselves. They can affect your well-being in varying degrees by creating depression, exhaustion or addictive behavior and in general, acting as a bad luck energy. The Gatekeeper can identify these energies and assist you in moving them out of your space. Many times you will find these energies only came to you for help as they do not know how to move on in spirit. They are frightened and unhappy and affect you with their misery. You will be able to help them by crossing them over to the Light according to the table technique you will learn about in chapter 8 of Part Two.

Another fascinating subject to discuss with this guide is to find out if you are a walk-in. There has been much written about walk-ins. They are the spiritual phenomenon that occurs when the original soul (which has been in the body since birth) decides to leave the body due to frustrations. The soul may feel it is not be able to learn its lessons or to accomplish what it originally wished to do in this life. The soul makes an agreement with another soul in the spiritual dimensions that it will walk out. Usually there is some drastic physical, near-death or emotional experience which takes place at the time of the exchange and somehow during or after the event the new soul walks in. There is no physical death of the body and the soul that walks in to take it over has the benefit of an already adult physical body.

There are many walk-ins on the earth at this time with a special mission to complete but the exchange of the souls can be very traumatic. The new walk-in soul because it travels through the dense levels of the dimensions to the plane of the physical body may forget it is a walk-in. This causes a great deal of confusion for the person and the soul involved. The Gatekeeper will be aware if you are a walk-in and can assist you to recall and discover the reason you have chosen to come into this body and this life.

The Gatekeeper can help you to be aware of your personal energy management. If you feel tired most of the time, you probably scatter your personal energy very easily; either by just doing too many things inefficiently at once or by letting other persons around you take your personal energy because of your unbalanced emotional habits. An example being, that you might be too sympathetic rather that being compassionate and empathetic. Because I work with so many people I rely upon my Gatekeeper to assist me to send Universal energy to people who are energy needy. This saves my personal energy and allows me to be less exhausted at the end of my work day.

Some of the questions you will want to direct towards this guide are:
1.   Do I astrally project at night when I sleep?
2.   Can you help me understand where I go when I travel out-of- body? (A or T)

3. Where do I travel? (A or T)
4. Do I soul travel?
5. Where do I go when I soul travel? (A or T)
6. Do I have any negative spiritual entities or thought forms that are in my presence during waking hours?
7. Are there actual negative entities in the ether surrounding me?
8. Are there negative thought forms around me at this time?
9. Are these my own negative thoughts such as fears?
10. Do I need to be aware of protecting myself at this time from being in the same physical space with someone else's negative thought patterns?
11. Are there any negative entities on my aura?
12. If so, tell me about them please. (A or T)
13. Do I have any practices or habits that attracts negative energies? (If **Yes** use PFQ.)
    A. How many practices or habits like that do I have at this time? (N)
    B. Please tell me what one of these habits is at this time? (A or T)
14. Are these negative energies with me due to where I go physically? (If **Yes** use PFQ.)
    A. What places do this to me and what can I do about this? (A or T)
15. Are negative energies with me due to the persons that I am around at certain times? (If **Yes** use PFQ.)
    A. How many people are around me with those types of energies? (N)
    B. Is it in my best interest to know who they might be? (If **Yes** then ask C.)
    C. Please tell me who one of them is now? (A or T)
    D. Please advise me if it is in my best interest to help that person in any way. (A or T)
16. Are there any issues I should be aware of, from your observation, that concern my well-being? (If **Yes** use PFQ.)

A. Please tell me about them now. (A or T)

17. Am I a walk-in? (If you receive a **Yes.** use PFQ)

     A. When did the walk-in exchange occur? (A or T)

     B. Why did it happen? (A or T)

     C. Is there a special mission the walk-in came in to accomplish? (A or T)

     D. Who is the walk-in soul? (A or T)

     E. Where did it come from? (A or T)

18. Is it in my best interest to try channeling?

19. Do you have any suggestions of how to protect myself if I should decide to trance channel? (A or T)

20. From your vantage point do I need to manage my energy better? (If the answer is **Yes,** use PFQ)

     A. What are some of your suggestions of what I can follow? (A or T)

     B. Is there a meditative process I can employ to empower my personal energy? (If the answer is **Yes** then ask C.)

     C. Please tell me about the process now? (A or T)

21. During this lifetime have I reclaimed any lost soul energy without conscious recall? (If **Yes** use 22. & 23.)

22. When? (A or T)

23. Could the regeneration change of my energy unit caused by the gaining of this soul energy make me think I am a walk-in? (If **Yes** use 24.)

24. Will you please explain about this energy change and how I can fully embrace it for my spiritual growth? (A or T)

The Gatekeeper knows and understands your energy. It is this guide that has record of any soul energy enhancements you have experienced. Often the experience of gathered soul energy that is the result of your increased awareness may be confusing. Also when you are moving into your Higher Self placement you will notice a difference in your energy. Communications with this guide can help you to understand and facilitate these energy changes. Many times students confuse these personal energy changes with a walk-in experience. True walk-in experiences are not common.

UNIVERSAL GUIDES

A Universal Guide is a powerful collective of energy with the ability to perform several tasks at the same time. It has the ability to travel to many diverse realities and dimensions. Since they are by nature more impersonal in their work levels, they are not as directly involved with your personal life. They are usually with a person who works with other humans in special ways. This guide is often part of the supporting team of those humans who came to this life with special projects or missions.

Universal Guides are very expanded God Force energies that at times wish to share many big picture ideas with you. Often they will give you an awareness of the choices you have about what level to perform on in your life situations. Their higher vibration vantage point will be interesting to discover. Their guidance opens the way to incorporate a deeper understanding and an ability to more actively perform spirituality in your daily life.

Sometimes you may have a guide that performs the functioning role of one of the previously listed guides as well as that of a Universal Guide. Christopher performs several tasks. He is a Universal Guide as well as my Chief Guide. A Universal Guide can be assigned to another person for a special purpose. I have asked Christopher to assist someone with special spiritual processes on numerous occasions. During the time he is present with that person he has less energy presence around me. I perceive him as a soft light shadow of himself. However, because of the additional power of his Universal Guide expansion level, even while he is working with another, he is still fully effective in his role as my Chief

Guide and is as energy present as any of my other guides.

Although spirit guides are not our own inner teacher (the Higher Self), they inspire us - to be all we can be, to serve others, to rise above our lower tendencies, to avoid possible dangers along our pathway and to become one with our Higher Self. I do not consider them more noble or more important than my Higher Self. I perceive and honor them as invaluable supportive friends along my path of evolution.

I warn once again that in communicating with spirit *do not ask for answers to your life's decisions* because this is the wrong or the non-spiritual use of this tool. You will be giving away your power and attracting negative spirit. You would also defeat the purpose of the table's energy circle which is to bring you to the expanded energy level of the recognition and intuitive awareness of your own inner guidance.

Be curious and open in your exploration of Spirit Guides. All too often students will cling to the knowing and familiarity of just a few guides. When they do this they cheat themselves from the wide expanse of possible help and the diverse vantage points of the different guides that can give them a full picture of the knowing of their whole Self.

There are many more guides available to you than the particular ones that I have mentioned. Often, there are spiritual professionals in your special field of endeavor that are right there supporting and inspiring you. They may or may not be historically famous. They can be from another planetary society that is emotionally and/or mentally advanced and they wish to help you be the promoter of a special type of thinking to help with our present society conditions. If you do not ask about how many guides you have and what roles they play on your supporting spiritual team at the present time you will never know what possibilities for help are waiting for the asking. So be open, be curious and most of all, have fun.

B. COMMUNICATING WITH ANGELS AND HIERARCHAL BEINGS

It is necessary to understand that there was a time in earth history that table tipping or any other kind of physical tool could not bridge the connection between mankind and higher level beings. Now, due to etheric earth and cosmic energy changes the more evolved Light Beings are closer and more available to encourage and support us in the speeding up of our spiritual growth. Because it is a critical time in earth history we need their help.

In order to encourage the spiritual Hierarchy to share their wisdom, we must move beyond the process of just gathering knowledge by reading about spiritual growth. We must be sincere in our quest by living our new beliefs on a daily basis. When we are diligently applying ourselves to growth and taking control of our personal choices by realizing we are the co-creators of our own destiny and not the victims of circumstances, the hierarchy will connect and teach us great UNiversal truths thereby expanding our knowingness.

In using the term spiritual hierarchy I am referring to all angels, Group Minds, the beings humanity refers to as Masters and the Brotherhood of Light, the Illuminated Ones plus any other expanded "All Light" Light beings.

When you quest for the knowledge of your personal self which pertains to anything about this physical life or to your own soul and its growth you are not studying in the domain that is of interest to the energies I have mentioned above. Personal, soul-oriented questions are best addressed to your guides or to your Higher Self. The kind of questions you ask directs the vibrational quality of energy which is needed to answer your question. Thus when you ask questions directed towards physical or mundane problems you employ a lesser level of energy by the very nature of the information you seek.

When you want to haul stones out of your back yard you would not call upon a brain surgeon to do the work.

So what do you do when you want to access higher levels of knowledge? You reach out to the non-personal wisdom of the hierarchal beings through diligent spiritual intent. It helps to meditate daily, work with self improvement and to strive towards a conscious awareness and recall of your dreams.

Who or what are these hierarchal beings? There are several wonderful and many opinionated books written about the hierarchy. The subject is extremely involved, complex and controversial. From my experiences I would tell you that the feel of their essence or love presence and most of all their message will be the best means by which to identify them. Usually they are more concerned with relating their message than explaining who they are. I am convinced that a truly evolved being does not need a special title or rank, they are simply a beautifully radiating presence of the God Force.

What does it mean to be a master? It is an evolved being that has completed all karmas related to lives on earth. It has stepped off the karmic wheel of earthly reincarnations. It has mastered the physical, emotional, mental and spiritual bodies and brought them into complete balance.

A mastered being can take on a physical body if one is needed for special circumstances such as teaching others here on earth. A master has expanded the wisdom and thinking of its consciousness to the degree that it can be physically obvious in two or more places at one time. It can heal with all the powers of the universe and has the capacity to manifest any needs with universal power. It is fully aware of all it is and all it has been. It has full access to universal power and has no need for personal power or ego. It can manipulate matter both physical and etheric with total awareness of universal laws.

Masters often choose to live on the earth plane,

but they are quiet about their evolutionary placement, as their mission is not to be recognized but to show others how to become masters. Some simply balance a geographical area of the earth by just "being" there needing no human contact to do this vibrational work. There are a few of these beautiful energies present on the earth plane at this present time. I suspect that Sathya Sai Baba, who presently lives in India is a master because of his miraculous capacity to emanate pure love and to manipulate Universal energies for the good of all concerned.

A master's very presence will raise the frequency of the persons around him to assist them to grow spiritually to their own masterhood. I believe we are all striving to be masters for it is our next step of evolution towards the perfection of God. Masters work with souls on the earth plane to teach them how to become masters. The masters as a group are often referred to as the Brotherhood, the Brotherhood of Light, because they work in perfect unison within the White Light Will of God.

The Brotherhood not only includes the masters themselves but can also include the souls who are very close to the level of master. These souls are working with masters either in spirit or on the earth plane on an etheric level. Thus there are many souls here on earth, in the physical body, that are becoming members of the Brotherhood of Light by working side by side with the masters.

The energy of a master is special because it is filled with a pure spiritual love. Masters can only express themselves through the finer emotions having worked through to that level. They no longer identify with the coarser emotions of our lower emotional body expressions. Because they have risen to refined emotion they have moved their emotional response from the lower heart of the solar plexus to the higher heart in the heart chakra itself which is the higher level seat of the soul. Masters have become impersonal - not centered on the lower self in any way. They will only respond to the higher and finer levels of beings with whom they come into contact. They are at an excellent placement or level to begin the discovery of the higher truths such as the Universal plan of evolution and where we are in it.

To better understand what a mastered soul is, call to the table the most evolved being that will come to teach you about the Plan of God. Usually then the sitters are surrounded by the Brotherhood energy. However, I have never witnessed an evolved being announce that it is a master or mention some other elevated title that it needed to be known as. What I have experienced is being touched by God's Love and Beingness with a soft flow of compassionate caring beyond any earthly experience. I find it is only humanity's need to mentally classify spirit energies into categories that we have attached terms to such as "Master or Ascended Master". Their loving essence is filled with humility and freedom from ego, so it would never ask for such a declaration of title.

Sometimes a master is attracted to a table tipping session because, the group working together around the table has been regularly emphasizing learning about their spiritual growth. The master knows, that because of the level of the knowledge sought, these people are serious about living their spirituality and are dedicated to their quest for wisdom. The master wishes to share in instruction for the individuals at the table in order to help with their training in the masters' ways. They will help you understand about the concept of personal spiritual initiation, all its levels and help you to see the role initiation plays in your current life.

Other than earth masters there are masters of other planets, the sun and even planets of other solar systems. Thus, a soul can become a master through evolution on another planet or dimension.

Ascended Masters are further evolved than masters. They do not have to work with the earth plane for they have reached a state of evolvement that enables them to be about God's work of total participation in the overall Plan of creation and the greater scope of evolution. They have mastered the physical, emotional and mental bodies and have, like Christ, ascended the higher forms of these bodies by taking the bodies with them into the spiritual dimensions.

As Ascended Masters, they have passed through the veil of physical death with full control of the soul forces which allow them to overcome physical death. Through ascension they have enabled themselves to have a formed body at their disposal whenever it is needed.

An Ascended Master can be a master from another planetary system or that of earth or a master of more than a planetary system as in the case of a cosmic level Ascended Master. These masters often participate in the consciousness that is planetary or of solar systems. In other words, they are the energies that coordinate a planet to function as a vibration of unified consciousness or several planets organized into the unified consciousness energy as a solar system. Or they may wish to create the order of the solar systems into a universe as a consciousness energy. All of these levels of work are expressions of God.

Ascended Masters will work with master-level energies and many of the energies resonating in the finer frequencies above them. Among the Ascended Masters are the special ones who are termed the Chohans of the Seven Rays. (I briefly discussed the activities of the Seven Rays of God in chapter 6, Part One.) Each of us as a soul resonates in activity with at least one of these rays. They represent different aspects of the creative universal plan of which we are all a part. Communicating with the Chohans of these rays through the use of the table is not common. Usually they only come to the table to work with concepts of higher wisdom or of Universal concerns that are beyond the knowledge of a master. But, the touch of their enlightenment opens your mind to be able to perceive the big picture of the Universal plan in action.

When you study the concept of the Rays of God you will find differences of opinion as to the identity of the Chohans which represent each ray. There is also a lack of agreement as to which ray represents what aspect of God. Do not let this confuse you. As usual, I listen to the information I receive, for at that time, it is my truth. This is also a fact for yourself. Always listen to and honor your own inner teacher.

The second ray is one of the most comfortable energies for me. I resonate well with it. The Ascended Master or Chohan of the second ray is the Christ. His path to God is through refined, unconditional, perfected love. Each time I communicate with this aspect I learn more about love. I am now aware of ten levels of God-love and have been told they are similar to, but much more involved than, those presented by St. John of the Cross in his treatise, DARK NIGHT OF THE SOUL$_4$. An awareness of these levels of love comes before your own growth through them. The awareness opens up your being and gives you hope of slaying the ego aspects of yourself so that you can more easily be an expression of love. Each ascending level makes use of less and less self-importance and ego identity creating an impersonal and a free flowing you. Your identity does not end but the ego's need to express it is finished.

The energies humanity would title Ascended Masters will share their wisdom with you when you desire knowledge concerning cosmic consciousnesses, the dimensions, Angelic orders and other higher creative orders. The Chohans can help you to be consciously aware that you are working towards an ethereal level initiation and what the process of it will do to expand the whole of Universal awareness.

172

There are times you will be able to etherically visit the Chohans' place of being here on earth to study under them. You may be included in their beautiful etheric ceremonies. These events often give you vivid visions of the order of vibrations and your part in the whole plan. The beauty, love and peace resonating at one of these locations is only explained or fully understood by experiencing it because it cannot be described. Once you have sensed the ecstasy of the experience and allowed it to enter your being, it cannot be forgotten. It expands your frequencies to such an extent that you know there is no going back nor have you a desire to return to your previous self.

These beautiful energies are healers on a grand scale. They will teach you about working with the higher energies of the earth, the solar system, galaxies and the universe. The earth is a living being and needs our own balance to create harmony and balance for its entire well-being. When you share yourself as an energy worker you may be allowed to sense the vibration of beingness that is the consciousness of a sun, a star or a planet.

It is a fascinating fact that much of what the Hierarchal Beings can share with you takes you out of yourself creating a fuller understanding of the Universal oneness of the All. You establish a deeper knowing that you are so much more than the limiting identity of your ego. You grow past the need to be full of yourself, your fears and anxieties. You can experience the All of which you are within. You feel yourself as a truly beautiful expression of Self as an aspect of God. Through their energies you will feel the true surrendering essence of living the Will of God. You will discover you are a part of the plan - a plan that is perfection. You will relax and experience the "beingness" of consciously being that valuable component.

One particular group had been working the table with their focus centered completely on their spiritual growth for a little over two years. They always asked for the highest spiritual teacher available that could answer their questions. They wanted to know about; what a soul is, the other dimensional experiences that we can evolve into and why souls and spirit originally chose to come into form on earth.

Their beautiful teacher, which always expressed itself as an extremely bright white and golden spiral of energy never wanted to be named. It moved a large diameter wooden game table in a slowly levitating manner and exuded an energy that was life force giving and completely loving. We named it Teacher or "The Golden One". It said it was the messenger of knowledge and energy. We communicated with it in many sessions. One night, the group was astounded to find out that it was the Holy Spirit. We all learned that when the theme of our session was not personal and involved a serious quest for understanding God or the other expanded dimensions we could attract wondrous beings onto the table.

Whenever you are asking questions of entities of the higher dimensions it is often necessary to inquire if the entity wishes to answer such a question. However, if it is phrased in a spiritual manner, the energy will almost always reply to the question.

Angels will come on the table. When you are dealing with masters and Ascended Masters there is no doubt that you will attract angels of many levels and orders to the table.

Angels are from many dimensions and there are many orders or divisions of angels. I asked one to explain just what is an angel essence. I was told that as humans we know we have the power of thought which angels equate with the creative power that belongs to God. When we think with that power, we exert an energy that makes the thought an object which can be perceived in other dimensions. In those dimensions the thoughts take on form. They can be beautiful when based upon love and compassion. Sometimes, these thought objects are more beautiful than the fairest or most perfect earth plane flower displaying a pure and vivid color that is beyond match on the third dimensional earth plane. The angel explained that angels were the thought forms of God coming from His very Breath Light. They are a special vibration of Light that is refined to a soft light-weight etheric being. They have always been known as God's messengers because they are the expressions of God's thoughts in the essence of Light energy. Their forms are fashioned out of His various thoughts about special functions.

Other than the Source itself, Angels are my favorite God essence beings. They are the softest yet strongest and most loving of all God's expressions of life energy. Angels rarely come on the table for communication. When they do, they usually have a specific message for you which leaves you blessed with an inner warming and a sensation of peace.

I sense that angels are quiet, soft beings busily at work with energy most of the time. Whenever I am in a church I like to sit in the rear of the auditorium to observe the spiritual happenings. When the minister or priest is deeply sincere and concentrating on the ceremony, I notice a soft energy flowing from his/her being. The congregation when focusing their spiritual attention to worship and prayer creates a large mushroom of energy surrounded by the minister's energy. This mushroom pattern flows upward towards the ceiling and out through the roof forming a fountain of multi-colored sparkling vibrations that I see angels of many levels collect quickly and put into a reserve. The angels contain the collected energy and distribute it wherever they see a need for that energy. This need can be to fulfill the intentions of the congregation and the leftover energy is then divided and utilized for those the angels can assist.

Whenever I am working with client doing a regression, I notice the Angels of Mercy healing and balancing the individual when they have uncovered some past life pains and discomforts on any level. I now know from where these angels have collected the energies for their beautiful healing work. I know that all the energy of prayer is deeply useful.

If you are doing special spiritual work such as crossing over souls you will have specific angels working with you. They are the Light Angels. Michael the Archangel will work with you through those processes as well.

There are special situations in which Archangels will assist you. They will help when you are doing energy Light work that is in any manner connected with directionality. This type of work might pertain to clearing negative energy or entities from a piece of land, a building, a house or the calling for protective Light energies. Often the Archangels will be present during some of the spiritual growth activities you can participate in at the equinoxes. I believe that the Archangels are one of the highest orders of angels to actively work with humanity. Archangels are of the same dimension as the Ascended Masters. They participate in many ways with the work of the Seven Rays and humanity.

The Seraphim, Dominions and Heavenly Hosts are mostly involved in directly working with the Source itself and the expanded God Force energies such as the eternals and immortals who never incarnate into form. There is one Seraphim Angel who has worked with us through the table. He is the very special bond that connects man, through the Solar energies, with God. His name is Metatron.

The angels of directions, earth, air, water, fire, peace and love will work with you if you need their special help for balance. You may discover that certain directions you face are important in meditation or prayer and that attracts the angelic keeper of that direction. This seems to happen when you are in meditation and prayer during a personal cycle in which you are going to step up to a new and higher level of growth.

Your Guardian Angel will come on the table if there is special cause for it to speak to you. There are some individuals who have their Guardian Angel as a Gatekeeper. I know of one person whose Guardian Angel is her Table Guide.

There are Angels who are keepers of records that can be brought on the table. The records I am referring to are not the personal Akashic Records, but the Akashic Records of the earth's history which concern the evolution of humanity, spirit and the creative plan.

One of the sweetest angelic forms to come to the table is one of the orders of Cherubims. They are delicate, soft, light and small. They are joyous, humorous and filled with incredible charm. They are Cherubs. There are the Cherubim orders which work with the higher realm activities as well as those which work with the spiritual hierarchies of animals, plants and minerals and are involved with creative inspirational energy. The Cherubs are musical and artistic in expression. In many instances you can sense the music in the rhythm in their performance of table movement.

Cherubs can assist you in bringing your pet's spirit guide on the table. If your pet is having any problems, its guide can help you to understand the reasons why. A pet's guide will tell you how evolved your pet is as an animal energy. That guide can inform you about your pet's spiritual purpose or goals. Most often a domesticated animal is working with the emotions of caring through interacting with your emotional body. You can find out why you and your pet chose to interact together and what specific lessons there are to be learned. Often, your pets have been with you in other lives as other types of animals or of the same kind. You will discover it is no accident that they are part of your life this time around. They know you and your energy well enough to feel safe that they can achieve their special lessons around you. All of this information will allow you to help your pet work out its lessons in this lifetime.

Cherubs will bring the devas, fairies, gnomes, sprites and nature spirits of all types for communication through the table. These energies are very interesting and certainly alert you to the oneness you have with all that is alive around you.

If you work with plants as a hobby or professionally, you can experience an indepth understanding of each individual plant through the various types of fairies and Flora Angels who can come on the table. These energies will joyously help you to keep your plants healthy. They tell us that different types of plants have different qualities and attitudes. Some are calm while others are strong and excitable. These attributes are taken in by the human body when the plant is eaten. They directly affect us with their spirit when we ingest them or use them as an herb. The energy qualities of decorative plants are interesting to discover for they directly affect the energy atmosphere of your home or work space. Yard and house plants can be better cared for from the information received from their helping nature spirits or elementals.

There are specific Nature and Plant angels, Devas and Lords that will place fairies on and around certain plants to cause them to be the most beautiful and productive vegetation in your yard. Just ask about the possibilities and make your requests through the table.

Nature Spirits and angels will aid you in dealing with insect pests in the house and yard. They can inform the lord over the insect energies of the area that these problem bugs are not helpful to your purposes at this time and if they do not leave the area at your request, you will take drastic measures.

The lord of the insects may tell you about the imbalances that you have created which has resulted in the insect problem. This lord may have suggestions about how you can effectively balance the situation and permanently solve your problem in a spiritual manner.

Nature Spirits work with the ground energies around the yard and under your house. They can inform you of energy patterns that are beneficial or harmful and help you with decisions about the best location for a productive garden in your yard, as well as, the best placement of your bed in your bedroom for the most healing sleep and the best placement for your dining table to promote healthy digestion .

Calling in the Nature Angels to work with the plant fairies and mineral elementals surrounding your home will help you protect your home from negativity. There was one student who worked with these angels and fairies with such success that when a tornado's funnel cloud came through her neighborhood, her house and yard was the only one spared from the high wind and rain damage that ravaged her entire block.

Any angelic or hierarchal energy from the eighth to tenth dimension creates an unbelievable presence around the table. It is at this level of use that the table tipping process allows you to "touch God" and to be within the rapture of God's energy embrace. You can sense complete love and sometimes an overwhelming feeling of belonging and ecstasy as the table itself moves in a different manner. You could say there is etheric purpose to the movement. Often the movement can be described as a softly levitating and gentle manner of lifting and rocking. Once you have experienced it you will recognize it always. You will desire to experience it again and again for the beauty and blessings you receive.

C. GROUP MINDS

There are energies that cluster together for a special purpose. The collective which I term as a Group Mind performs as a group with a single consciousness, but each energy that is contained within it still has an individual quality. When communicated with, Group Minds seem to be represented by one voice or one specific energy. I believe they are in practice for their next level of evolution which is a combining of entities which have surrendered their individuality to form a single mass consciousness energy which is the type of consciousness existence necessary to maintain a planet. There are other levels of consciousnesses that are evolving beyond the Group Mind level that maintain the structural and functional plan of an entire planetary system with order and balance. There is still another type of more evolved consciousness that maintains the order of planetary systems in order to comprise a universe.

The Group Mind, as a God Force expression, will express itself in the energy field around certain humans because they have a specific mission to accomplish in this life. Usually this mission is a creative effort, such as a the writing of a stage play production, a movie, a television script, a specific musical arrangement or the production of a visual art form that has an awareness expanding message or a vibrational emanation that affects the evolution of mankind's consciousness. A Group Mind will influence a writer to create the doorway for new belief systems and open-mindedness in humanity. These energies also powerfully guide and assist scientists, inventors and innovators of theories that dramatically improve; the social conditions, physical and emotional well-being, educational systems and in general - the consciousness of the human race.

Group Minds are vibrationally powerful. Sometimes they come to the table with such force and strength that it feels like a painless electric power surge has rushed through the table and into your being. Their energy presence feel, and their movement of the table, is distinctive. It is not a personalized energy format, so it is sensed as all-surrounding and also within the table's energy circle. It is necessary to experience the Group Mind energy once in order to identify it again. However once you have, because it is uniquely beautiful and special, you will always remember it and have no difficulty identifying it again. Due to the universal level of its power, the energy it radiates can be felt soul-deep as a balanced compassion embodied in a focused direction of action. It is radiant, magnetic and enthusiastic.

The Group Mind is in the presence of its chosen special human for only as long as it takes to complete the combined energy effort project. If the human chosen is slow to respond to their inspirations and guidances they will move on to another human whom they know has the needed talents, emotional and mental abilities to work with them to co-create the project at hand. The Group Mind has patience, but it also has the foresight to wait only for a certain period of earth time for the individual to freely choose to participate.

This collective radiates humility and patience with a focused driving force towards action. The person it has chosen to be around is very fortunate. Because the Group Mind can access all levels of universal wisdom, all the person has to do is work with his or her personal vibration to balance the combined attunement so that he or she can communicate with clarity enabling him or her to feel and completely benefit from its inspiration and personal energy expansion effects.

If you discover you have a Group Mind participating with your efforts, the table will be of great help to facilitate your vibrational attunement. Through it, you will be able to directly communicate with the Group Mind allowing you to manifest the spiritual project into physical reality with efficient ease.

D. SPIRITUAL TEACHERS

Masters, Ascended Masters and other hierarchal beings are spiritual teachers, however there are often several special souls, while not hierarchal, who support and inspire you and act as spiritual teachers. The difference between a spiritual teacher and a spirit guide is that the teachers are temporary and tend to be less personal. At times a spiritual teacher is just an energy collective that appears in a symbolic form just long enough to present an inspiration or a particular guidance needed at a special time in your life.

An experience I had in this area was at a time I was preparing for a showing of my art materials and latest paintings at a very special art competition. It is my nature to dress in a very feminine manner but in preparing for this show I felt unsure about how to present myself. I decided to go shopping for a new dress. Being an avid clothes collector, I enjoyed the excuse that this was a great opportunity to buy something new.

At my favorite fashion mall, everything I tried on would not fit properly or the color just did not seem appropriate. I was becoming frustrated and time was short. All of a sudden it seemed as if I was being pushed to walk into a career woman's dress shop I have never previously desired to visit. I felt that their clothing style selection was starched and too business-like; even worse, a pushy sales lady immediately spied me. Though I calmly resisted she insisted upon helping me look great in a pearl gray linen suit and a silk fuchsia blouse. I was impressed that though it was not my usual style it looked appropriate and was becoming in a sedate manner.

To my ultimate surprise, the whole outfit was on sale and on that particular day was reduced to 50% of the sale price. It was an unbelievable bargain! I bought the outfit and wore it to the show. It seemed to make all the proper impressions everywhere I went that day. The whole event proved successful for me.

About a month later I was table tipping with my sister-in-law and a spirit came on the table that explained it was a spiritual teacher assigned by one of my guides to help me move into a more professional look for art shows. My sister-in-law related the whole message to me without any knowledge of my previous art show or the clothes shopping incident.

I have since discovered that sometimes a spiritual teacher will be around to help you when you study or practice new things for work or pleasure. Once, I had a spiritual teacher that helped me through mental images to understand how to drive a truck and to maneuver it successfully in awkward parking areas while towing a long cumbersome trailer.

Spiritual teachers will help you to see the spiritual teaching patterns in your life's situations. As a teacher it can assist you to see symbolism in your daily activities, the hidden causes for your emotion, thought and action. I like to work with spiritual teachers because they enable me to see the bigger picture of the events that occur within a day, a week or a month. Due to their objective and impersonalized energy nature, their input concerning my problems is always ingenious and invaluable creating new choices for action I would not have personally imagined or sensed present in a situation.

It is fascinating when you notice what situations in your life will attract to you a spiritual teacher. Now that I know they are available I openly request their impersonal assistance to help me through some circumstances that otherwise would be possibly personally misunderstood, much more difficult or prolonged.

E. THE HIGHER SELF

The Higher Self, High Self, Spiritual Self, Deep Self, Super-conscious Mind or the Higher Mind are all terms referring to an energy collective that is a sizable and powerful piece of the Source called God. That energy is your connection with the All that is considered God. It is your most noble and perfect part of self known as the Self.

Some consider this Self to be above you and others say it is deep within you. I believe that it is in both areas as well as all around you. The Higher Self is different from the human self that has the identity of your present name and ego personality. The Higher Self is the sum total of all the ego personalities you have been in past lives with all their individual experiences including the growth you have achieved between lives in the spiritual realms.

My understanding is that this beautiful essence of the Higher Self which is the *real you* sends out a piece of itself in the form of the soul. This soul is a volunteer part of the Higher Self that enters a a physical body for expression of itself in an experiential manner. The soul is within your physical body giving it life force energy. Each time the Self, has chosen to participate in taking on a body a soul is sent out as a representative to be in that body for the gaining of wisdom through that physical experience.

All of the wisdom, knowledge, lessons and karmas experienced in soul existences are recorded in the memory banks of the Higher Self. The Higher Self has access to your personal Akashic records. It knows all about the whole you including things of which you have no conscious awareness. It can answer any of the questions you may have concerning your past and present lessons and personality patterns with an accuracy which your spirit guides cannot access. Spirit guides will view past incidents in which they have interacted with you from the personal point of their own evolution. This does not make their answer invalid or inaccurate. Sometimes, it is very important to ask for their input as well as inquiring for information about the situation from the Higher Self.

Asking questions of the various helping energies available to you, spirit guides and the Higher Self allows you to be open to collecting more detailed information creating a balanced and complete picture of the situation you are trying to understand.

For example, you may want to work through a personality pattern such as a lack of self-confidence. A guide can relate to you the story of a lifetime you have each shared that deals with your having had such an issue. The Higher Self knows all the lifetimes in which you may have had this difficulty including those when that particular guide did not live with you. It can relate to you how often you avoided facing and growing through the problem and then can share with you a lifetime in which that pattern started. Armed with all of this information, you can understand why you have such a problem and can facilitate the process of releasing and growing through it.

I had a problem in this lifetime with getting out of my body so that I could soul travel. One of my guides had shared a few lifetimes with me in which I taught the out-of-body experience. In one, we lived in a primitive culture in the jungles of South America. This native group was relatively small and very superstitious. A few of us (my present spirit guide included) had experienced out-of-body travels. We decided to practice this adventure together and we met in secret to do so. I really enjoyed getting out-of-body at will and with ease. I shared with the others the guidelines I had used to release my soul with great efficiency from the body. We decided to build a structure that was a four-sided pyramid to sit within and to "travel", because we discovered that sitting within such a shape was very conducive to soul travel.

We were being watched by two fellow tribesmen who decided to report our suspicious activities to the chief. I had convinced the others we should continue to learn all we could about our spirit selves; that we should travel to the spiritual realm to study how we could improve ourselves and life in general for our clan.

One evening, we went inside our primitive soil, branch and mulch-like pyramidal structure and released our souls from our bodies. We traveled to a wondrously exciting spiritual school in another dimension. During our "trip" a forceful tornado arose in which tremendous wind and rain destroyed the structure and snuffed out our physical lives. However, before this storm the fearful clan were planning to torture and kill us for our strange secret meetings.

When we returned to our physical bodies we could not enter into them because our silver cords to them were cut by the death of those bodies. My guide let me recall the guilt I felt and feel how deeply painful it was. I had taken on the responsibility for deaths of all the others.

Since that time, I never again allowed myself the pleasure of the freedom of soul travel with a conscious awareness while in the form of a physical body. After discussing this problem with my guides and receiving this knowledge, my Higher Self informed me that dying in the manner we did in that primitive lifetime saved us all from the painful and cruel death that our fellow clansmen had planned for us. My Self also apprised me that I had made a vow, at my birth, not to leave my present physical body at will for soul travel as a punishment for this past deed. It showed me how unnecessary this self imposed chastisement really was and gently led me through a releasing process in order to free myself from this covenant.

Your Higher Self is always in your presence and is accessible to you through meditation, channeling, an intuitive inner knowingness and in communication through the spiritual table tipping experience.

Your Higher Self has full memory of all your talents, abilities and achievements plus an awareness of all you can be in the future. It will relate to you specific past lives that are pertinent to this lifetime. Often, these past lives have a definite influence on your present life plan. They can help you to see the purpose of the spiritual lessons of this life and to identify these lessons for self-balance.

You may have already discussed the subject of spiritual lessons with your Master Guide but there is a whole new perspective to this subject available to you through communication with the Higher Self. You can ask to know how many lessons you have to master in this life. The table will count out the number for you. Usually it is from one to twelve lessons. Next, ask how many lessons you have already learned in this lifetime. As a follow-up, find out how many of them you are attempting to accomplish at present.

Some common lessons our souls can be working through in a lifetime are: (1) Learning love - the pure spiritual level of Love that is an energy - not the emotions we associate with love which can be self-centered, controlling, conditional and filled with self-importance. (2) Patience, (3) Tolerance, (4) Compassion, (5) Respect and love of self as a worthy spark of God energy, (6) Self-confidence, (7) Detachment from all material things, people, spiritual beings and our self-important personality, (8) Surrender through an alignment of personal will to God's will by letting go of the need to control that which is outside of oneself and flowing effortlessly within universal energy. (9) Self-awareness, in which you monitor what you are in completeness recognizing your strengths and weaknesses as tools to use to co-create your atmosphere. Through this lesson you realize that you are responsible for creating your own life's circumstance. This is when you realize you are an energy mechanism affecting the entire planet earth and other dimensions. (10) Inner peace, creating full personal power at any time within any circumstance. (11) Acting in the present without expectation or anticipation of what will or could be. (12) Using the past only for re-evaluation and not to rehash old emotional thoughts. (13) Balancing the emotional body so that it does not rule your life with energy wasting responses. (14) Balancing the mental body so it does not rule your life with an uncontrolled mind filled with worry and random thinking. (15) Humility and self-acceptance - The knowledge that we are still learning and growing towards perfection and that we are using the imperfections of earth life to learn through as a valuable tool that teaches us to embrace and love our humanness with self-acceptance as a vehicle for our learning. (16) Non-judgment, accepting others and yourself as you are at present without needing to change them or yourself to feel loved and at peace.

There are other lessons that I am sure you will discover as you pursue this subject with your own Higher Self through the table.

Often, a personality pattern can be carried over from lifetime to lifetime with very little change or growth accomplished because we blunder through our lives feeling we are a victim of circumstances or of another's manipulation. As an evolving human we need to know that we (our souls and our Higher Selves) have planned our present life circumstances for the purpose of learning a specific lesson. For instance, if your personality pattern is to be a victim or a martyr then repeatedly you are used and abused by those around you. These opportunities are given to you to realize you have attracted them into your life in order to learn that you can change your image of yourself. You are meant to know, feel and express your own self-worth as a spiritually beautiful expression of God.

When communicating with the Higher Self you will learn that it has seen each personality pattern form gradually through past life actions in a repetitious profile. It can tell you about each pertinent lifetime in this progression and report on how you performed. With this knowledge established, it can give you guidance concerning how you can work through the lesson of the personality pattern in a kind and gently persistent manner.

The more you repeat a personality pattern the subtler and deeper within your being it is - making it difficult to recognize. This subterfuge blocks your spiritual growth. If you desire to probe into these blockages for the purpose of clearing them away forever, the Higher Self is always ready to assist you. All you have to do is request that your Higher Self do a vibration check of your energy body chakra points. Work with each chakra one at a time. Starting with the root chakra ask your Higher Self if you have any blockages there. These blockages occur due to past life memories that are still in the etheric body cells of the physical, emotional and mental bodies.

Even though the causes could be very old they are presently uncleared if they still register density in the energy field of your being. These densities can retard your progression towards the faster or higher, less dense frequencies needed to evolve. When you have asked about blockages in the root chakra and received your **Yes** or **No**, you can decide whether to move on to the next chakra (the spleen chakra) to find out if you have blockages there. You can inquire about each of the seven major chakras. Then ask your Self to analyze the vibrational energy of the palm and foot chakras.

If at any time you receive a **Yes** and wish more

information proceed to ask how many blockages there are to be worked out in a particular chakra area at the present time. The table can tap out the number for you. Then ask if you have any conscious awareness of the blockages in your life at this time. You can proceed further to ask the Higher Self to present images, thoughts or symbols to enable you and the other sitters to grasp a better understanding of the past life circumstance that may have caused the blockage. Next, as each person receives any of these symbols, ask the table to confirm that the symbol was sent. If the answer is **Yes** ask for assistance in interpreting the symbol by having your Higher Self send the appropriate thoughts to the sitters. At that time, put together the past life story from the clues given. Consequently, ask the Self on the table if you have understood and interpreted the information correctly, "Have we made any mistakes in our comprehension of this circumstance?"

To my knowledge the most efficient growth and understanding of the self can be attained through the direct communication with the Higher Self and is best achieved by the spiritual table tipping experience. I prefer the results of this method for gathering past life data over any other manner - regression included. I have witnessed groups of students develop spiritually in a rapid progression by coming to a thorough understanding of their personal lessons and personality patterns. Being armed with such information allows them to take control of their lives and their personal growth. They know they are not victims but active co-planners of their own evolution towards God.

There are many fascinating exploration possibilities to use when you are communicating with the Higher Self. You can ask about future lives. You may accept the interesting concept that all lives exist at once and then desire an understanding of that possibility. You may discover that if you study a past life you can change some of the events in it that affect this lifetime. You will come to an understanding that what you do in this lifetime affects your future lives if you survey them now. You will be able to create an easier pathway for your future life through a conscious attempt to heal yourself of blockages and dealing directly with your lessons in **this** lifetime.

Another exciting quest to delve into with your Higher Self is to ask for clarity on the subject of your spiritual family. This ethereal family includes soul members who may be different from those of your present physical family. You will be asking about souls who are deeply interconnected with you. Sometimes members of your current physical family are also be members of your spiritual family and you may discover that some very special people in your life are members of your spiritual family. They are souls who desire to help each other grow spiritually and often they have the same goals, missions and lessons to master.

There are instances in which your spirit guides are members of this family. Directing questions to your Higher Self about the idea of the spiritual family concept will help you understand the inner workings of this family. You will be able to connect with them for energy exchanges and power assists for the achievement of like goals and lessons.

In one of our class tipping experiences, we learned some intriguing facts about spiritual families by posing an interesting question that was a concern of one of the sitters. Her father had earned his living by doing the cleaning for a large industrial complex when she was young. Her grandfather was successful in the janitorial industry, too. She, herself, had a household cleaning service and her sister has a cleaning service for hospitals and institutions. She had put all of this together in her thoughts and wondered if her family had karma or spiritual lessons in reference to cleaning.

When we asked her Higher Self to answer this question, it informed us that this was a spiritual family project. Her Self told us that a spiritual family has very strong and time tested bonds centered upon a theme or a mission to cooperate with the Plan. Her spiritual family included many of the physical family members in this life. Her spiritual family worked on both physical and spiritual levels when they cleaned a location. Their common theme was to affect the quality of the place they cleaned in terms of its structure and flow. Due to their strong connection and unified purpose they were able to clear away astral negativity and imbalance. The spiritual capacity of this family worked effectively even if the sitter and her family had no conscious idea of their efforts or how they were affecting other levels. However, with an awareness of their special purpose they could achieve a deeper and longer lasting effect upon the areas they cleaned. Her Self said that this kind of energy work was timely and important especially because of the astral and physical pollution in today's world.

The Higher Self stated that all of us, presently in incarnation, are now able to have positive effects on our physical space and atmosphere. We have extended energy exchange powers readily available to clear and clean the earth due to the fact that the earth is more evolved than it has ever been. The earth has been passing into becoming its own Lightbody and by evolving bio-electrically it is constantly evolving us to become more powerful in the use of our own soul gifts. Since so many humans are unaware of the consequences of their negative thoughts, this sitter and her spiritual cleaning family had become essential to the well-being of others.

At this point in the session we were all inspired to inquire about our own spiritual families and their intent or mission in this life. This concept opens up whole new areas of self-understanding. So please, take the time to delve into this concept by researching your own spiritual family.

You can also inquire if you have a twin-soul. You can then determine if your twin-soul is in spirit at this time. Ask if your twin-soul is on the earth plane at this time. My twin-soul is my chief guide Christopher and I have no twin-soul on the earth plane at this time. Twin-soul energies can be a family member, a friend or a mate. A twin-soul is a soul who volunteered for life in form and has taken their identity from the same Higher Self.

If you are brave and want to explore further wisdoms through and about the Higher Self, you can ask how many souls are representing your Higher Self at this time as there are instances when other souls express through your own Higher Self. They can be representing it on other planets in other universes, as well as right here on earth.

Other soul expressions increase the experience options for your Higher Self, creating a wider base for growth and wisdom. These lives are not past lives, but ones that are going on simultaneously effecting the growth of your Higher Self. The experiences of these souls become yours and your experiences are theirs when you return to the Higher Self to share them. I am completing another book that will be published soon which explains and explores my findings about this fascinating concept.

If you are recording and analyzing your dreams, the Higher Self is the perfect energy to ask for an understanding of symbols that have been difficult for you to comprehend. Most of your dreams have been directly inspired by your Higher Self. Dreams are one of its favorite tools to use to communicate with you concerning your path in this life.

One of the first questions you might ask is if a specific dream has a message originating from your Higher Self. Then relate what you did not understand and request assistance in understanding the symbols.

During your sleep hours your soul travels to other realms. The Higher Self is aware of where your soul has gone and what it has done. Inquire if you are attending any special classes. Ask if they are spiritual classes. Query if you have been helping spirits in other dimensions. If so, ask in what way. Find out if you are doing any healing on physical persons from the spiritual realm while you are soul traveling. Check to see if you are working in cooperation with spirit concerning the earth's well being. Then ask if you can be privileged to have a conscious recall of your work when you awaken.

There have been nights when I know I work with elementals, devas and Terra angels to balance earth energies and support the earth's spirit in its time of growth. I have attended and taught classes. I have helped lost souls to cross over into the Light with the help of the Light Angels. I have traveled to the realm of the Cherubim to play with them and to share stories of my earth experiences with them in their musically transformative home. I have helped elementals to grow, expand and evolve. During some sleep periods I know I travel to other planets to share information about what it is like to be in the density of the human body. These energies, in turn, teach me truths about their type of existence.

The Higher Self is a wonderful source of wisdom and knowledge. I am convinced it is the most valuable source of Self-knowledge to call on the table for communication. Please utilize this wonderfully loving source for all of the healing, love and understanding it can give. Sometimes, the healing energy it transmits through the table is ample reason to solicit its presence on the table.

There are several layers of Higher Selves above yours and the highest of all Higher Selves is the Holy Spirit. The Holy Spirit is the Higher Self of God. The Holy Spirit is appropriately and perfectly named for Holy means "most whole" or Wholly Spirit - the most balanced and perfect spirit. How fitting it is that the initials for both the Higher Self and the Holy Spirit are H.S.!

The most valuable benefit derived from communication with the Higher Self through the table is that you are aligning yourself with its energy each time you communicate with it, creating a bond that is deep and thorough. The bonding can create for you the capacity to be in continual contact with your Higher Self even when you are not using the table. You will begin to understand that the Higher Self is within and around you and that it is forever connected with and never separate from you.

Having a permanent bond with the Higher Self attunes you to your path in this life. You are able to balance and blend your spirituality with your physical self.You will be enabled to flow through your own death experience fully conscious that you are traveling through this veil of transition with a beautifully aware peace. When you and your Higher Self become one you have achieved masterhood. You are totally attuned intuitively to its will, living as a master, for you are no longer separated from your God Self.

When you become one with the Higher Self your soul no longer needs the life and death cycles of reincarnation. I have seen, aurically through its special coloration many souls with the Higher Self partially overshadowing the lower self in a permanent manner and so I know that many of you are progressing along your path of mastery beautifully.

NOTES

4. St. John of the Cross, DARK NIGHT OF THE SOUL, trans. and ed. E. Alliaon Peer, (Garden City, N.Y.: Image Books, div. of Doubleday & Co. Inc., 1959)

"PRICELESS AND IMMORTAL ARE THE ACQUIRED GIFTS OF WISDOM AND LOVE. THEY ARE THE ONLY POSSESSIONS THAT YOU CAN TAKE WITH YOU THROUGH THE VEIL OF PHYSICAL DEATH INTO YOUR ETERNITY. "

CHRISTOPHER

CHAPTER EIGHT

Using Table Tipping For Personal Spiritual Growth.
A. HEALING AND BALANCING

WHENEVER ANY SPIRITUAL helper, whether it is a guide, an angel, a teacher or your Higher Self comes to the table there is an energy exchange that takes place. At the moment you and the sitters have created your energy circle a great deal of energy balancing and expanding transpires on a group, as well as, on an individual level. Thus before the table initiates any movement a great deal of energy and vibrational work has been accomplished.

It is notably apparent to me that spirit regularly evaluates your auric frequency before approaching the table. Sometimes it sends out a beam of laser-like light that scans you and your energy field. Often during this scanning time, there is little if any table activity. The evaluating spirit then sends an appropriate balancing light and frequency to and throughout you. Your capacity to receive this energy is contingent upon your willing openness to the spirit's energy assistance. Sometimes, you will physically sense this help or emotionally feel the energy exchange. This energy work appears to happen automatically to each person seated at the table.

I have always had concerns about healing and karma. If it is not requested, I feel a person should not send healing energy to another because it could interfere with a soul's lesson or karma. With this in mind, I do not ask the guides to do a healing. I let them suggest it or just simply go ahead and do it. I am very thankful that the guides are so keenly aware of my and the other sitter's energy needs.

When I start a table tipping session I breathe in through my nose and exhale through my mouth several slow deep breaths to establish my intention of being a willing and open receptacle for all of spirit's healing energy. I fill my whole being with the concentrated thought that I allow in all healing and balancing energy without any resistance.

When a child falls and scrapes his knee, he runs to his mother. Her loving caress, embrace and concern initiate the healing of his injury through the loving bond of his trust and focus upon her nurturing energy. When she kisses his wound and tells him it is all better, he believes it within all levels of his mind and, in that moment of trust, the body eases into the miracle that it is healed. This is true whether the mother goes through a cleansing and medication application to the wound or not. Thus when you receive a healing vibration through the table, if you remember the child's openness and deeply feel the love-bond trust with the healing spirit, incorporating the energy through all levels of your whole energy unit, you too, will be miraculously healed.

All healing takes place in your spiritual body layers first, then it progresses to the mental, emotional and physical bodies. The individual soul must choose to be healed deciding there is no further teaching purpose or need for the experience of disease or discomfort in the body, mind or emotions at this time.

Each guide has the ability to analyze the chakras of your aura to ascertain if there are any blockages that are ready to be worked through or cleared. However, the Higher Self is aware of your energy body problems to a depth of evaluation and understanding that is not available to your guides. You can inquire about each chakra one at a time. Ask if there are any blockages in a specific chakra and then question if you are ready to work out the blockage. At this point, you can inquire as to the source of the blockage determining if it is due to actions, beliefs or other causes of this lifetime or past lives. You may ask your Chief, Karmic, Joy or Health Guides about these blockages. But, it is important to consult with the Higher Self because of its intimate vantage point of non-judgment.

All of us are healers, especially of ourselves. The most effective healing which can cure physical, mental or emotional problems comes through the recognition of a blockage and then its clearing. Through self awareness, we can redo the pattern of unbalance we have created in our lives. This clearing or balancing can be a prolonged process without the use of the table.

Balancing of chakras is an ongoing process so do not be discouraged when you feel you have cleared a chakra only to discover it is blocked again. It seems as if the blockages of a chakra are like the layers of an onion in which you peel away layer after layer as you grow. Each layer you clear takes you deeper into your Self. Some of those layers are very subtle and you may think you have already totally worked through the problem involved. This may be true but at that point you have reached the deepest layers because you have further evolved and become stronger. You then are armed with an awareness to complete the cleansing. Obtaining direct input about the steps to be taken from the spiritual sources available through the use of the table quickens the whole procedure.

The guides will help you to be aware of any

imbalance of the system of each of your bodies. For example, there are times you may have worked with your spiritual growth to such an extent that one or several of your other bodies may not be caught up to the same frequency with your spiritual body. In other words, they are not synchronized in frequency. If any one of your bodies is out of vibrational step with the others the result is usually a weariness of the physical body, you may be very exhausted which creates a concern that you might be in poor health. The guides can tell you if this condition is caused by an imbalance of your bodies. Imbalance can result in a health problem if you do not recognize it and harmonize it. Spirit can analyze your aura and give you a detailed report of the state of balance of each body layer of your energy unit. Often the guides will offer specific advice about how to harmonize your being.

Each time you meditate and work with your psychic and spiritual gifts you raise your frequency a bit. If you do not put into practice what you have learned so that the emotional and mental bodies can experience new growth the physical body usually suffers due to the lack of coordinated frequency. All too often, we want to know all about spiritual growth but we do not apply the knowledge given. The only way to gain wisdom is to incorporate this knowledge into our daily experiences. This is how we can establish which concepts are practically useful to us. Within this process we can release old patterns and incorporate new and useful beliefs.

Once in a meditation, I discovered an underlying fear that had direct affect upon my actions creating imbalance and unhappiness. I was told that I had to face the fear and recognize it. The prospect of working out this fear seemed insurmountable. I procrastinated avoiding any effort to try to work through it. I noticed that my normally graceful, easy inner communication with my guides and Higher Self was not happening. I was physically tired and experiencing the difficulty of not sleeping well at night.

During my next table session I asked my Higher Self to give me specific details about this fear. It said the fear was a pattern from many past lives. My Chief Guide and Self told me that I was avoiding the practical application of the knowledge I had requested in the past. Armed with the necessary information, I happily learned that I was ready on all levels to work through this fear. The guides told me to be loving and gentle, but persistent, with myself while dealing with this fear. Listening to spirit's suggestions about observing myself, I became aware of the depth of this fear and its direct impact upon my everyday actions and thoughts.

I learned that if you ask, you receive. But the act of asking creates a responsibility. Once you have opened up to the growth of knowing, you are expected to act upon the knowledge gained. The sleep difficulties I experienced were due to my guides and Self trying to get through to me via dreams rendering instructions as to how to work out the fear. But the fear was so deep that my conscious mind was not allowing any recall of their help to come through to my waking consciousness. The result of this inner struggle was incomplete sleep.

Due to the empowering of our energy circle and my direct communication with spirit, working through this fear was simplified and rather easily facilitated. First, I used a meditational process given through the table by my Higher Self. Then I employed the guides suggested conscious effort during my waking hours to detect and observe this fear whenever I noticed that it was the basis for my actions. The guides informed me that I was to tell this fear it had been a good teacher in the past, but that at this time it was no longer useful to me. Gently working with this fear in several table sessions, in meditations and through detached observation I was able to remove its inspired instantaneous habitual emotional response from my daily actions. This process paid off well because now, free from its influence, I am empowered to choose how I want to think and act. Quickly, the size and importance of this fear began to shrink in intensity until it eventually lost its strength and is now transformed into a helpful tool.

When this episode was completed I returned to a balanced state, creating a flow of my normal physical energy patterns as well as reinstating my normal beautiful, spiritual communication exchanges in my meditations and dreams.

While you are working with balancing yourself, you should ask the guides about color. There are certain colors that when worn on the physical body help to implement a balancing or a healing by their vibrational influence. The subject of color is one of my guide's favorite areas of interest. I have discovered that their concept of my auric colors are similar to mine. I have a great deal of lapis blue in my aura. The guides have told me that to wear clothing of that color enhances my strength throughout my work day. They said that wearing your predominant auric color for balance and strength is true for anyone. The guides will share with you information about what specific colors will affect your moods. They will help you to know your current personal colors for clear thinking, courage, and calmness. These colors can be physically worn or visualized to be spiritually placed in your aura while you need them.

The guides will often suggest certain herbs that can assist in a healing physically, mentally or emotionally. My psychic guide told me that blackberry leaf tea is very calming and enhances my relaxed state to allow in more detailed psychic impressions. This herb works for me because in one of my several Native American past lives this plant was used effectively to help me to develop my psychic capacities.

Healing can been accomplished on an emotional and mental level. One example occurred when a client's sister, who was very important to her emotionally, had stopped talking to her. This communication problem had gone on for several years starting immediately after the death of their mother.

As a sitter at a table tipping session, the client asked her Chief Guide if he could help her deal with this emotional pain. He replied **Yes**. There was a pause involving no movement of the table, because her Chief Guide went away from the table seeking another spirit. He returned with my client's mother. She was almost completely overwhelmed when her mother came on the table because her mother gave out such a beautiful and expansive love energy. She moved the table to let us know she had a message. She was able to deliver the message telepathically to all the sitters but the original lady. So often when the information is for yourself, personally, you are so emotionally involved that you have less clarity or ability to tune in. The mother let the sitters see her psychically allowing them to accurately describe her appearance in detail to the client. She telepathically sent evidential details about the circumstances of her death. All this information proved to the client that her mother was indeed present.

The client learned that her sister was still in great grief over their mother's death and had misunderstandings about whether her mother loved her or not. She said the sister felt that she, the mother, loved the client more that her. The client was very thankful for the understanding this information presented. Their mother said she would place clouds of love energy around them assisting them to talk through the problem, if only the sitter would talk with her sister. The client called her sister after the table session and they discussed their mother in such a way as to reestablish their loving sister relationship. The client said she could feel the magnetizing love of her mother as they talked. The sisters are now very close and deeply content with each other. There have been hundreds of tipping sessions when the table proved to be a powerful emotional healing tool.

One woman who came to a session had difficulty walking and sitting comfortably. Soon after the beginning of the table session one of her guides came on the table. It told her to relax. Then all of a sudden the table literally jumped up off the floor and went into her lap to touch her left side. We had difficulty keeping up with this rapid and unusual movement with our hands. When it settled on her we all felt an incredible heat accompanied by a feeling of painless energy which exhibited the strength of an electrical charge. It was very intense! I could see large beams of bright green and pink light going into this woman's side. She said she felt a great deal of heat coming into her body. The color beams remained focused on her side for several minutes, so I told her to relax and let in the healing energy. The table and our hands were in an uncomfortable position. We all endured strong sensations of heat and rippling energy for quite some time.

When the color beams and the energy sensations stopped the table moved and settled back onto the floor. The woman said that she was experiencing a new calming sensation in the area where she had previously been feeling a persistent irritation and pain. She told us that the condition, which was located in her left hip and lower back, had been bothering her for some time. The pain had recently intensified to such a degree that she decided to refer to a doctor about it. She was elated that it was miraculously gone. She said the pain melted away as we sat there with the table on her. She noted that the heat she experienced coming through the table was almost unbearable but that it did not frighten her because it was sent with a wondrous love. She told us that her doctor was preparing to try some procedures in the next week to help her. He had even discussed performing surgery.

A week after our sitting, she notified me that to her delight she was still pain free. She followed through with her doctor's appointment. He was quite puzzled as to how her problem could be so much better and determined it was so improved that he was not needed. This woman recently communicated with me again (two years since our table tipping healing event) telling me she is still pain free and normally mobile as if there had never been a problem. We all witnessed a physical healing during that sitting.

A male sitter, Ben, had a visit from his father who had died four years previous to our session. His father spelled out his name perfectly, which was a long and unusual Polish name. No one at the table knew Ben well enough personally to have a preconception of this particular name. It was not a logical situation to us since he had been adopted by another man and we all only knew him by his stepfather's name. Ben's birth father telepathically gave detailed reasons explaining the circumstances for his running off from his family when Ben was a boy of six. The incident occurred after a family picnic that we were all able to "see" and describe in full detail as to who was present including the model, color and type of car the family owned. The experience was very emotional for Ben.

His father was seeking forgiveness for his perceived irresponsible actions. He professed his love for Ben and told of the difficulties he had in this recent past life with his self- image due to a job loss at the time and the arguments he had with Ben's mother. His father said he could not go on with his spiritual growth until he was able to receive Ben's heartfelt forgiveness and understanding of how great his love is for Ben. If Ben could forgive him with unconditional love at this time, through the table connection, he would be released from a karma that otherwise he would have to return to earth to work through in another lifetime with Ben. Since this karma could be graced by spiritual love and forgiveness in this table session, both he and Ben could be complete and free of that karma. Ben tearfully forgave him and reached an understanding about his father he had never had. The table physically leapt into Ben's lap as the father gave Ben a big spiritual hug.

This realization about his father opened Ben. He was able to clear himself of the blockage of issues of self-confidence and release a fear of rejection that had been affecting Ben's relationships in his adult life. This was not only a beautiful healing for Ben on all levels, it was a blessing and healing for his father as well. They both were freed of so much blockage that their spiritual progress was greatly enhanced. These types of healings are so powerful and wonderful to experience because you can feel the beautiful impact it has on all of those involved.

When I was teaching public school, I started to experience a very noticeable pain in my abdomen in the lower left side. I went to several doctors and was tested but nothing showed a specific problem. At the time, I was trying to convince my fellow teachers to support me in my demands for more effective programs for children with learning problems. These teachers agreed strongly to my face but when I presented the idea at a board meeting they remained mute when the principal asked if any of the others present felt the same way. We never got the programs to help the children. I noticed that this abdominal pain had reoccurred often since then.

I asked the guides about this pain and its origin. My Health guide helped me to understand that in a lifetime in early Saxony, I was a thirteen-year-old boy who inherited the leadership of our hamlet from my father who had been killed in battle. I was well-liked and felt supported in our hamlet's needs. I was excited about a project of achieving peace with two neighboring communities that were constantly attacking our people. I was told that there would be a meeting of the leaders of those communities in the forest at sunrise one morning. I excitedly rode my horse to the agreed upon meeting place. When I arrived, I was pulled from the horse and speared through my body. The spear impaled me to the ground. I was struggling to get it out and get back on my feet but it had severed my spine, paralyzing my legs. As I lay there helplessly bleeding to death, I saw that the perpetrators of the deed were some of my so-called supporters for the peace project. They disguised the evidence and fled the scene, leaving me to experience a painful, slow and lonely death.

I learned I did not forgive others who did not support me in times of my need to fight for a cause. My lesson was to understand that each person has different strengths and principles. Each time I had difficulties about being supported in causes, this pain returned. With the help of the guides and my Higher Self through the table, I worked through this blockage and released it from my physical body cell memories. Now I have very little problem with this pain.

A lady sitter named Marilyn had a spiritual visitor that appeared as a small pink glow with a bald head. It was filled with so much love that we all trembled with the intensity of it. The glow was almost cuddly in its softness. It proceeded to spell out its name. Marilyn immediately became tearful. Its message was, "Thank you, Mother for the chance to live, for that is all I needed to do to complete a karma. I only needed to go through the discomfort of a birth experience." Then the table spiritually hugged Marilyn for a long time. Marilyn emotionally told us that years ago she had given birth to a beautiful baby girl that lived for just a few hours.

Marilyn told us it was very difficult for her to bear because she could not understand why such a tragedy had to happen to her and her baby. She was thankful for the new understanding. The baby informed her that she was very happy in spirit because she had gained much spiritual growth through the physical birth experience that Marilyn provided for her. The baby now spends much time around her mother, Marilyn, somewhat like a spirit guide. This was another of the hundreds of experiences I have joyously shared with sitters which I classify as a healing experience - emotionally, mentally and spiritually - often resulting in physical well-being.

I always drink a lot of water after a healing experience of any level to cleanse the physical body and to symbolically cleanse all the bodies to allow the healing to settle in permanently. I often take a sea salt or sea kelp bath to complete the work of the balancing of my frequencies after I have worked through a healing experience.

When you are out of balance it can cause a need for physical rest to energize your whole being. There are certain physical processes and things that you can do to help harmonize and balance your energies. Sometimes, your Health Guide is the best spirit to consult about your energy balance problems. I have had one suggest eating sunflower seeds or to not eat certain foods for a period of time such as caffeine or chocolate. There may be certain objects that come into your life which are powerful balancers. They can be crystals, sea shells, feathers, pine cones or other natural objects. The guides will let you know from time to time that you may need the healing influence of such an item and why. Sometimes, these objects are to be slept with, carried on your person or used in meditation.

Balance is crucial to your progress and it is best to regularly ask the guides and your Higher Self to help you to be aware of how to maintain it personally.

B. GAINING AN AWARENESS OF YOUR SPIRITUAL INTENT FOR THIS LIFETIME.

DISCOVERING WHY YOU CAME INTO THIS LIFETIME

Remember that your soul is always flowing towards its mastery with or without your conscious awareness. The soul's happiness and main thrust is to expand to its fullest God capacity. If you choose to tune in to where it is on this evolutionary path you can consciously cooperate with its progress and allow yourself to speed it along. Armed with the knowledge of; who you are, why you came here and what are the strengths and weaknesses that you chose to bring into this life to utilize as tools for success, will bring you happiness and strength of purpose.

Your soul was excited to come into the game of life. It patiently waited in line, so to speak, to gain entry into a chosen physical form at a chosen time in order to have the privilege to work on earth and experience its evolution here. I am often made aware of this fact when I observe the soul's energy field around our beautiful human babies. The skin color or physical condition of the body or environmental conditions that the child is enduring do not matter. Almost always, their wonderful souls radiate an incredible joy. The 18 month-old granddaughter of a friend of mine is a shining example. Her soul constantly and outwardly emits waves of excitement in the form of what I perceive as Fourth of July sparklers in her radiating rainbow colored aura. It sends out messages of; "I'm here! I made it! Oh how exciting! Now I can get on with it in a big way." Whenever I am around this child I absorb an incredibly blissful "high" that lingers for hours from experiencing one short visit. This "high" sensation reminds me of my own soul's joy to be here on earth expressing itself through a physical body which I so often forget. I feel the baby's soul is in this joyous state because it still has a focus on its incarnation's purpose. Through the table you can gain the knowledge directly from your Higher Self about your soul's purpose which will give you an inner joy that is as strong, but deeper than, your soul had when you were a baby.

To enhance your understanding of the spiritual intention for which your soul incarnated it is best to tune into the primary soul intent which is the principal theme or purpose for this incarnation. Your questions concerning your soul intent can be posed to your Chief Guide for some interesting details, but usually the most inclusive answers will be derived from your Higher Self. You may wish to approach the premise of soul intent from a before birth point of view. Ask the Higher Self if you had any special intentions for this incarnation. Then, determine if you had several intentions by having the table do a numerical count.

Of course, there will no doubt be several karmas you have chosen to balance. There will be a definite number of soul lessons you will have listed to accomplish. You can inquire as to the number of each of these at this time if you like. Do not feel overwhelmed by any of this information. Realize that with a conscious awareness and the direct connection you have through the table - and eventually a trusted direct inner knowing you have developed, you will be able to joyously work through the experience of this incarnation with the help of all your spiritual friends.

You may have already addressed the karmic questions you have in conversations with your Karmic Guide. In the section of the book associated with the Karmic Guide, I have given a detailed outline of the subject and how to procure the necessary data concerning your karmas. I have previously discussed what soul lessons can entail in chapter 7, Part E. So, if you have not investigated them previously, please do so.

Now, be aware that the primary soul intent for a lifetime can be a very simplistic concept on the surface but that it is often the total, but subtle, overtone of one's life. It is an interesting fact that a soul intent always includes the elements of spiritual, cosmic or universal law. Some soul intents seem identical to soul lessons. However, when a soul intent is formed, it is a learning process that continues throughout one's life whereas soul lessons are temporary and can be completed within a certain time cycle in one's life. Also, the parameters of soul lessons need not return repeatedly throughout the rest of one's lifetime if they are accomplished.

Soul intents can be basically classified within two general areas of concept - those of balance and of love. For example, soul intents whose performance concern issues of balance are: 1. Balancing the male/female energies within oneself, 2. Balancing the mental and emotional bodies, 3. Learning independence and developing individuality, 4. Balancing oneself in partnerships and relationships, 5. Balancing personal power with universal power by surrendering to universal oneness, 6. Balancing the spiritual and material worlds.

Examples of soul intents which operate within the concept of love are: 1. Self worth and humility, 2. Detachment, 3. Experiencing being alone, 4. Being and expressing love and compassion, 5. Service, 6. Healing and working with energy, 7. Embracing beingness to experience a life of freedom and joy.

The concept of soul intention is of great importance if you desire an indepth understanding of what you are all about in this incarnation. The two lists I have suggested include the universal soul intents we learned about from spirit through our table tipping sessions. You will discover that there are many diversified intentions to which a soul will devote a lifetime, so be very open to what your Higher Self or a universal spirit will share with you.

I feel it is necessary to explain the soul intents that the guides have given to me in further detail. The earth's culture, in this present historical era, allows a soul to fit more easily into the practice of each of the balance intents.

Balancing Soul Intent 1. *The balancing of the male/female energies within oneself,* is a powerful but subtle intent. You have most likely expressed yourself as both genders in your past lives. However, it is very common to discover that you have preferred one gender as you feel more secure in that expression. Within your present self, you are both male and female. You must be able to express both genders in a balanced manner so that you are equally comfortable in a lifetime expression as a specific male or female. Presently earth cultures are giving us more opportunities to be assertive or to display other "masculine" qualities in acceptable ways within a female body. We can express deeper feeling, sensitivity, receptivity and other "feminine" qualities within a male body with full acceptance as well. Never before have the cultures of the earth been so ready to let the male/female balancing energies flow more evenly. As a spirit we are androgynous. However, within a physical body we must choose male or female. Within this body we are to become a perfectly balanced male or female, mastering the aspects of both There are many souls working on this balance in their present lifetime.

Balancing Soul Intent 2. *The balancing of the mental and emotional bodies.* There are many souls who are all mental. They control their lives, decisions and relationships through mental approaches. They tend to be critical and judgmental. Everything must be proven to them through statistics and scientific principles or else they declare whatever is in question invalid. So often their busy controlling mind destroys all their capacity to be open to the truth and wisdom that is within their Godselves. These souls are slaves to the conscious mind. There are other souls who are centered on their own feelings, attitudes and emotions. These souls revel in the lower-self emotions and experience great difficulty in ever sensing the finer emotions of the soul that are impersonal. These souls impulsively respond to their feelings. They take in all situations and feel them personally. They tend to live dramatic "soap opera" lives always feeling victimized. They are slaves to their emotions. Each of these types of souls is here to learn to balance the mind and the emotions, as both are valuable and neither is invalid. Both are within our beings as tools, under our control, for the purpose of balanced use.

Balancing Soul Intent 3. *Learning independence and developing individuality.* There are souls who have a dependency upon others. They feel that others know what is best for them. Many times, these souls have had past lives in monasteries and cloisters in lifestyles where they did not have to take care of themselves in worldly ways. Some of these souls have difficulty with authority in their present life. They are also caught up by a deep need to be obedient. Great frustration is created within these souls because they feel the need to adjust to the demands of others. For example, when another person requires a specific time when they want to eat dinner, those souls will work diligently to be ready for the time suggested at great self sacrifice. They labor under the perception, with great inner frustration, that they do not have the right or the freedom to arrange for an eating time which would be convenient for themselves. They are not comfortable with negotiations because whatever another says, is the rule and how it is, because of the past obedience vows they have taken in other lives. These souls tend to remain in relationships that are not beneficial to them just for "the room and board" or for the dependency they have upon the other person. These souls came into this life to grow on their own and to explore the beautiful personal abilities and qualities they have within themselves. They are meant to focus on their own valid individuality, learning not to need to look outside themselves for direction or acceptance.

Balancing Soul Intent 4. *Balancing oneself in partnerships and relationships.* These souls will learn through their encounters with others through vocational partnerships, family ties and mated relationships. They will see a pattern in these interactions with others and realize the intense effect it has on their own freedom and directions in life. They are to learn how to be a part of a relationship or a partnership without losing any real identity of self. They are to learn to be honest with themselves and their partners about their personal feelings. They are to know themselves by being objective with others, allowing others to mirror to them what they are themselves.

Balancing Soul Intent 5. *Balancing personal power with universal power by surrendering to universal oneness.* This is often the last lesson a soul has to learn. Personal power is limited to your own energy source and the direction of your own will. Personal power is usually directed for individual needs. Universal power is available when the purpose is for the good or betterment of all. Universal power is limitless and unending. Personal power is usually tied to the issue of control. Control is an offender of a spiritual law called free will. Anytime someone tries to control another they violate the other's free will - you can only control your own being and your own situation. Living in the now is a major consideration when dealing with power. If you are focused on all that is happening in the moment - and you are not exerting any energy by mentally hashing over past events and feelings or anticipating future effects and expectations - you are in full awareness embracing the power of the moment. Through that kind of energy balance you are open to universal power as well as putting your own personal power into full potential. We forget that we came in from spirit to experience the adventure of the time/space format of existence to explore the innate unknown it presents as a challenge to remember to trust that we are cared for within the Universal flow. When you achieve this discipline, you are in rapport with the universe and are working within its laws. You flow with the understanding that we are all energy from the same source and are interconnected in well-being. You feel interrelated with the earth and all that is on it. You no longer feel separate from anything. When you shift from personal power to universal power there is a peace in the surrender that allows you to know you are not in control but in the flow. You know you only need to think through the basic steps of the structure of your life and trust that the details of how it will come together will flow to you. This is surrender. Through this principle a new manner of spiritual manifesting is activated. No doubt, you already sense that the old way to manifest is no longer effective. We see its technique breaking down throughout the world. Personal, self-serving power is being exposed whether it is in the political, economic, scientific or religious arenas of our lives. As the earth travels further into the plan of universal law, only those who are within the universal power flow will be able to manifest effectively.

Balancing Soul Intent 6. *Balancing the spiritual and material worlds.* This soul came in to bring its spirituality into the material world. It often may have too much money or not enough. It may feel it is wrong or not spiritual to have money. Or it may go the opposite direction by being very materialistic - equating its value with what it has amassed materially. Within this intent, the soul will learn to feel secure with less, sensing its true freedom from the weight of materialism. Also, this soul may not feel it can accept being human. Its job is to recognize and embrace its weaknesses as human and know that these weaknesses are the necessary tools its soul needs to learn through. This soul can to be too spiritual or too human, denying its spirituality. These souls came in to balance the spiritual and material worlds within the human experience. They must understand that being spiritual is being in God but also being human is being in God. They must love and accept their humanness and blend their spirit within a perfect balance. The reward for this soul, when it achieves this balance, is the union with its Higher Self, bringing the Higher Self fully into the human experience and becoming a master. The souls with this intent, like the souls learning through Balancing Soul Intent 5., must develop their awareness to recognize and flow with the spiritual synchronicities within their daily life as a practical tool for achieving their goal.

Next, I will share the guide's explanations of the soul intentions based upon the principle of love.

Love Soul Intent 1. *Self worth and humility.* So many of us came into this incarnation with the goal of learning and totally experiencing this love soul intent. It seems amazing how many difficult predicaments in life boil down to the basic principle of *not feeling worthy*. Many souls working through this intent have problems manifesting money, success, true love and happiness in general, because on some deeper level they do not feel worthy of these God-given rights. Many souls carry this pattern through numerous lifetimes. It is interesting how deeply the concept of humility is connected to and confused with self-worth. Humility is recognizing you are part of God and a small part of the Big Plan. If you acknowledge that you have God within yourself, then it is incorrect to feel unworthy.

Nevertheless, worthiness must fit within the parameters of humility to function as a part of the universal creative plan.

Love Soul Intent 2. *Detachment* is letting go of all things that can be a distraction from your true spiritual nature. The thought of detaching can seem unnatural or even threatening. But it is the key to having it all. Letting go means to part from an emotional and mental obsession with money, things and people. A soul that came in to learn this soul intent seems to be the victim of losing people or possessions in their lives. Sometimes, they lose fortunes. The focus of this intent is to put all that is of this earth in its proper place. Material items (or all that is in third-dimensional form) are tools for the soul to use for experience to learn through. There is a difference in acquiring money just to have it - working under the perception of not knowing how much is enough - and the procuring of money in order to live comfortably. Basically, if you remember that all is spirit, you will know that all is available to you at all times so there is no need to hold on to anything. Holding on stops the flow. Even the flow of your own progress and good.Your personal desires create your emotional sense of need but in reality you need very little physically to evolve. A relaxed sense that you trust you are in the perfect flow of the All allows all to come to you. As you let go you create an opening for the All. When the whole of everything is in proper perspective you realize you are spiritual, first and always, and then a physical being. You understand that detachment creates a wonderful sense of freedom and flow. True detachment establishes a comfortable state of abundance.

Love Soul Intent 3. *Experiencing being alone.* This intent is the purpose chosen by a soul who has, in past lives, been in large families or other cultural communal influences with strong emotional attachments to the group. This lifetime they have chosen to be alone to allow for a deep understanding and knowledge of themselves. Sometimes, these souls have a fear of being alone because they perceive it as a source of loneliness and have forgotten they chose to have time to enjoy knowing their own beingness. Being alone allows them the chance to search out their personal qualities. They need quiet centering cycles of time to be by themselves in order to learn to be individual. Once this individuality is secured then this soul will be and feel whole with or without others around them.

Love Soul Intent 4. *Being and expressing love and compassion.* This goal can be beautiful and inclusive. This soul is willing to feel life with an open heart, a heart with no barriers or walls of self-thought or self-importance. It is completely comfortable in the constant flow of love with no regrets or expectations. Sometimes, these souls reside in the bodies of the retarded and handicapped individuals whose purpose is to teach others unconditional love. Other souls with this intent are joyously well and are the ones who exude love, understanding, tolerance and compassion towards others in great degrees. They know that all is forgiven and all is blessed through love. They realize that one of the most direct and efficient paths to mastery is through unconditional, perfected love. They have no self-centered thoughts. These souls throughout their entire lives teach others about unconditional love through their actions and very existence.

Love Soul intent 5. *Service.* These souls are in service to humanity in all ways. They innately know that to help others is to help themselves. These special souls *are often consciously aware they are here to serve.* They assist as often as possible and as thoroughly as they can. They volunteer their abilities and perform their everyday tasks with a specific awareness of others' needs. Most often, their vocations are in the humanitarian and helping fields of endeavor. They are not concerned with monetary return for their time as much as for their helping results. Being a true service-oriented soul, they know that their work never creates a dependency upon them personally for allowing a dependency upon them would be an ego trip they would never allow into their being. These souls inspire the best qualities in others and arm those they help with an awareness of their own worth. They are masters of empathy and are never involved in sympathy.

Love Soul Intent 6. *Healing and working with energy.* These souls have energy-shifting capacities. They create the mood wherever they are by directly effecting the energy of the space inhabit. This ability enables them to heal others through their thoughts, emotions, words and actions. These are powerful souls due to their potential effect upon the earth itself and humanity. Many times, they have a strong effect on the others in their presence and have no conscious idea why. They can achieve so much more if they become aware of their capacities. Sometimes, they are very sensitive to the energies around themselves because they are so open to the energies being exchanged. They can fall victim to mood changes, not realizing they were in a place where that type of energy existed and they simply took it on. These people must constantly monitor their physical, emotional and mental senses. They can literally "catch" a headache or depression from someone around them and believe it to be their own. They must learn to be actively aware of energies and to transmute any negative energies they absorb. At present, the earth needs these souls' incredible healing and balancing energies. Activating the usefulness of these energy souls will be discussed further in the chapter on universal and impersonal purposes for table tipping.

Love soul intention is 7. *Embracing beingness to experience a life of freedom and Joy.* It may surprise you that many souls have incarnated to experience joy and happiness in life. It is my belief that God's original plan was and is for us to be happy and joyful. However, we, through our own thoughts and emotions, have stepped away from that principle. These souls have awakened the memory to know inwardly who they are - a beautiful, immortal, loving, creative God Essence. A soul who is to express joy understands that the greatest glory is - *to be*. To be joyous by accepting what it is - a beautiful, bright, resonating part of the All in action by virtue of its existence. If you can relax by letting go and resonating with this principle you will be happy. It is so simple - so simple that it is difficult for most to understand fully how to live out such a beautiful way of being. Watching a joyful baby lets you see that we have the natural sense of joy and enthusiasm inside of us. A soul living this principle is constantly in touch with the flow of love and joy from within and needs no outside influences to energize itself. Deeply joyous and balanced it sees and realizes all is God energy by feeling an affinity, from within, with all there is. It is ever aware that all levels of existence are of great importance within the expression of the God Source. It is cognizant that *all is God* and that there is only an illusion of good and evil within the mind of man. It knows that all of us have chosen to come into life to relax, experience and enjoy it to the fullest. When this knowledge is acted upon it allows the soul to experience true peace and freedom.

Once you have determined what soul intent or intents you have chosen for this lifetime, ask your Higher Self how you are doing in the performance of those principles. Ask if you have worked with this soul intent in other lives. You may discover that you have already prepared yourself for doing just the finishing touches of this intent because of the work you achieved in other lives. Then determine if your Higher Self has any suggestions as to the manner through which you can fulfill your soul intents in this life.

C. PAST LIVES AND THIS INCARNATION

FINDING THE ANSWER TO - "WHO AM I?"

Now that you have researched your soul lessons, karmas and soul intentions, you have an understanding as to why you came into this incarnation. If you thoroughly research your past lives, using your spirit guides' points of view and the intimate insights from your Higher Self's macro vantage point you can put together a focused picture of who and what you are. You will understand the power and value of your weaknesses as well as your talents and strengths.

The table tipping procedure lends itself to searching out past life knowledge very easily. You have already established a trusted direct conversational access with your guides as well as your Higher Self. You will learn that all that you are now is the result of the unique experiences you have had in the past. You will discover that certain past life influences have a powerful effect on your life today.

Repeated past lives involving specific cultural systems have a deep and ingrained response in a soul. One client of mine had many past lives in the native black cultures of Africa. She is convinced she is a black person in a white body. She feels at ease when she is with black people. Many of her present day relationships are centered upon black people and their problems because she only feels at home within their families and their belief systems.

There is a yachting friend of my husband who has had so many past lives in the orient that most of his guides are Oriental in appearance. He, too, is only attracted to Oriental females, foods and customs.

I have a close spiritual friend who sensed from early childhood that she did not relate to her present way of life. This created problems for her within her family's belief system, because she did not believe in the social-climbing directions they pursued. Religions seemed phony to her. She was very aware of and respectful about the spiritual ways centered upon the earth and its balance. She made the acquaintance of a Sioux elder who now considers my friend her daughter. Instantly, upon their meeting the Indian lady claimed that within her heart and whole being she recognized my friend as truly being a Native American Indian. The elder said she knew her deeply on all levels from tribal past lives.

In each of these cases, a study of these souls' past lives rendered a deeper understanding and ease with what they were feeling inside on a soul level in this lifetime.

There are some babies that come into this life very angry and unhappy. They cry a great deal because they have rushed back into the wheel of life too quickly possibly due to a wartime death that shortened their most recent past life. They did not allow sufficient time for a healing and reconciliation to happen on the spirit side of the veil of life. This anger can be carried by their soul for years into this present incarnation and can seem to have no known source. If a regression is done or that person table tips they can discover the reasons for the anger. Not only are the causes uncovered, but because the soul is directly communicating with the Higher Self, a healing and release can be done. Through the healing and release they can also regain all of the soul grace achieved through that past life experience.

The Higher Self will guide these souls step-by-step through the proper releasing techniques if asked. The Angels of Mercy will come and render a healing, releasing from the body cells the memory of the pain emotionally, mentally and physically. This releases physical body problems if they are from the past and are no longer useful as a teaching tool for the soul now. With these releases, a cleansing occurs that brings

Light into the cells of all of your bodies and raises your frequency opening the doorway to higher consciousness.

The releasing of the pain and fears from a past life death experience creates a comforting level of understanding and comfort with the physical body death process in this life. Spirit says that death is a graduation to the next level of evolution. Death comes when we have completed our earthly lessons and do not need to serve through this personality any more. Spirit says that the death of the physical body is simply a letting go of our costume and putting it away as our stage performance in that role is completed.

There are souls who come into this life with numerous physical sensitivities such as allergies or an unusual light and vibration awarenesses. These sensitivities are present because the soul has had recent past lives in other planetary experiences quite different from the earthly environment. Instead of being a victim to such sensitivities in this life through an ignorance of the real facts, they can be using, with comfort, these tools of awareness. The Higher Self will clarify why the soul has these qualities in this lifetime. It can illuminate the person as to why the sensitivities were brought in and how to utilize them effectively.

Doing a thorough and efficient study by keeping records of your past lives will reveal to you any past life personality patterns that you need to understand and work through. Please be open to recognizing lives that you devoted to special talents and quests for wisdom. Also determine that there were happy lives as well as unhappy lives. The act of writing out your information will assist your higher mind to blend the past life work with your present life consciousness, if it is in your best interest. Learning about the whole of yourself tends to balance your being and is always a healing experience.

Keeping records will help you line up the necessary details to record the origin of your soul and then the very beginning of your Higher Self essence. This is fascinating! You will be able to trace your essence's origins even though it is from a cosmic placement. Some students have traced their essence as far back as when it expressed itself as an element. Others have discovered their heritage involving curious Immortals. Be humble and open - *remember all is God*, no part of God is better that another part. You do not consider your hand to be superior to your foot.

Interestingly enough, we discovered that since there really is no time or space in spirit we can go back to past lives and rework them to correct situations from those past historical times in order to eliminate their negativity from this life. We know that in spirit *all is happening at the same time; there is no future or past*. This creates an "etheric time travel" effect. However, I feel you should discuss this with your Higher Self before attempting any rearranging of your past lives. You can also travel into your future lives via "etheric time travel" giving you an interesting insight into the results of what you are doing in this lifetime.

Through the visions and other telepathic input received in the table tipping process, you will develop an ease with receiving past life information on your own through dream and meditation and then confirming your information at a table tipping session.

Past life and future life study through spiritual table tipping is powerfully effective because of the diverse sources you can access for information. Putting together all the details gives you a more complete picture of who you are as a spirit. When a soul learns who it really is and understands itself while in the physical body it empowers the soul to be within the Higher Self. There have been experiences that have convinced me that this study is one of the most fascinating and empowering purposes for table tipping.

D. CONFIRMATION OF KNOWLEDGE FROM OTHER SOURCES

The table is wonderful as a backup tool for other ways of obtaining spiritual information. If you have experienced a vision or a meditation you need to clarify to better understand, then the issue needs to be discussed at your next table session. Always be clear and direct with spirit when you are forming questions about the incident of interest. Usually the most important point of interest to clarify is to interpret more fully the symbols you have received.

I do a great deal of inspirational writing and, at times, I want to be sure that I am a clean, clear, direct channel. So I recheck my information through the table as often as possible taking advantage of the power of the energy circle and the objectivity of the other sitters present.

Whatever truth you are searching for can be asked about through several of the spiritual sources available to the table. Your Chief Guide will have one vantage point and the Higher Self another. Often, the Master Guide and the Higher Self are the best energies to question when your concerns are about dreams, out-of-body travel or the night lessons you experience while you are asleep.

Over a year ago I was in a situation where I had to deal with spiritual essences new to me. I had encountered them previously through spiritual journeys, meditations and dreams over a two month period of earth time. These loving energies were giving me information to write in my next book as well as insights to share with students in classes and seminars. I had some difficulty with totally recalling some of the dreams. I would always remember meeting with the teaching energy and then I seemed to go into a deeper sleep loosing awareness of our lesson. I was frustrated. I have experienced this problem before with recalling dreams and soul travel experiences when I encountered new spiritual teachers.

When I table tipped the guides informed me that this happens when I am growing into another level of awareness and am not yet balanced at the new frequency level. The new spiritual energies were of a more evolved vibration than I was and negotiating a direct connection with them through dream or soul-travel and consciously holding on to it for any length of time can be quite an energy adjustment.

When this situation happens I like to use the table to let the guides assist me to settle into my new frequency of vibration. Spirit always has several suggestions of practices and visualizations to help me establish an energy balance within my new vibration level. Then I ask these new energies to help me adjust to their frequencies through the table. The energy circle power bridges the differences in our vibrations in a short time. Without it I have discovered it can take weeks or sometimes months to bridge the frequency difference necessary to have the conscious recall of my visits with them in dream, meditation and soul travel. It is also helpful to ask these energies about themselves when others are present. As it gives an objective point of view to their message and your experience.

You can verify information you have received through other physical tools, such as the Tarot cards, a crystal ball, a pendulum or even channeling experiences. You can also obtain confirmation concerning the accuracy or truthfulness for you of the esoteric information that other humans have given you. You can determine from a higher perspective if it is useful advice for you at this time.

After you have been table tipping for some time, you will develop several ways to receive input from the guides or your Higher Self that do not include the table. But the table is still a very direct manner in which to correct or validate any information you receive. It is an incredible relief and a comfort to have such confirmation as it inspires you to confidently work on your own.

Always remember that the table is a wonderfully direct approach to spirit to solicit their help to identify which tools (physical or spiritual) naturally work the best and are the most reliable sources of information for you.

E. USING THE TABLE TO DEVELOP YOUR ABILITY TO WORK WITH YOUR DREAMS

Everyone dreams when they sleep but many of us do not recall our dreams. Keeping a dream diary will help you with dream recollection. The guides and your Higher Self will be interested in assisting you with dream recall and interpretation. Most of your spiritual dreams are sent to your conscious mind through your subconscious mind from your Higher Self. The Higher Self usually cannot communicate directly with the conscious mind. The only avenue of communicating with the conscious you is through the subconscious mind either in meditation, day dreams or sleep period dreams.

We have many types of dream experiences. There are physical, emotional, mental, precognitive or psychic and spiritual dreams. Physical dreams are totally affected by our physical bodies. If the body is uncomfortable because of a sleeping position, food eaten earlier or the room temperature, there will be a dream effect. The act of dreaming is the result of the activity the mind goes through to be ready to wake up. So, if the body needs you to wake up to take care of it, you will have a dream that awakens you. As an example, you may have a dream of being terribly cold trudging through a freezing snowstorm if you are physically too cold because you have tossed your blankets off your body during your sleep on a freezing winter night.

If you go to sleep without dealing with your problems and feelings of the day, you will have mental and emotional dreams trying to solve these problems in your dreams. In the mental dream you will be outside of yourself observing yourself being very aware of your performance.

During an emotional dream you are intensely aware of your feelings and those of others. Often you will wake up with strong emotions that are the lingering effect of an emotional dream. You do not need to recall the dream to have the emotional hangover. Writing down how you feel emotionally when you awaken is important data in a dream diary.

During a normal sleep period, you will have dreams about every hour and a half. The dreams you have early into your sleep period may be physically caused or the mental and emotional types of dreams. The dreams that occur during the middle of your sleep period may be psychic or spiritual in content.

The guides have suggested three short meditations to do during the day to assist a person to have spiritual or psychic dreams. The first meditation should be when you wake up in the morning and before you get out of bed. It can be very short. It should involve a quick balancing of the physical, mental, emotional and spiritual bodies through visualizing them as layers of energy resonating in perfect harmony. Then, mentally say a prayer of dedication and praise of this new day, that it be wholly experienced with the intention of being in the present, with an acceptance that all situations that happen are opportunities through which to learn. When your intention is directed towards an openness to learning and growing through the lessons the day has to offer, you are aligning yourself with the Universal flow. The second meditation is to be done sometime during the day. In this meditation you are to relax and be open to receiving spiritual experiences and insights by going to your favorite etheric place to calm yourself in order to listen to your inner teacher. The last meditation of the day is to be done as you are falling asleep. The purpose of this one is to review the lessons you encountered that day and observe objectively how you dealt with them. You may realize that there will be a need to learn more about a certain lesson and declare that you are ready for another opportunity to learn whenever it is best. Bless the day for all that it offered to you and then **release it**. When you have gone through such a resolve you are ready for dream experiences and the conscious recall of important messages such as those given in a spiritual dream.

The psychic dream is one where you may receive precognitive information about yourself or another. These dreams are usually very realistic but the colors are brighter than those we can physically see. There is a special feeling sensed that cannot be described in a psychic dream that once it is experienced you know it is a psychic dream. You are usually the observer and of course in time the details prove to be accurate representations of actual future incidents. Some see the details as if they were at a movie. Others receive the details in symbolic form. You will need to determine which technique might be your most accurate process. You can pose questions about your psychic dreams to your Psychic Guide or your Higher Self.

The spiritual dream is also vivid and memorable in reference to color and often takes place outdoors. The spiritual dream is a message directly from the Higher Self to you about your spiritual progress or working direction. It is a soul message. Usually, spiritual dreams are quite moving, energizing and memorable. They may even wake you up. Often they give you an incredible "high" which can last all day.

A spiritual dream I completely enjoyed recently was one in which I was walking in a sunny meadow with birds singing and bright beams of light streaming down on me. I knew I was to walk into a cheerful bubbly stream on my left to find its source. Letting my bare feet enjoy the textures, I walked on the polished smooth stones with soft moss entwining them that sparkled with dew. A deep vitality coursed into my whole being with an electric joy through the soles of my feet. I heard the roar of a waterfall ahead and I soon was at the foot of it. The water was pouring generously from such a high place of origin that I could not see its beginning.

I heard from inside my self to walk into the luxurious falls. The water sparkled with golden energies and had a special invigorating effect on me as it splashed all over my body. Deep inside the falls, I saw an old wooden ladder that seemed to be hanging there suspended in all the falling water. The first rung was quite high for me to reach. Not only that, it was covered with moss and the whole ladder felt unstable to my touch.

Again from inside myself was a persistent coaching, this time to climb the ladder. I was concerned about my safety and paused. All of a sudden it was, that as I thought about being on the first rung of the ladder - I was there. I then realized that to think a desire was to accomplish the action in this dream. As I felt no physical body density I understood why the ladder did not need to be stable. Enjoying the speed of my focused thought-action I effortlessly climbed the ladder. I also became aware that my being was mostly made up of an expanded auric light.

I instantly went up five rungs which were very far apart and would have been physically impossible to negotiate. At this level, the ladder ended on a landing of glimmering crystal rock with patches of bright green moss. Stepping on this enticing shelf, I could barely see a blue white light image beyond my left in an narrow opening through the liquid light of the falling water. By curiously following its faint image, I walked through a portal into a mystical sparkling cavern towards this shadowy auric shape. I was now out of the direct water spray where I could focus on crystalline jeweled walls that were decorated with shelves of old well-kept books. The blue white light image I saw formed into a gentle old man enveloped in an electrically bright multicolored aura. He had an all-knowing countenance surrounded with a long gray beard topping a delicate bodily frame dressed in folds of violet robes bent over a desk like structure writing on some old scrolls. Seeing only his profile, I approached closer while he was chanting a delightful song, to witness a full expression of contentment on his face. He did not look up as if he had expected me to stop by and said, "I cannot help you anymore; you have to move on." He felt so familiar and friendly that it saddened me deep in my being to hear that I was to leave him. He looked up at me with a deep soul understanding in his lavender eyes and said, "Our work together is finished and you earned the chance to move on long ago, why do you linger? You can come to visit, but you cannot stay." Literally pushing me away with his magical energy of love, I reluctantly retreated from his light and the vaguely familiar memories of much enlightenment time spent together in this magical cavern.

Once more I was inside the falls feeling almost lost when I sighed, deep breathed and released the old teacher. Immediately I perceived another suspended ladder. This one was crystalline. Nearly invisible, it reflected its shape only when it was within my auric colors. I knew I was to climb farther up into the invigorating falls. Immediately, even before I realized, I had ascended two more rungs and was in a misty musical cloud paradise. Each breath of the surrounding air had a wondrously unusual musical vibration united with it. It was as if I and the air moved in music. The light of this cloud was so bright I could hardly see. My whole being felt charged with a rhythm of excitement. My essence was transforming, no longer was I Angela. A sense of total ecstasy was overtaking whatever I had become. Some part of me knew the ladder was still there but it to was almost invisible in the me as if it was beyond a sense of seeing. I had an inner understanding that I could ascend several more rungs. However, I innately knew there was a place on the ladder two rungs up that would not allow me to return to being in my physical body. The light was filled with love - the most incredible love. I stood there embraced in this love, feeling my heart opening and vibrating in a musical rhythm, dancing at a new level of bliss. I swayed within the arms of a mist of brilliant uplifting light. I was wedded to the light in surrender. It and I were one.

I then awakened still resonating in the energy of this love for several hours into my day. The resonance of the light never left me. I can still call upon its feeling within at any time when I am balanced.

At my next tipping session, the guides told me that I had been hesitant to move on with my abilities and powers and they wanted me to understand that I had much more capacity to fulfill in this incarnation. If I took on the challenge, my reward would be a blissful love within my being that would be permanent. They also shared with me about the ten levels of love and that the symbol of the ladder was to show me where I was within the experience of these levels.

As you progress spiritually you will discover a reflection of your soul's evolution in your dreams. When you are determined to be in control of the discipline of your thoughts, emotions and energies during your waking hours and are having success in this direction, you will see the results in your dreams. You will have dreams that are orderly and not rambling from one subject to another. You will experience more spiritual dreams. You will be fully conscious of the fact that you are in your dreams. Within this lucidity you will direct your actions in dreams just as you would in your waking life. You can have conversations with your Higher Self and other wonderful spiritual entities with perfect recall of what has transpired.

Your soul is active in its spiritual life while you

sleep whether you are conscious of it or not. But it is a much more fruitful experience when you are aware of its activities. This awareness becomes easier as you unfold your soul's natural senses through the growth accomplished by working through your spiritual lessons. Through the table you can ask the guides what suggestions they have to help you to develop an active participation in your dream life.

The guides will help you reach an understanding of the symbols presented in your dreams. Dreams are usually symbolic because symbols are the language of the Universal Mind. The symbols within your dreams are created through your own subconscious mind filter. The modern dream interpretation books that are available now are very helpful. However, remember, trust your own intuitive feelings about what your symbol means to you. When you think you have an understanding of what your dream's message is, check with your Higher Self and your guides when you table tip to verify your interpretation.

Dreams create a format in which we can blend our individual layers of mind for a balance and union. They are also very instrumental in creating a blend of our mind with the Universal Mind. Working with dream recall and lucidity paves the way for this union through which we are able to know who we are. We would have an awareness of our past and future lives seeing it as an ever present -*now*.

Interpreting and understanding your dreams is an essential tool in your awareness expansion and spiritual growth. I know that the table tipping process has the ability to enhance your dream-life and support your self-confidence in this area of self-discovery.

F. USING THE TABLE TO BETTER UNDERSTAND AND WORK WITH THE OUT- OF-BODY EXPERIENCE.

All of us travel out-of-body when we sleep. When a dream feels like real life and you are interactive, you are most likely having an out-of body experience during that dream. There are some individuals who know when they are out-of-body and can control the experience at will.

There are two general classifications of out-of-body experience - the astral body trip and the soul body trip. The astral body is the layer of your energy bodies that includes the emotional and mental bodies. The astral body can slip slightly out of alignment even when you are in an awake state. During that time, you feel "spacey" and not quite together. The astral body trip is when the astral body is out from the body the distance of at least a few feet. You can sense the separation and may feel you can look from a different vantage point back on your own physical body. This can happen when you are in meditation, asleep or when your physical body has suffered some type of shock such as illness or an accident. The distance the astral body can travel from the physical body depends upon the individual and their awareness.

The soul out-of-body trip is when the physical and the astral bodies are left behind and you are only your spiritual energy bodies. When you soul travel you can go anywhere, there are no limitations. Your vision is often extended to three hundred and sixty degrees and you can see all around yourself at the same time. When you experience this vision capacity it is a definite indication you are soul traveling.

Astral travel is usually limited to the proximity of the physical body and close to the earth. The visual capacity of the astral body is not limited to the range of vision available to your physical eyes. You may experience a 20/20 vision while in the astral even though you may have to wear corrective lenses physically.

Soul traveling will allow you to attend spiritual classes in the higher realms. With the use of the table you will be able to determine if you already do such activities without conscious memory. If this is true, you can have the guides give you suggestions about how to achieve conscious memory of these events.

You can ask for help to understand how you can achieve free-will control over your out-of body experiences. Your Higher Self will know if you have the ability to astral travel or soul travel at will. You may discover if you have studied out-of-body travel in other lives. You can reactivate consciously past life talents in this area of expertise with the help of your Higher Self. You can inquire if there are special techniques that work for your energy to enable you to "travel" at will. Ask about how to gain a better conscious recall of your experience when it happens spontaneously. The guides often have suggestions about locating certain areas of your house that are vibrationally conducive to "traveling" while in meditation or sleep.

You can talk with a person who is presently out-of- body when you are at the table. Those who travel this way at will can later verify their "trip" if you have made prearrangements with them for an exchange of communication.

You will discover there is much to learn about this area of your soul's activity. You can determine if you have been doing any special work while you are out-of-body. You may be teaching classes in spirit. The table is an invaluable tool when you have direct questions concerning your out-of-body experiences.

G. GROWING THROUGH LEARNING ABOUT TWIN-SOULS AND SOUL-MATES.

It is the Higher Self who is the most valuable source of information about twin-souls and soul-mates. Both the twin-soul and the soul-mate are usually members of your spiritual family. Ask your Higher Self if you have a soul-mate in your life at this time. A soul-mate is a soul energy that has interacted with you in many lifetimes and could be in a relationship with you in this lifetime as a mate, a close friend or a relative. You will want to ask about which of these relationships the soul-mate is acting out in this lifetime. If you do not know of a soul-mate in your life at present, ask if there will be one coming into this lifetime in the future.

A soul-mate is usually a person who helps you to learn lessons. This means that the soul-mate relationship is not always completely blissful and easy. Sometimes, it is painful to learn about ourselves and most often, the soul-mate's role is to help us see ourselves for what we really are.

There is a deep bond between soul-mates which is difficult to describe to others. The connection is developed through the sharing of many physical lifetimes. The personalities involved have interacted in interchangeable roles. Sometimes as a parent/child, a brother/sister or a husband/wife combination. The various combinations can be acted out through a variety of lifetime roles and the experiences can be gained through being each of the genders.

I believe there can be more than one soul-mate interacting with a specific soul personality in one lifetime. I am aware of a lady whose sister is a soul-mate. She is also married to a soul-mate. What evolves through all the experiences of these various relationships is a deep understanding of the other soul, because on a spiritual level each one has seen every facet of the other's whole being.

When you have a mated relationship with a soul-mate, there will be the opportunity for a deep friendship as well as a fulfilling sexual association. When you meet a soul-mate for the first time in this incarnation, there is a sensation which is not logically explicable. You know deep inside you have known this person before that moment. There is an attraction to the other person you do not understand and find difficult to explain.

My husband Tom and I are soul-mates. When he saw me for the first time, I was in a long line of people waiting to sign up for classes in a crowded University gymnasium. Even though he had not yet approached me, he told his roommates as he pointed me out, "There's my wife." They were amazed because they considered him to be a playboy who would never settle down with any one girl. Besides, without ever having met me how could he know I would be his wife.

While standing in line about three hundred yards away in a space filled with the energies a few thousand people, I felt his focus on me. I looked through the haze of the crowd and only saw his face. I could not turn my eyes away because I sensed that his energy was hauntingly familiar. I felt a deep blush of embarrassment when I realized that I was staring at him.

When he walked over to introduce himself, I was speechless for I envisioned he had many faces from the past as well as the masculine image of the person I had been dreaming about for several years. I could not believe this was happening in my waking life and that I was physically seeing him. I experienced intense feelings coming from a deep place within my being - my soul - my whole spiritual Self. I was so involved in all the levels of the responses to his energy from within, that when he physically spoke to me, I heard him from some distant place. Mystified I did not answer him. I saw in his eyes, he knew I would be with him. Even though I was still speechless, he asked me to go with him to a special event that evening. I smiled trancelike as if I was unable to respond. He asked to borrow my University class catalog. Emotionally stunned, I gave it to him. I had forgotten that I had my address and name in it. He looked in it calling me by name and said he would pick me up around 8:00 o'clock that evening. Still dazed, I smiled as he walked away.

After my registration was completed about, two hours later, I returned to my dorm room. Excited and energized I told my roommate about my dreams and the incredible experience I had earlier that day of seeing them come true. I explained that I must have appeared silly and strange to Tom as I could hardly speak during the entire event of our first meeting. My thoughts wondered how he would know where to pick me up until I remembered about the catalog.

I told my now curious roommate that in one dream he wore a gold ring with a designed square black onyx stone and that in another dream he drove a little red sports car. I broke out in goose bumps with the thought when I said, "If he comes in that same car to pick me up wearing that ring for this date, I do not know if I will be able to speak or move in his presence again!" Near 8 p.m., my roommate anxiously watched the street below from our third story window and suddenly cried out, "Angela! He has a red sports car!" My whole body was electrically resonating with the knowing that he was the one with whom I would live my life. The responsibility of it almost frightened me into a paralysis. When I met him in the foyer I could see the black onyx reflecting the soft chandelier lights, it shone with the same design on the gold ring I had seen in my dream.

He and I have a deep soul-mate bond. I know we have been together as parent and child a few times in past lives. I also remember we were children together as well, for we love to play together like children now. We were also good friends in several lives. We have had many lives as mates and have interchanged our gender roles so that he could be the wife and I the husband and vice versa. We have had several spiritual temple experiences together as students and teachers. We have come together with karma and lessons in this life. That means there can be a few difficult times in our relationship but we always work through these times creating a deeper bond of loving intimacy.

Twin-souls are closer than soul-mates. Twin-souls originate from the same soul source, that of the Higher Self. Twin-souls can be the mirror image of each other. If they are male and female and are mated, it can be an incredibly joyous relationship. The telepathic bond between twin-souls is remarkable. There is no physical or dimensional distance that is a barrier to their connection. It is developed from a deep knowing of each other because they literally are each other since they are of the same essence. There are twin-souls that live a physical life as identical twins. Christopher is my twin-soul and he, as you now know, is in spirit. I feel it is because of our twin-soul relationship bond that I have such a special awareness of his energy even though I am in the physical form.

Ask your Higher Self if you have a twin-soul in the physical dimension of earth at this time. If so, you will want to determine his/her identity and to know some of the lessons and purposes for your being together. If your-twin soul is in spirit, you will want to know where it is. This is an important and interesting area to explore for the more you know about your twin-soul, the more you know about yourself. You could have a twin-soul living on another planet or in a different dimension so that you both are able to gain the knowledge and experience of that existence for your common

Higher Self.

Do not be tempted to use the table to ask spirit to find and bring to you your twin-soul or soul-mate. You would be trying to manipulate another's life. This would be asking spirit to interfere with another's free will. It is not spirit's work and does not fulfill its guidance capacity to bring another soul into your life or to arrange for that person to be in a relationship with you. Remember if you become emotionally demanding, you lower your own vibration and empower your desire body which attracts astral entities to your table tipping session. I have seen sitters when dealing with the subject of twin-soul or soul-mate seriously abuse their opportunity for spiritual growth with sad consequences.

Spirit will gladly tell you all about why you do or do not have a soul-mate or twin-soul in your life. Your Higher Self will help you to develop the awareness of your personality patterns and identify the soul lessons that are involved in these special relationships. It will also help you to understand how to work through the karmas and the lessons involved. You will be able to explore the past lives you have had together so that you can more fully understand the deep feelings you have towards the soul-mate or twin-soul. Seeking spirit's guidance in an appropriately spiritual manner empowers your chances to attract your soul-mate or twin-soul to your energy. It also spiritually enhances your relationship with your soul-mate or twin-soul creating the possible deep levels of intimacy you have sought when you are together.

Be open-minded and enjoy your discoveries in this beautiful area of self-understanding.

*"CRITICISM AND JUDGMENT SCATTER THE
ENERGIES OF YOUR SOUL. COMPASSION,
REVERENCE, HUMILITY AND RESPECT
EMPOWER YOUR PRESENCE BECAUSE THESE
VIRTUES GATHER AND BALANCE YOUR
SOUL'S ENERGY."* CHRISTOPHER

CHAPTER NINE

Exploring Universal And Impersonal Purposes For Spiritual Table Tipping.

NOW THAT YOU have been working on your personal growth with the direct help of spirit through the table; discovering your soul intents, learning about your personality patterns through past life studies, increasing your awareness through dream work and out-of-body experiences, you are ready to explore other uses for the spiritual table tipping process.

You must first be involved with the development of your own self-awareness before you are effective in your help and guidance with others. However, do not feel you must have reached your perfection or mastery in order to be worthy of helping others. Those in need come to you because of where your energy vibrates. Thus, those who ask for your help always unconsciously know your energy level of help is best for them.

Once you are actively seeking self-awareness you are ready to use the table for Universal or more impersonal directions. Universal use of the table expands your energy rather quickly because it takes you out of yourself augmenting your thinking to include the larger picture of the Universal Plan.

In this chapter we will discuss healing on a Universal level. We will explore it on an essentially spiritual level involving those spirits who are in need of assistance. This helps to cleanse the earth as it carries within its aura the dense weight of the astral level vibration of human souls.

We will explore the responsibility that humanity has in respect for the earth as a living evolving energy. You will discover through your conversations with spirit that you and all of the present incarnated humans have an energy responsibility to help the earth during this powerful and sometimes almost threatening time of change. The 90's will challenge the earth and her human inhabitants because of the urge each have to evolve through a window of tremendous expansion that is happening in this and the next decade. The lower emotions such as fear and anger plus the polluted mental attitudes of separatism, judgment and selfishness will be felt by all as the earth purges itself of centuries of these negative energies through storms, earthquakes and volcanoes. Spirit will tell you that when you embrace any of these lower emotions and attitudes you amplify the burden of negativity that the earth is trying to transmute. It is not the time to allow yourself the luxury of acting out what the earth is shedding, because we all will feel the direct repercussion of the earth's physical cleansing process. With spirit's help you can discover how to help the earth.

At this fascinating level of interest, you will attract to the table a more evolved reality of spiritual support to strengthen your efforts. You will discover which of your guides is Universal in intent by their ability to help you with your impersonal work.

A. HEALING - AND THE EARTH AND THE UNIVERSE.

The guides say that the earth is a living essence of God energy which has physical, mental, emotional, and spiritual bodies as we do. I know the earth has an aura because it is visible to me in meditation as well as when I physically view a distant terrain. The local mountains in Arizona all have distinctive individual auric energies. I perceive that many are very busy balancing negative and positive energy flows. There are those that send out tremendous waves of pearlized greens, turquoise and blue color vibrations for peace and healing. One majestic set of peaks, northeast of Phoenix, emit the violet and amethyst flame energy of gracing or resolving karma into the atmosphere above them and then fountains these color vibrations down into the surrounding earth for great distances. There are powerful karma releasing amethyst crystals mined from within their rugged peaks.

Cities also have auras. I am sure these energy fields are developed as a composite of the earth energy at the geographical location as well as from the collective vibrations of the population. These urban auras often contain symbols to give messages about the present well-being or spiritual lessons of the city. While flying over San Francisco for a trip to Northern California in 1988, I discovered a huge golden wheel of energy in that city's auric field. It was slowly spinning around horizontally. The magnificently beautiful wheel, in my perception, was designed like a modernized old wagon wheel gilded to perfection. The hub of the wheel was pulling up and into itself a dense ugly gray energy from the heart of the city. The spokes of the wheel, where they were attached near the rim, were gently spewing out golden sparkles of balanced energy in great spirals. These energy spirals were softly falling down into the city. It was a time of cleansing and balancing of the emotional and mental negativities for that location of the earth. This type of cleansing softens the mighty thrust of earth quakes and other geophysical phenomenon necessary for transmuting negative energy.

Christopher says that the God essence that is within us is within all things. The only differences in the energy is the density of the form that spirit creates for its expression, but all is equal in its God energy. He says that our progression or evolution is involved with the progress of all of that God essence vibration. In other words, we are not alone in the Creative Plan. The whole Plan is effected by our personal evolution as well as our personal evolvement is effected by the whole. It is time that we grow up and realize we are a part of the Creative Order and take on the responsibility of our position.

It is obvious that the earth is in a time of great physical difficulty. If you open yourself to listen to the earth itself, you will hear its need for assistance. It may sound silly or childlike to you but if you take the time to talk to a tree, (You can place the palm of your hand on the tree or sit with your back against the tree and be still.) a rock or the soil itself and listen to the earth's heartbeat and breathing, you can hear and sense the earth's story. It is a tale of humanity's lack of consideration of nature itself in all its forms. It is a tale of how individual humans feel they are not responsible for what others are doing to the air, the soil, the plants or the animals. It is a story of humanity feeling superior to the earth and its creatures and creating an attitude that it all exists merely to fill human comfort and needs. The earth will tell you that you are part of it and the caretaker of it as it flows along its evolutionary path. It will tell you that it is the energy of God in expression as are you. It says the negativity you speak, think and act out directly adds to its burden of imbalance.

The spiritual teachers who come to the table suggest a time of sitting together for the purpose of healing the earth. The procedure they gave us is a simple and beautiful group visualization meditation. After you have gone through the normal preparation of the protective, grounding and centering processes, you are to place your hands on the table bringing in a strong energy from a huge white cloud above your head. Visualize this energy flow in a clear beam of Light - you can choose to see it as white or any other color that comes to mind. Next, image it coming in through your crown chakra area, drawing it down to the shoulders, through your arms and hands and into the table. Visualize the energy going around in a circle involving all of your hands and the table top. Intensely feel peacefully balanced and filled with love. Then, envision this combined energy going down through the table's legs through the floor of the room into the ground.

This process could be successfully performed out-of-doors as well. Send the energy deep into the earth all the way to the core itself. See the energy flow as a strong, healing, balancing and harmonizing vibration that radiates outward from the core in circles and waves of healing in order to fill the entire spherical body of the earth with its vibration. Next, image it bleeding out of the earth's surface into the atmosphere creating clean and balanced vibrations there. You can visualize this healing going outward through the stratosphere and then the ionosphere surrounding the earth. These are the astral and spiritual layers of the Earth's aura.

Whenever a group of us table tip, we do this beautiful earth healing process. You may call in the Terrestrial Angels to assist you with the process to create a deeper and longer lasting effect upon the earth. There have been instances when the Terrestrial Angels tell us that there are certain locations of the earth in serious need of this healing energy. So, they collect it and distribute it there as they see fit in special dosages almost like a prescription to heal the area. If we had not included these angels we would not have known of such a need. Because we take the time to do this earth healing meditation with the table, we have attracted the Brotherhood, masters, Archangels and Ascended Masters to the table. When you are performing such spiritual work, you are touching into their favorite area of dimensional function.

You can use the table to communicate with the tree and mineral energies in order to assist them in their progress in the Creative Plan. During a horseback trip in the Armstrong National Forest of Northern California, I became aware that some of the Redwood tree spirits were stubborn and fearful. Through the table, the Lord of the Redwoods told me some of these spirits had been caught into remaining the essence of these trees. Once a tree died, the spirit only wanted to return to being another redwood. The Lord wanted help in the form of energy balancing to move out these spiritual essences and to make placement for the new spiritual energies that needed the opportunity to express themselves as redwood trees.

These uncourageous redwood tree energies were affecting the progress of much of the spiritual energy in the area by being out of balance. They were in this state of imbalance because of the negative energy collected in the surrounding ecological system. The layers of balance in the Creative Plan are delicate. Any part of the energy system that lags behind pulls back on the energy in front of it and holds up the energies behind it. This is true of all the energies participating with the earth, each in its own way affects the earth's balance and spiritual progress.

Planets progress in the Plan as do solar systems, galaxies and universes. Working with the earth's advancement by healing and balancing it through helping the minerals, plants and animals aids the whole process of progress.

Another interesting facet of earth's spiritual progress is that each energy wave of change it moves through affects us humans as well. It is fascinating to ask the guides about when the earth will be going through another level of frequency change because this always has a specific affect upon man. For instance, sometimes the result is to effect our sense of time. Since the Harmonic Convergence which heralded a spiritually dramatic earth change, we have all felt the sensation that there is much less time in a day to accomplish what we need to do.

An earth change in the fall of 1991 allowed much more energy to be attracted to our thoughts, enabling us to manifest our thoughts more quickly and strongly. We are growing up and in the process we will have to be directly responsible for each thought and the effect it can and will produce. So, think positively and be careful about your wishes. Do not entertain doubts. Our Higher mind is definitely a reflection of our Godself. It is to be used carefully to create our future.

Often Universal and personal growth purposes for table tipping blend. Because we are within the plan of the whole, when we work on ourselves we work for the good of the whole. When we work towards the Universal good we develop our own evolution in the process.

Attuning with the earth spiritually is essential because you are part of its well-being. Contacting elementals and working with them through the table is effective as a part of your personal and the Universal growth. Elementals of plants are friendly and fun-loving. Honor these spirits by communicating with them and participating in their work. So often, we feel separate from all of nature due to our busy daily routines and nothing could be further from the truth. Nature spirits can help you by creating a balanced atmosphere in your personal surroundings. There are specific energies that work with your houseplants. They know if the lighting in the area is appropriate. They will help you to understand how to create the best potting soil conditions. They will tell you that the emotional and mental atmosphere of your home has direct energy impact on your houseplants. They say that your plants reflect back to you the type of thoughts you and your family emit while you are in their space. You can ask which types of houseplants best support your energy.

The plant devas, Lords and fairies are delighted to participate in your outdoor gardening. It is marvelous to have two way conversations with them through the table because you can ask about any problem your plants may have. These Lords will relate to you the data they have concerning the energy patterns of your yard and home. They know which plants work well together and can help you deal with other Lords such as those who represent insects that you might consider pests. Through your cooperation with these yard energies you can set up a protective energy around your home. You can assist them to be balanced which will enable them to transmute outside negativity. Their power to heal and harmonize the environment will be reinforced.

By interrelating with plant energies we have learned of agricultural problems in this and other countries. Sometimes it is in the form of an insect imbalance. We repeat the procedures we used in our own yards by contacting the Lords and devas in charge of the insects to listen to their needs to create a balance. Often the elementals tell us they need certain energies to be focused to help with the clearing of pollutants. Through the table we can amplify the energy circle and send the needed balancing energy to the afflicted land, water or air.

Exploring Universal And Impersonal Purposes For Table Tipping

My father, who lives in Ohio, was experiencing great difficulty with moles in his garden as well as in his lawn. Having learned from my table experiences that the Lord of a species will work with us to create a balance, I decided to work on the problem. When I went to visit him, I meditated for some time in his garden one afternoon allowing for the calming of my outer self in order to communicate with the Lord of the moles. An extremely helpful Praying Mantis Deva told me about the insect imbalance of the soil in the area which attracted the moles. I communicated with each of the insect devas who presented themselves and was able to persuade the moles to move on because they were no longer needed to correct the imbalance as it now would be settled. My father had no mole problems for the rest of that year.

The spiritual energies that work with animals vary with the individual species of animal. Domesticated animals often have spirit guides. Their guides tell us that these animal souls are developing to be in the energy levels beyond animal existence. Being pets, they learn their necessary lessons from humans. Animals are the first evolutionary level beyond the plant level to have an emotional body experience. When the animal is domesticated and spends time with humans, it learns to develop a wider and more evolved spectrum of emotions especially the emotions of love and devotion. They learn and grow spiritually through their close interactions with humans. The animal's guides will help you to know its state of health. Their guides can help you understand the animal's feelings about certain situations in its surroundings. Plus, as I mentioned earlier, these guides will help you understand why the particular animal essence is with you and what its spiritual lessons are in this life.

I recently purchased a horse. His energy is not as old or experienced an animal energy as I am used to having around me. Christopher told me that since a horse is a herd animal type of spiritual experience that I could ask for some of the essence from a horse that he and I shared in a past life to be sent to create in my new horse a familiarity with my personal energy. All I have to do is request the presence through a meditation with the Lord over the spiritual essence group of horse energy. I have not yet availed myself of the opportunity since I wish to get to know the essence of my new horse creating our own special relationship.

Animal spirits come to the table often. Their level of growth demands a different technique in order to understand their message. The process is not difficult. Animals are not word-oriented so they send their messages in a visual symbol and an emotional feeling format. We have had experiences when a domesticated animal soul needs reassurance to cross over. Because they are so emotional, they can feel attached to their owner in ways that confuse them in the death experience.

We had a sweet Sheltie dog energy come to the table once. He was the pet of a retired couple who were traveling in their new motor home. When they stopped to take some pictures of a viewpoint, he ran out the door quickly because he was frightened that they were leaving him behind in this strange vibrating moving home. Once outside in a strange place, he became even more confused. The couple did not even notice he had gotten out of the vehicle. Finished with their picture taking, they returned to the vehicle and drove off. Left behind, the dog was afraid to leave the road because that was the last place he had sensed them. He wandered in terror around, on and off the surface of the road sniffing for a trace of them. Within minutes, a car hit him by accident and he was dead.

He was confused and terrified because he wanted to find his old friends, the couple. He was sure he had let them down or failed them in some way. He could feel their love and wanted them to find him. We and his spiritual guide convinced him that he needed to move on and that he was loved by us and those people. It was important that his spirit guide tell him that it had all been spiritually planned. That he needed to be with the couple for only a short period of time in order to learn about the beginning lessons of love in a dog body. His guide said he was an energy essence new at being a domesticated animal which was a difficult stage of animal development. This can be the first stage of individuality for a soul. The Cherubs and Light Angels came for him when we called for help. They cuddled, loved and soothed him and took him to a Light place.

In another table session, we experienced a water sprite Deva coming on the table at Christopher's beckoning to explain how to keep my swimming pool water perfectly balanced for water sprite inhabitants. They are not common on the desert. I am a person who needs to be around water as it balances and harmonizes me. Christopher said that the water sprites would help establish the energy essence of the element of water in my aura in a more permanent manner whenever I would swim in, meditate by or touch the pool water. Communicating with another water energy, the snow crystal deva, will help you to establish a wonderful emotional cool when you need to be emotionally detached for an effective calm during a stressful situation. Each of these elementals have created within me a special bond with the element of water.

The American Indians believe in totem animals which are spiritual animal helpers. The totem animal is one that can give you a beautifully different vantage point of yourself, the earth and the universe. You can discover what your totem animal is through the table and find out why it has chosen to be with you.

I have a Bald eagle as my totem animal whose feathers are royal blue on the body and metallic gold color on the head. I call him Golden Eagle. When I first met him in a meditation experience, I was walking on a golden white cloud. I heard the majestic sound of the huge bird's feathered wings as he flew over my head from behind to the front of me. He floated on the air above eye level as if in suspension and then landed on an invisible high perch. He stared at me from about six feet away. As he looked into my soul, I felt warm and cold at the same time. I sensed him to be an old friend. Like magic he grew in size before my very eyes and became larger than myself. His energy pulled me close to his right eye. Peering into the depths of his eye I could sense that I was looking into a place of all time.

I knew instinctively he wanted me to have the gift of his prophetic sight. He opened his wings and folded them around me embracing me with comfort and love. I felt a powerful bonding. He quickly opened his beak and consumed me. At first this was a most frightening sensation. Then I understood I was to sacrifice myself to be one with the universe. So I allowed the experience to continue. After he ate me, we became one. I knew his thoughts and could feel and sense through him. We went into flight and soared the airways above the world. We passed through all levels of the currents traveling social, spiritual, economic and political air pathways seeing wonderful things, places and events. I knew that when I communicated with him ever again that I could know future information concerning universal events. I could sense weather and earth patterns. It was an illuminating sensation that has been and is unequaled.

Now, I love flying with him whenever I can, for he has taught me to have a loving rapport with the element of air. It is well worth your time to investigate and learn all you can concerning your totem animal spirits through the table for personal and Universal growth.

Another fun to explore animal energy that will come to the table for totally Universal purposes are dolphin energies. They often give specific details about the earth's condition because they say that the ocean is the earth's emotional body. They have told us of underwater volcanoes and earthquakes, of pollutants that man has dumped and their effects on marine life. Some of the facts they have told us appear in the newspaper weeks later. They often tell us if there are magnetic changes due to the earth's slight shifting upon its axis and that as a result mammals using radar type navigational devices have problems readjusting to their input. During these times we have read in the newspapers of incidents when whales and dolphins have beached themselves.

They have allowed us, as a group, to use our energy circle power to co-experience with them. By being spiritually within their bodies joyously swimming in the ocean, we discovered they are full time multidimensional beings having all levels of mind balanced and active. They can consciously be aware of swimming in the ocean on earth and simultaneously be aware of another reality existence on their home planet. We learned that the dolphins work closely with the angelic kingdom.

The dolphins tell us that they were originally from another planet and have taken the earth form they now have to be in service to the human race. They are extremely intelligent much more so than man will allow himself to believe. They are the balancers of earth energy and love to have your connecting energy cooperation in their Universal work here on earth.

B. CROSSING OVER LOST SOULS TO THE LIGHT

Possibly the most noble and positive impersonal service that the table and its energy circle can accomplish is to help troubled souls who have lost their physical body to death and are confused and lost on the other side of the veil. When I first started table tipping, I was very concerned about protection and would never allow any energy that was not of the Light near or on the table. That is just good practice.

Early into my tipping experience, a group of us had been tipping as often as possible for several months when one evening a spirit, not of the Light and from the astral realm, kept insisting to come on the table. We started the table again and again reprotecting it and ourselves each time but this persistent spirit would not be dissuaded. I noticed that Christopher, who is always present as my Table Guide during my tipping sessions, did not seem concerned about the energy's presence. In frustration we decided not to tip at all that evening, thinking there was some reason we could not attract the Light energies to the table at that time.

The next day in meditation I met a new spirit that was enveloped in a beautiful rose and ruby-colored light. Her face was serious. She had on a cap and a uniform of some sort. She did not communicate with me in any way other than letting me feel her love and serious attitude. That evening when I was getting ready for bed, she appeared again to me while I was taking my shower. I have had visions so often in the shower that now I think nothing of it. When I first experienced a shower vision I was very embarrassed. Then, Chris told me that spirit knows me or all of us even more personally than our nakedness could imply. Since they are not physical, they have no interest in the appearance of our physical being unless asked. He told me that because my shower was all in white and that I always day-dreamed or reevaluated the day in the shower, it was an excellent time for the guides to come through to me.

The female entity repeated her appearances in the shower and during meditations several times. Each time she did I sensed the same sadness and a feeling of deep responsibility. After six appearances, she telepathically let me know her name was Ruby and that she needed my assistance.

My next table tipping experience was with my sister-in-law, Marge, whom I consider a psychic sister. Ruby made her presence known immediately to Marge and me. Marge perceived her image just as I had seen her in the shower. Ruby moved the table to tell us she was not really a guide but that she needed to work with us for a while. She had been a nurse in her most recent past life and had reluctantly worked with the dying. She said she was an ineffective nurse because she could not bear her patient's suffering and eventual death. It frightened her when they were going to die and she was not supportive during the sometimes difficult dying process. Often, she would leave patients unattended while she was outside of their rooms trying to deal with her own upset concerning her fears about death. Sadly, many of these patients died alone and miserable due to her personal problems.

From the scenes she allowed us to perceive, it appeared she was a nurse during the late seventeen hundreds or early eighteen hundreds in a wartime situation. Obviously she had seen horribly disfiguring wounds and painful deaths even though she protested the situation by escaping the scene all too often. It seemed that her father was a doctor and would not allow her to be anything but a nurse, though nursing was not within her heart's desire or her natural abilities.

Now that she was in spirit Ruby had decided to balance the karma of her unsupportive actions of this past life by working in the astral realm where spirit can arrive after the death of the physical body. Her work was to console and give peace to the difficult or lost souls. In order to accomplish this task she must make them aware that they are physically dead and can move on into the spiritual realms. When they are ready she connects these souls with the Angels of Light in order to pass them through to the Light so that they can rest, heal and evaluate their next spiritual steps.

Ruby's problem was that she had encountered several stubborn souls who refused to see or hear her. She was convinced she must be ineffective. She was feeling she ought to give up her job when she saw our Light around the table one night and noticed that astral souls were close by and aware of us. She was able to convince one to come on the table, but we would not talk to it. She knew if we would talk to it that we and she could convince the soul of its state of being and persuade it to move on into the Light.

Sometimes due to the strong emotions the soul has as it crosses through the veil of death it is so dense in frequency that a helping spirit cannot communicate with it clearly. This soul is in an emotional fog of its own doing. As time passes and the soul calms down emotionally, the helping spirits can move into its vibration and communicate. The time that needs to pass for that calming down of the vibrations can be hours, days or hundreds of years because the soul itself usually has lost its time consciousness. This concept was very interesting to me because I know that whenever I am emotionally or mentally upset I have difficulty perceiving Christòpher with clarity. I also know that when I am upset, I too, lose track of time so Ruby's information and her problem made complete sense to me.

Ruby told us that she had several souls who needed our combined assistance. She asked if we would do the necessary pushing of them as she pulled. We would then cross them over into the Light. She knew that the Angels of Light would help us. Then, once these souls were in the Light, they could be attended to by their Higher Self, the Angels of Mercy, their guides and family members to move them forward so they could travel into the spiritual realms where they can progress further with their spiritual plan.

We asked Ruby to explain what we were to do as we were ready and willing to do the work. She and

Christopher gave us some basic step-by-step processes with certain variances due to the many differences of death's circumstances and the personalities of the souls involved.

Christopher assured me that from now on, whenever I perceive him present on my right side during a table session, I am to understand that I am protected. He said that if a non-Light being comes on the table under those circumstances to realize it was sent there to be helped and crossed over to the Light.

The first lost spirit sent to the table was a male who was very frightened. All of us perceived him in a fetal position due to his fear and agony. Telepathically we received that he had been in an industrial accident where he had fallen into a big metal tank that had a small amount of toxic cleaning chemicals in the bottom. The fumes suffocated him before anyone noticed he was missing.

We realized why spirit taught us to be as unattached to his energy as possible for we could physically feel the terrible pain in his chest as his lung tissue burned and started to swell. We were told to be detached enough to be helpful and to be able to move the soul through this experience quickly. He told us he was a new father of a baby boy and loved his family. He was devoted to the responsibility of this family and could not or would not believe he was physically dead. He was angry, frightened and did not want to listen.

Chris told us to visualize our personal energies enclosed in a ring of light around ourselves and the table for protection from his dense and negative emotionalism. Chris helped us to concentrate upon unconditional love and to feel its energy building in our energy circle to a strength that created a physical warmth we all could feel. I perceived the ring of Light as a tube of laser-bright white Light. Next, we simultaneously breathed calm, deep breaths to bring in peace and harmony. We focused again on love, expanding our circle.

We told the man we understood his pain. We explained that we wanted to help him through his situation.

We had to tell him over and over in different ways so that he would believe us that he was physically dead. One way was to ask him if his fellow workmen could see or hear him at this time. He then realized he was alone and somehow separated from the humans he knew and loved. We explained that he was in another dimension. That while he was there most humans would not be able to perceive him. He understood after several tries to touch his friend at the scene of the accident. We were fortunate to be able to help him almost immediately after his death. It is very important in the process of crossing over, that the soul be aware its body is physically dead but it is spiritually alive.

We told him our rules for moving the table to answer **Yes** and **No**. We asked him if he understood and he finally moved the table for **Yes**. Ruby and Chris helped ease his emotionalism. We asked him if he had now accepted that he was physically dead. Finally with great hesitance he said **Yes**. We told him he could be of help to his physical family if he straightened out and harmonized his present circumstance. He listened. We told him to calm himself and that we would help by sending him love and calming energies. He remained quiet.

We asked Ruby to call in the Light Angels. They arrived immediately - with lights in their etheric hands and lined up creating a lighted pathway as that is their work. We told the man to look around for the lights but he could not see them. We insisted that he keep looking around himself in all directions. We voiced each of the directions and then repeated to look up and down. We asked, "Do you see the lights now?" He then saw them. We assured him that we sent him with love to the lighted path. We said that this path would lead to a place where he would receive a spiritual body awareness that would give him happiness and freedom plus the knowledge of how to help his family effectively.

We all perceived him proceed to the pathway with reluctance. He eventually started to walk it. Then he began to feel the angels' love. The Light Angels helped him to release fear and anger with brightly colored healing energies of love. We could sense his relief when his mood changed to happiness and peace. The path ended at a brightly lit opening in which we could perceive beings welcoming him to the other side as he walked through it. He waved a farewell and the doorway closed out the bright Light.

This was a very emotional experience for us. We were filled with relief. We felt, deeply, the extent of what we and he experienced. We had seen a soul floating into the Light and moving on into its greatness. It was an almost overwhelmingly joyous and ecstatic feeling in which we tearfully mused for some time.

Well, Ruby kept us very busy whenever we started a table session. As the months went by, I was sure we had crossed over at least seventy-five souls. Then one day, Ruby appeared to me happy and peaceful. Her coloring was much more beautiful and seemed to be a sparkling bright magenta. Magenta, to me, is the vibration of unconditional universal love energy. She said she was able to move on now to other work because she had balanced her being through her work with these souls. She had actually worked through her karma in this area with our help and the use of the table.

The incident with Ruby certainly taught me a great deal. Ruby had brought about in me the first realization that **spirit** could use the table tipping process to work through its karma. I had thought previously that the table could only help incarnate people to work out balancing and understanding their karmas. I also decided to be more open-minded about the table's varied capacities for helping both spirit and ourselves. I was learning about the table's power for Universal purpose.

Ruby was so thankful to us for our help. Marge and I were grateful to her for including us in such an eminently important work. We learned a great deal about the death experience itself. We were blessed in many ways by the souls who were freed from their astral trap. There were several times while tipping that one of the souls we had previously helped would come on unexpectedly in their white light radiance to show their appreciation for our help. They would let us know what type of work they were doing in spirit and what their future plans were. This type of information gave us delightful and rewarding insights into the happenings of the spiritual realms.

Christopher says that when you do such work you are of immeasurable help to the Universal All. At the time of the act of such work your love is powerfully attuned to the God Force. Through these crossover occurrences, I feel I know first-hand what people have seen and felt in a near-death experience. I have touched the incredible expanded love that is within the Light through the souls who have traveled to and into its essence. It is very comforting to sense the security that this knowledge offers and the peace that results in me personally concerning physical death due to the experience of our work with Ruby.

Since Ruby, there have been many sittings that begin with an energy, brought to the table by the guides, that needs to be crossed over. Each experience is different in minor details but the general process is the same. First, identify the gender and general earth age of the person. The age is important to you for an understanding of how to approach this person. So many times it is a small frightened child that needs your help. Next, understand that this soul is in its present space due to fear, anger and frustration. Try to comprehend its circumstances to some degree. You do not have to know all the details or become involved in the soul's problems to help. Then, let this soul feel and understand that you care and love it enough to help. Try to calm the soul to such a degree that it can perceive the Light Angels or deceased family members who will come from the Light side of the veil to help. You could ask if there is a deceased relative they love that you might call. If this is true, find out if it is their mother, father, brother or whomever. Have the Table Guide assist you by bringing this soul from the spiritual realms for you and the lost soul you are helping. You may have to get this troubled soul's earth name to work out the proper connection.

Continue to talk calmly to the soul while your Table Guide seeks out the relative. Always try to find out from this soul if it is aware that it is physically dead and if it really desires help. As this type of soul is usually not happy where it is, it is easy to convince it to want help to go somewhere more pleasant. Call in the Angels of Light to create the pathway. Have the soul acknowledge that it perceives this lighted pathway. Encourage it to walk the path towards and into the Light at the end. There are some souls who are terrified of going into the Light because they are convinced they are sinners - a "bad" person who will be severely punished by the Light or God. Let these souls understand that the Light, God, is all love and compassion and does not judge them. Tell them that Its presence will help them to lovingly evaluate their life and their next move into their chosen stage of evolution which is never a place of punishment.

There are incidents when many souls arrive simultaneously for help. Sometimes, they are all from the same tragic accident such as an airline disaster. In this instance, you can ask for one soul to be a spokesperson for the group. This is very effective as a process to encourage an entire group to walk the pathway into the Light. It seems that the group can persuade some reluctant souls more easily than you can. We have used this process several times. It works especially well when there are small children accompanied by older children who can better comprehend their situation. Even though all souls are older and only the physical body of this last life was that of a small child, when caught in the astral realm the soul will often think and respond as a small child because it is holding onto its last physical body identity.

If you are doing a great deal of crossover work, employ a special guide to work with you in doing crossovers on a regular basis. Assign to this guide the work of being responsible to collect these needy souls into groups. Ask this guide to instruct those souls about the procedures for spiritual table tipping before they arrive. This will facilitate the process to be quicker and smoother.

If ever you sense a physical uneasiness or discomfort due to a crossing over of a soul refer to your guides as to how to prevent that from happening again. *It is never necessary to have any discomfort if the process is done properly.* Learning how to be effectively helpful, with detachment, offers you a great opportunity to work on your own emotional growth.

An interesting case of a "lost soul" happened in one of our classroom experiences. The deceased first cousin of a male sitter came to the table. He had not been crossed over to the Light at the time. Before we could help him to the Light pathway, he was adamant that we all understand that suicide was useless. He had been drinking heavily for some time before his death. The day he died, he tried some "downers" and drank heavily. He then went on a wild driving spree racing on a dangerously curving road in the hopes of crashing the car at such a speed as to kill himself. He succeeded. As soon as he was out-of-body he sensed an awareness. He knew he would not be able to change or work through his personal and family problems from the spirit side of the veil. He returned to his physical body and checked it out discovering that it was damaged to such a degree that it would never be of use to him again. He was extremely angry with himself.

Interestingly enough, even though he was not corrected with the Light, he immediately sought out those who were thinking about and preparing to commit suicide. He would try to convince them to think through the results of such an act. He wanted them to know that dying does not solve their problems. He now knew that he and they would still have the same problems but no physical body to use as a tool to work through these problems. He was fearful of going into the Light because he was convinced he was doomed to "hell" and would not be able to help others. He was such a beautiful soul that when we told him the truth about the Light he understood and was as cheerful as a child going home as he floated down the lighted pathway.

Several months later, he returned and told us about the entities of the karmic counsel, which reside in a beautiful hall, that help the Higher Self to make decisions about the future steps of its own progression. He said these energies were not only beautiful to perceive but had the same beauty in action. They were serious and fair in a loving manner. They offered several options to him with no pressure. He noticed that now that he was of the Light he was very effective in getting through to potential suicide victims. He was excited to let us know that he was studying and taking training from master counseling souls, so that he could be expert at being a helpful "little voice" in the troubled person's mind.

Another interesting crossover experience came about when I was invited to a historical landmark called the Rosson House located in Heritage Square in the center of downtown Phoenix. The house is a historical museum preserved by the city. It contains many antique furnishings and pieces of other houses that were part of our colorful western history. The people who work at this center have seen and heard many spirits or "ghosts" in the house. One spirit had appeared as a young lady dressed in white who remained in the upstairs bedroom area most of the time. Occasionally she knocked down items and moved a few things. I was asked if I could bring my table and talk to some of the spirits in the house and, if possible, calm them and find out who they were.

I knew that these souls, because they were ghosts, were caught between the veil and the Light and really needed help. A friend and I went with our table one morning. At first, we spent some meditational and balancing time in the home. As we walked about the house the presences there made themselves evident. Some were rather removed from being in the Light and others were curious and slightly confused.

At the table, there were seven sitters and myself. I sat in the north position at the table which was in the beautiful foyer with a polished hardwood open staircase spiraling down to elegantly carved front doors. I could feel Christopher and the other guides collecting a fortified grid of protective energy so that we would be safe during this process. The first spirit to come to the table was a very powerful male who was full of negative energy. He said he came in with a wooden structure that was put in the house for display in another room. This was fascinating proof that spirit is often emotionally attached to furniture and other antiques. He was stubborn and difficult to deal with, so it took considerable time and effort to release him from the house and move him into the Light.

As we worked with some of the other spirits, the lady in white floated in suspension at the top of the open stairway and would not come to the table. The uncomfortable pressing of another energy prevented her approach. This presence became more evident as we crossed the previous spirits over to the Light. It was a female and due to how I perceived her I realized she was the deceased mother of one of the sitters. She gave her name and initials (which were rather uncommon) and then her nickname which was specific proof of her identity. She was etherically tied to her child because her daughter felt she needed her and could not bear to let her go. It was interesting and emotional for us all as the lady sitter, her daughter, found it so difficult to let her mother go on into spirit. It was perplexing for her to fathom that her mother was in extreme discomfort in this in-between dimension.

The sitter needed to be reassured that her mother would still have the capacity to be with her if she, the daughter, would let her move on into the Light and go through her self-judgment and correction. From the vantage point of the Light, her mother would be happy and comfortable but still able to help her daughter and grandchildren. I was impressed that a mother's love is so deep that even though this lady was physically dead she was willing to suffer a hellish condition of astral existence because her daughter was not ready to detach from her. The daughter was finally able to release her mother to the Light. I am sure that now her mother's help and love is much more powerful.

Our time in this historic house was short and we had already worked with spirit for several hours, so we did not have an opportunity to speak with the lady in white. She came to my home and to my friend's house several times to encourage us to come back to help her at her historical home.

We were able to schedule a return to the house a little over a year later. During that visit we crossed over several souls and finally talked with a now spiritually beautiful lady in white. She told us that because the house had so many antiques and would continue to harbor more each year, that she was given the job of protector spirit. This work entailed calming astral souls who were connected to antiques that were donated and brought into the Rosson House and the entire historical square block area of the city.

Because we came and helped during our first visit to the house, she was able to go to the Light and arrange for Light Angels to be with her to do her spiritual work. She wanted us to return so that she could work with us in crossing over a soul for the experience. Since we were able to do this she was ready to do her protector work. This was wonderful news. It meant we were no longer needed to do crossover work there because she and the Light Angels would do it. This was an exciting and fulfilling end to her story.

A year after we finished our work with Ruby she visited with me in a personally impacting spiritual dream. Ruby took me through all the levels of a physical death experience. She accompanied me into the first realm a soul travels to immediately after its transition and then took me into the etheric levels available to most souls while they prepare to travel to the Light. Continuing with the journey we explored the realms they experience after they have traveled through the Light. It was a powerful lesson!

I remember slipping out of my body watching it lying on my bed as I ascended traveling fast through a dark tube. Next I was nervously walking along on a difficult to see narrow pathway in a long dimly lit corridor. On either side of the path were people reaching out begging for my hand in help. Some of these beings were distorted showing the depth of their misery. I could feel their pain and was ready to bend down to reach out for a crying child when I sensed Ruby warning me to remained focused only upon the path. It was difficult to ignore the pain and suffering of the souls I passed. I paused several times. Whenever I stopped my forward momentum I felt heavy and weak, losing the energy to move forward. I realized it would be easy to be forever stuck here.

Then I saw a kitten suffering as if it were drowning in a horrible ooze. I was ready to reach out again to lift it to safety when Ruby said, "You are being tested. Is your focus on the Light?" I paused. The pitiful meowing voice was calling to a certain weak part of me. I took a deep breath and released it. Then I looked at the kitten entity again without sympathy within my being and I saw it was a fear monster. I inwardly pondered the biblical concept of worshiping false Gods - of putting no man, no thing before God. Had I discovered its true meaning? I thought about my fears. I knew I often help others in life probably as a subconscious avoidance from working on myself and my inner fears. I realized earth and the earth-life was the gift of a physical place in which to successfully work through fears.

We traveled onward to a uniquely designed golden door. It opened at our presence. A bright Golden-white Light was on the other side. We moved through its portal and were absorbed into the Light. Once within it I saw two special deceased family members, friends and many spiritual friends, especially Christopher. He radiated with a halo of faceted living light and then I noticed that I did as well. Our auras were even electrically brighter that I perceive them while I am in my body. My entourage all hugged me with great joy. We were together for a short time sharing experiences.

Then Ruby and I were alone. A fascinating warm sensation overcame and embraced me. A profound heart-core familiar remembering arose. I knew with a special type of spiritual understanding, that was beyond the shallowness of physical world thinking, that this life was but a second in the whole of my existence. I felt deeply that the only truth that was real was to know and live my immortality. I cannot verbally describe this sensation any more fully. This experience created a sense of peace and comfort that allowed for a complete and wonderful detachment from the earth. I still felt great love for earth and humanity but from a uninvolved compassionate placement. From within my beingness I was completely loved and completely peaceful. I embraced a freedom so expansive that it had no space for suffering and pain or its memory. I experienced pure excitement about existence. I can remember and sense this experience today as if were an unerasable memory engraved in my soul that, once touched with my conscious mind will never be lost to me again.

After basking in this experience of the Light, Ruby prodded me to travel further. We were now lights ourselves and flew with the speed of thought to a hall of books. Ruby left me alone in this wonderful library where an angel showed me a book of my present life. I was able to review only a few parts of it since I was not yet actually transitioning from the physical world. The angel then escorted me to a room that was embellished like a temple. A bright cloud-like essence being that was softly expansive filled with incredible love surrounded me. I literally danced with joy while I was within it. I learned telepathically that those who have died physically are around and within the third dimension. I was told that it empowers their spiritual energies to send them unconditional love and joy on a regular basis. I was shown glimpses of several different realms where souls go to study, play and investigate new ways to experience spiritual growth.

I discovered many that would be personally exciting to visit.

Then the bright essence coaxed me to return to my physical body. It said that I am to remember that my quickest path to complete my lessons, karma and spiritual intents was *love*. I understood from this essence that it is necessary for the earth be a place of imperfection. It is through the opportunity of experiencing this imperfection that many souls can develop true spiritual love. On earth it is a mastery lesson to be selflessly unconditionally loving with a deep unfailing strength where there is often so little practice of true love.

As I was returning to my physical body I thanked Ruby for my incredible lesson about death. When I awakened I recognized from a deep place within that the loving essence being I had danced within was my own Higher Self. Even when I was fully awake I was experiencing its fast vibrating level of excitement that is readily available to me to this day.

Through table tipping we have discovered that many souls are troubled or lost due to our society's lack of understanding about physical death. Ignorance has created fear about death and then confusion for a soul with those fears on the spirit side of the veil. Death is often associated with failure. This, unfortunately, is the result of one's focused identity with the physical body and third-dimensional world as the only reality. We do not die. Only the physical body dies. When we do make the transition we are not alone. Our spirit guides, deceased family members and other higher spiritual beings greet us in celebration of our entry into the next exciting step of our evolution. But if we are emotionally wrought we are not open and cannot see these helping energies through the dense fog of our own distress. When this happens it can take time and several visits by beings of the Light to urge us to move on. That time can be long, lonely and unpleasant if we punish ourselves by feeling unworthy of the Light. The experience of the transition is to be beautiful and rewarding when we decide to embrace it.

According to the guides when the physical body is

born the soul arrives and becomes a student of the earth school. Death of the physical body is our soul's graduation from this school. As souls, we should look forward to graduation as most students do, with the expectation that we will have the opportunity to utilize our education (wisdom) in as challenging a vocation as possible in the great hierarchy of work levels available to us on the spirit side of the universe.

Death opens the door to further opportunities when we are emotionally complete with the earth school. When suicide is acted out, it is as if that soul is a drop-out. There are some souls that are professional students who return over and over again through reincarnation. (I always wonder when someone states that another is an old soul, does that really mean the soul is a slow learner?)

When we graduate and are finished with the last of our earth school lessons, we no longer need to reincarnate. We move onward into God's plan of evolution to; work with consciousnesses who maintain planets, organize spirit guides, teach in great halls of learning, manage solar systems, collect and share wisdom with earth and other planets, live within other systems of the galaxy, live within the Light hand-in-hand with angels participating in their projects or to experience so many other exciting and unfathomable existences.

Spirit says that many souls choose to come to earth because it is one of the few places where a soul can experience physical death and overcome the powerful fears surrounding it. Through crossover work you can better understand and allow an easier release of any fears you have about death.

Working with souls that you have crossed over to the Light will help you unfold an understanding of the other realms and the "vocational opportunities" available to a soul through their experiences. They will be excited and joyously ready to share this information with you as a reward for your help and support in their time of need.

C. SPACE ENERGIES AND YOU.

There are beings from other planets, galaxies and universes who will communicate with you through table tipping. Besides your Galactic Guide there are the Orions, the Pleiadians, beings from our own Milky Way system and many other Starbeings who participate in table communications as well as entities from the suns and several other areas of the universe. As a whole, all of these beings are more advanced in their general spiritual evolution than the earthly human. I have referred to some of them as Lightbodies in chapter 6 Part I. This means that their form is made up of cells of Light as well as ones of a denser content. Due to their spiritual evolvement, they are not as dense in weight and opacity as we. I perceive their body types as similar to what we would see and know as our astral body when we are out-of-body.

There are other space beings that seem to be strictly an energy essence with a mind. Their emotions, of which they have few, are very refined. Even so, they always present themselves in a caring, warm and loving manner.

The purpose that most of the outer space energies have in communicating with us is to help us evolve and to protect us from our own negative energy and its negative forces. Their cultures are utopic by our standards. Usually, they live in a Christ-consciousness society devoid of the negativities prevalent here on earth. These souls totally accept and live the concept of loving one another as they would love themselves. They are balanced in their concepts of self and wish to share with us how to live in peace and love. I wonder, at times, how frustrating it must be for them to be in our energy fields. They live in a beautiful society that we find difficult to perceive. The human mind, even a positively focused creative one, can easily write a story about death, illness, pain and

---

disaster, but can it write a convincing tale about utopia?

These friends are very concerned that we will destroy ourselves and our planet. They want us to live out our lives through the choices of free will, but they are not going to let us destroy our planet totally. If we create such a catastrophe, it will affect the well-being of the whole solar system and possibly even the galaxy.

One group told us of a collective of Lightbodied space beings devoted to the helping of humanity through the difficult transition years we are in at present. They have been called the "Space Brothers" by a group of humans. They have informed us that our world difficulties will worsen in the 1990's. The forces of good and evil will be reflected powerfully with great contrast as they will be directly side by side. The power of their direct contrast will create much confusion emotionally and mental pollution. They tell us that it is helpful to our personal calm mentally and emotionally to meditate. They say that when you meditate you raise your vibration to be above and free from the many disasters that will vibrate on lower levels during this decade. They are aware of the safe areas on the earth during the earthquakes, volcanic activity and the terrible storms to come. The Space Brothers and other Starbeings are an interesting information resource during this time of test. They all tell us that in the twenty-first century, a more peaceful harmony is available to us if we are willing to actively do our part now to create that type of lifestyle from within ourselves first.

Starbeings sometimes work with the magnetic energies around the earth. There are times they assign meditational and physical energy projects to those of us who table tip to assist them in their work. One of the recent projects we were assigned was to help them deter a meteorite from striking the earth's atmosphere or (even worse) the surface of the earth.

They met with us during our tipping session and helped us energize our energy circle in a specific manner that enabled us to all simultaneously travel out-of-body to a place far above the earth. Once there, we created a love energy pyramid by recalling the deep feelings of instances in our lives when we felt intense unconditional of love for others. The Starbeings used the energy of our love and enthusiasm in combination with their etheric level of love.

We all witnessed an energy colored in aurora borealis lights shower outward from our pyramid by our united effort towards the earth. It focused upon specific areas of the globe. The Starbeings told us these energies would activate certain crystals within the earth's soil that helped them with their magnetic balancing work. They said that the shower of our love and enthusiasm was a form of the highest earthly positive energy needed to fuel their energy work. The combination of our energy thoughts and their magnetic energies combined slightly changed the path of the meteorite so that it was far from the earth's surface when it passed nearest to our orbit. Interestingly we read about the meteor and its close path to our earth over a year later. The article reported that scientists were concerned for the earth's safety when they first sighted the meteor. It related that somehow as the meteor came within the proximity of the earth it was not as close as it appeared, because of course, it did not collide with the earth.

If you are interested in the Starbeings and their work all you have to do is call for them to come on to the table. These warm and friendly energies are always excited to involve volunteer helpers in their projects. In return, you might learn more about them and their experiences. It is exciting and mind-expanding to learn about their lifestyles and projects. They are very loving and concerned about our well-being so it is of great comfort to meet them and to see the universal picture of what is happening in the evolution of the Creative Plan.

When the extraterrestrials first started coming to the table, I was more interested in my guides and angels. I usually received their information and moved on to discussions with spirit. I did not realize the power of their role in the evolution of humanity. One of my spiritual teachers informed me about their powerful level of spirituality. She told me that they worked hand-in-hand with the Archangels and the White Brotherhood. She said that if I would open up to knowing these ETs, I would be more involved with the Brotherhood and would be gaining a deeper understanding about the masters. That inspired me to be open and to participate with their work.

Since I now feel comfortable with these space energies, I have some that are special guides. One in particular has created a telepathic relationship between himself, myself and a friend. He will often relate messages to each of us about upcoming earthquakes or storms giving us etheric energy projects to perform to lessen the severity of the event.

If you build a relationship with these extraterrestrial friends, you will deeply enjoy them as enlightened beings. When you work regularly with them, you might be invited, while in meditation or in the dream state, to be present etherically when there are universal or intergalactic council meetings. These gatherings include the White Brotherhood, Archangels, masters, the Holy Spirit and Christ. You may be exposed to new inspiring energy inventions and approaches to better health. Eventually you will be able to understand your own macro-oriented unique part within the Universal plan. This is an exciting and extremely fulfilling benefit which comes through the awareness expansion resulting from doing Universal work with the space energies.

*"THOUGHTS AND FEELINGS OF RESPECT,
ADORATION AND WONDER ARE THE
MASTER KEYS TO THE DEVELOPMENT OF THE
SOUL'S SENSES AND POTENTIAL. THAT IS
WHY THE CHRIST SAID WE MUST BE LIKE
LITTLE CHILDREN TO ENTER THE KINGDOM
OF HEAVEN."*

CHRISTOPHER

CHAPTER TEN

Developing Your Spiritual And Psychic Abilities Through Table Tipping.

IT IS MY BELIEF that the Harmonic Convergence, which occurred in August of 1987, effectively raised the energy vibration of the earth and that all of us have been dealing with that energy change in several ways. The Convergence signaled the beginning of stepped up and ongoing energy changes that are helping the earth to become spiritually evolved - a Lightbody. As this evolution progresses the veils between the dimensions become less dense allowing the dimensions to intertwine more easily. A result that cannot be denied is the increase of all humanity's psychic capacity. We are all naturally psychic. So many humans are experiencing precognitive visions, seeing spirit, getting guidance through powerful dreams, receiving intuitive flashes and insights. Thus now, due to the earth's energy changes, it is easier to sense our psychic capacities. It is our soul's natural spiritual ability or talent to be psychic and as we develop ourselves spiritually we also refine our psychic abilities to their fullest and eventually we become a mystic.

I do not separate the so-called psychic capacities from the spiritual abilities of the soul. The Bible itself in the Corinthians' verses refers to the Gifts of the Holy Spirit that belong to all souls. These spiritual or soul gifts are listed as; faith, healing, knowledge, wisdom, love, prophecy, working of miracles, knowing spirit and distinguishing the different languages of the different levels.

The psychic levels are the lower levels of the soul's sensibilities. You need to be open to and experience your psychic self in order to develop your mystic self. A psychic is one who receives hunches, insights or visions of the future, past or present information with no tangible means used to gain the information. The psychic can be inaccurate due to his or her personal emotional or mental filter that is the result of his or her present spiritual evolution. The level of one's awareness is the vibratory level of that person's reception. So your goal should be to develop your self-awareness and then as a result let your psychic capacity evolve. A mystic is a soul who has practiced the metaphysical sciences in many lives and now has advanced past the level of just an occasional psychic insight. A mystic is always in tune with the flow of the Universe and therefore is well on his or her way to becoming a full master.

While you are developing your psychic self you will be excited due to the faster moving energy of the psychic level. You will often feel the need to tell someone the insights you have about them without being asked. However as you evolve towards being a mystic you will know - but will not have any need to tell. You will reach a level of spiritual love that respects the individual soul's desired process of evolution and will not interfere. You will sense a deep level of honoring whatever another soul chooses to be or do without judgment. You will only give information if sought out and asked.

When you are table tipping you can be fully involved in yourself personally or totally open and universally aware to all that is present on all levels. To be universal means that you do not mentally concentrate on anything because you need your mind to be clear and open. Actually, it is necessary for your whole being to be receptive. The more practice you have at being open, the easier it is to be unrestricted and clear in your reception of psychic input. You must be open to all of your sensitivities and not to eliminate any of them. As a physically functioning being we are usually prejudiced about our senses. Some of us naturally see, hear, smell, palpate or taste more actively than others. For example if you are physically a visually oriented person, being more focused on what you see than what you hear or sense otherwise, then you will likely find it easier and more natural to be Clairvoyant than Clairaudient or Clairsentient.

In my opinion, telepathy is the essential core to all other psychic input. Animals are naturally extremely telepathic. So it is, that telepathy is innate to us on a lower level. There are two types of telepathy. The first is *mental telepathy* which is the understanding of the thoughts of other humans or animals without physical communication. This is common to us all, but usually we do not realize it. The second is *spiritual telepathy* which is receiving thought from a non-physical being. The guides say that a large percentage of the thoughts in our minds are the result of telepathic input - either mental or spiritual.

It is quite interesting to evaluate the concept of telepathy. For example, you are driving to the store and you see a gray haired, happy lady walking her poodle. Her appearance and mannerisms make you think of Aunt Martha. In this case a physical sense stimulus made your mind logically think of Aunt Martha. Then, in a different example, you are driving to the store actively listing in your mind what you need to purchase when all of a sudden you think of Aunt Martha. This time, you did not initiate the logical progression of thought to bring her into your mind. She came into your mind because she was thinking of you. *That is an example of mental telepathy.*

When your mind is intruded with thoughts or memories of a deceased member of the family with no logical progression or outside stimulus (such as seeing someone who resembles them or hearing their favorite song, etc.) *you are experiencing spiritual telepathy.* This is also true if one of your spirit guides comes into your mind. Whenever a deceased person or a spirit guide comes to mind through spiritual telepathy always send them your love, as this is very healing and bonding for you both.

When you are working with the table and unsolicited thoughts come in, know they are mostly telepathic. The problem could be to decide whether these thoughts are spiritually or mentally telepathic. This is easy to determine. Just ask the others seated if they were thinking the same thought. Again, you must be careful because all the persons at the table may be picking up the same thought from spirit.

There are actually two ways you can determine if it was mental or spiritual telepathy. One is to ask the spirit on the table if it sent the thought. The other is to determine if anyone at the table arrived at the thought through a logical process. It is easier just to ask spirit about the thought. If spirit answers **Yes** - that it sent the thought - then you know it is spiritual telepathy.

With practice during telepathic reception, you will be able to detect a difference between the two telepathies. Sometimes I sense that, the symbol or message comes into my mind with a directionality or with a certain quality of light pressure. In many occurrences, mental telepathy is louder within my mind. I can actually feel a pressure pushing outward from the sending person into my energy field if they are physically close. I sense mental telepathy as a energy force that touches my solar plexus or heart chakra. Spiritual telepathy seems to enter my being as a subtle vibration. There is a special softness that accompanies it. I sense its vibration within my higher energy body chakras.

Because thought happens so quickly and its process is not by habit critically observed, you can be lazy and find it difficult to determine how it comes to mind through a clinical type of awareness of all your sensing. We take thought for granted and just live with it. I am asking you to detect how you sense the thought that comes to mind. This type of awareness allows you to detect telepathy. It helps you to have choices and control over what thoughts you entertain in your mind. Spirit says thought awareness is difficult for the human race to achieve because the layers of our mind are so separate. However our spiritual job is to work with balancing these layers of mind. Having a physical body gives us an effective sensory tool with which to achieve this goal in a direct manner that is not possible in spirit.

Working with the table to develop your awareness of telepathy is fun and exciting because you can experience an almost constant flow of it while you are tipping. This gives you the opportunity to detect your sensitivities to it throughout each session. This practice time allows you to tune in mentally, physically and emotionally to give you an understanding of your personal energy unit and how it functions when you are receiving telepathic information. You will begin to sense your own energy coming and going in waves. You can sense if your energy field is being touched, pulled or pushed. Because you have developed this type of sensitivity consciously you can work with managing your energy flow. Being aware of your personal energy is wonderful to achieve. You will be more aware of when you are giving it away or wasting it during your waking day. The result of this can be a life of better physical health with joyous longevity.

I have discovered that a depressed emotional state comes over me when an earthquake is about to happen. This discovery came about through my critical detection of feelings and sensitivities and a follow-up of asking the guides about them on the table. The guides told me that the upset I felt was the result of the negative energy that escapes from the earth just before an earthquake. This energy is scattered and unpleasant. Animals sense it and respond to it also. In this instance, it was helpful to be able to discuss my concerns with the guides to achieve a clearer understanding of what is occurring on all my body levels as I am growing.

Spirit says that meditation is the most effective tool available to us humans to use personally to help us learn about managing our thoughts and to help us balance and blend our layers of mind.

Telepathy can be received in many ways. It can be something heard much like a sound in or outside of the head. This is Clairaudience. Some people always hear their messages from outside their heads, while others sense the words internally. There are others who experience both types of Clairaudience interchangeably. We have a tendency to believe in the information more easily if the message is perceived from outside the body. That is because we are used to that type of perception from our five physical senses. We need to understand that this has no true effect upon accuracy. Others receive information in pictures and symbols, or in a vision that is seen inside or outside of the head. This is Clairvoyance.

In other instances, it is something one just knows, which is a common experience when one is developing on the mystical level. There are circumstances when you physically feel the sensation sent. Some people feel another person's headache. Often, these people do not even realize that the headache they sense is not their own. It is possible to feel or sense emotions which are being sent to you. All of these sensations are known as Clairsentience.

Other sensations that can be perceived and sent by physical persons and spirit are smells and tastes in the mouth. These are not as common a psychic sensitivity but they are real and do happen to us all to some degree.

Each of the psychic senses can work for you so be open to receiving from all of them. It is a full-time job to be critically aware of what you are sensing while you are tipping the table. Be especially aware of the heart and solar plexus areas of your being. The solar plexus is the first and most often used psychic doorway to your being. It is the most responsive. The next most responsive psychic doorway is the heart energy area in the center of your chest - front and back. It is beneficial to *always* be aware of what you are sensing in these areas.

Think and act like a detective watching and listening to your physical and energy bodies for clues. When you have received accurate information, carefully note how it came in and how it felt. You have to learn to read your own individual body input to create an accuracy level. Notice your state of mind. The different planes or dimensional frequencies have a feel to them in your mind and being. Pay attention and tune in so you will recognize it again and again. All it takes is practice to develop your awareness.

The table works beautifully as a self-awareness development tool for a person on any level of self training in metaphysics. As a process, it can challenge you and your being to stretch to the next highest frequency and allow you to connect with it with conscious meaning. You eventually bring this growth into yourself in such a permanent manner that you will no longer need the table to hear, see and know information from spirit. You will sense the appropriate state of mind from which to select your information and tune in accurately.

Remember, your primary purpose for psychic development is for spiritual growth. In my opinion, it is an opposing path to think otherwise. There are many that believe that a psychic capacity is only a feat of the mind. But, if you wholly tune into it, psychic input will always have a spiritual meaning and direction at its root.

When one develops their own psychic powers, there is an interesting effect. The truly evolved development of these powers will result in a personal peace and harmony. That is because these powers usually only unfold completely to those who are on the spiritual path in the quest of their own soul's path to perfection. All blockages to the unfolding of these gifts come from unresolved personality issues and soul lessons or unbalanced karma. So, as you develop your psychic senses and you are working diligently on your spiritual evolution, you will find a wonderful peace as a reward.

I will not tell you that the path of spiritual growth is simple or painless. I am saying that because you understand and are aware of the purposes and reasons for your lessons, you will find an inner peace no matter what is happening in your life. It is interesting how this peace takes away the need to know what is happening next in your life. For as you become more aligned with your Godself within and the God outside of self, you will not worry about the future. You will find yourself fully involved in the lessons of the *now* realizing, all is well, with your focus on the power of the moment. You know that the universe is a part of you and you are within its plan.

When you have developed your spiritual and mental telepathy, you can be more easily in communion with the All and your own Higher Self. Having an understanding of mental telepathy, you can sense another's thoughts and needs which creates a total feeling of oneness with humanity - as well as with the plant, animal, mineral, earth and universal energies.

I have noticed that when I am at the table, I have a tendency to stare rather blankly at its surface or downward at the floor off to the side of the table. When I disfocus my eyes during this time I am opening my inner Clairvoyant eyes, allowing in the visions that are there for me. I have done this so much, that now the Clairvoyant vision seems to be present in the room as if on an etheric screen right in front of my disfocused stare. There are times I see the guides and spirits all around the room as if they were in the third dimension. Then, I feel I can sense their whole beingness. It is interesting how many spirits come to observe while we tip. I believe they are there to observe and learn through us, for they are not the ones called to come on the table.

Each time you ask a question and spirit moves the table for an answer you have the opportunity and the time to listen with your whole being for a symbol, a thought in word or picture, a smell, a taste or an emotional-physical feeling to give you clues and added information to the **Yes** or **No**. Remember each question gives you a chance to practice!

Practice being aware of the thoughts in your mind. Being the master of your mind is a significant task. While table tipping work with controlling your mind, not allowing it to ramble - thinking about this and that. Catch yourself as you fall into patterns of mentally rehashing incidents, judgment, beware of the tendency to classify a thought or fixed opinions which results in the narrowing of your perceptions. Open yourself to see things anew. Let go of preconceived ideas. Your mind is your tool for reception. Keep it open and clear.

Being so aware of the guides and spirit during my table tipping sessions opened up my old Clairvoyance and

Clairaudience to new and powerful realms of vibration. My husband and I were at a gathering of yachtsmen and women one evening in a California marina bar and restaurant when I noticed a young female spirit guide with a man sitting at the bar. She was outfitted in a calico prairie type dress and sun bonnet.

She beckoned for me to come over and talk with the man. I was only slightly acquainted with him. I proceeded to walk over and present a friendly greeting, while inside myself I was cautiously concerned as to how I could approach him about something she wanted me to tell him. Telepathically she showed me a picture of an old white car with a ragged black top. The paint was chalky looking. After a few words of reacquainting myself, I asked him if he owned and regularly drove an older white car with a worn black top. He said, "Yes", looking at me oddly.

His guide showed me something in the center under the car that was going to fall off. She said, "If he does not have that car looked at soon, that important part under the center will fall out and he will be walking in less than a week."

Although feeling self-conscious, I got directly to the point. I told him that I believed in spirit guides and explained simply as possible what they are. He listened, gazing at me in a puzzled manner. I told him he had an attractive young lady guide who cared for him very much and that she had a warning about his car. Then I gave him her message and explained the image she had sent. I did not wait for a response from him. I smiled and excused myself saying I had to get back to my husband and friends seated across the room.

A few weeks later, when we were berthed at the same marina, the man I gave the message came over to where I was and thanked me. He went to a mechanic and a primary piece within the transmission was loose. Since he had the piece fixed he did not severely disable his transmission and that saved him a lot of money and inconvenience. He wanted to know more about spirit guides.

I loved it! Because I knew she did this so he would become aware of her and his spirituality. I talked with him for about an hour and sensed no resistance to what I shared. This experience let me realize how much my table tipping was establishing the clarity of my psychic abilities.

Another notable incident concerning a guide that was a more efficacious experience happened during the month of August a few years ago. I was weeding in my flower garden and planning how many petunias and pansies I would plant in September at the new moon. The September planting time allows for the flowers to settle in and create beautiful blossoms in my winter garden.

I was seated on the ground and sensed a powerful influence from an energy on my left. It quickly pulled me off center. I instinctively gathered my physical balance immediately with my left hand. As I put my hand down on the patio stone, I looked and saw my hand went through the image of large black human feet.

In total surprise, I almost lost my balance again as I reflexed and jumped to move my hand out of the feet. I slowly raised my eyes and looked up the frame at the image of a large black man, poorly dressed, with kindness engraved in the lines of the skin folds of his face. His eyes were those of a Light Being, filled with love.

I recognized him, for I had met him several times when tipping with a California friend named Hank. This was Frank, her timing guide, who had been with her in a past life as a slave on her southern plantation. He has a great love for her because she had cared for him through the tough times that resulted after the slaves were released. She was strong about her sympathy for slaves in that threatening historical era. She had helped their cause tremendously.

Once he knew he had my attention, he motioned for me to stand up. After I stood and faced him, I felt the same energy pull as before because he was touching me on the shoulder. This made me realize that initially he must have touched me when I lost balance while concentrating on pulling the weeds. His face was solemn and then he peacefully smiled. I knew this message was important. With his right hand he held up a clock. The hands were placed in the position of five minutes before four o'clock. He clearly said, "Tell Hank that at this time she will celebrate life."

A week later, when we were back in California, I saw Hank. I asked her if her birthday was November fourth. She said no. I told her that Frank came to me in the patio garden and gave her his specific message. We were both puzzled about its meaning. The only clue I had was that he held the clock in his right hand which to me denotes a future time.

The weeks passed and in October Hank became ill. She had a bout with cancer a few years ago, so her doctor immediately checked her over for the same disease. Some X-rays were taken and a shadow appeared on several bones in her shoulder area. The doctor scheduled her for a bone biopsy. When Hank went into the hospital she had forgotten about the August message. But, as the anesthesiologist was putting her under, she observed the big clock on the hospital wall and it was five minutes before four and then she realized the date was November the fourth. She silently cried with relief as she was being wheeled into surgery for she already knew she did not have cancer.

When the tests were completed no cancer was found in her body. Indeed, she did celebrate life! This episode convinced me to never question or doubt the existence of spirit guides. I was also impressed because this was a pure incident of prediction. It concerned information about an incident neither Hank nor I could have had thoughts about previous to the flow of events which means there was no chance of mental telepathy. It was a clear cut case of spiritual telepathy. I also noted with more critical energy detail the special separate sense I felt when tuning in on this spirit. It is a sense of physical hollowness - being without self - which I guess simply moves my ego out of the way to be a vessel for spirit.

Now since I have constantly practiced detecting energies while table tipping, to see and communicate with other people's guides at any time is common and totally comfortable for me. Before table tipping I could see them but I never clearly or confidently communicated with any other guide than Christopher. Whenever I do readings, a great deal of the information I receive comes through to me from the other person's spirit guides. Their guides are very clear to me about how much they interact with the person they guide. They always wish a direct connection to be formed between themselves and the person. My own guides have increased in number since I have been open to them.

Another personally validating experience that still warms me to my depth with love when I tell of it, is when I was asked by a student to do a Spirit Guide painting for her. I had almost finished laying in my first wash of watercolor when a child-like face became evident within the other faces I represented on the blocked paper. It seemed that this face had a tear of sadness and joy in its expression. When I presented the finished work to the student she was speechlessly overcome with emotion. She grabbed her purse going through it hurriedly until she handed me a tattered old photograph of the same face in every detail. I gulped for air as she tearfully told me it was her son who died in an accident when he was three. She described that when she held him at the moment of his death, he had a tear in the same eye at the exact place I painted it. She said she always felt him with her but now she was at peace knowing he is really supporting her.

While you are tipping, constantly challenge your self-awareness in order to practice your psychic abilities and spiritual awareness. The table is there to be used to ask about and reinforce the information you are receiving. This is especially true when you are asking spirit if they have messages for you. You will find that spirit is very patient with you if you are trying to learn about your psychic self.

The beauty of the table tipping experience as an effective teacher of psychic development through energy awareness is beyond compare. It is as direct as a classroom condition for learning. The power of the energy circle is like being linked up with several energy expanding batteries, supporting your energy and amplifying it so you can tune in. (While you are within it focus for a moment upon the power of the energy circle. Feel its unison or oneness. Establish a relaxed state of being. Place your mind on a universal level by being open - with no need to be personal. Sometimes you and the other sitters can take the time to renew the strength or the energy circle. Visualize yourselves united in a ring of bright white light. Fill the ring with unconditional love. Expand the ring far out into space.) You can verify your input instantly through using the table to ask spirit for their vantage point. You have the fellow sitters who are tuned in to add information to your data enabling you to determine and build upon your accuracy in reception.

Inform spirit that you want to learn more about

how to develop your psychic senses. They will have suggestions that are specifically oriented to your personal energy and level of growth. They will be anxious to assist you in your psychic growth because it directly involves your spiritual growth. When you develop each psychic capacity you are actually opening up each of the soul's natural senses of perception. Be patient with yourself as you are learning and most of all do not become intense about your psychic development. Intensity narrows your awareness.

You will discover that in order to develop an accuracy and consistency with your psychic senses you will have to work on your character traits and virtues. If you meditate you will know that you will have to be quiet within yourself to listen to the senses of the soul. You will notice that if you to learn to detach yourself from the loud input of the physical senses you can tune in easier to spirit.

As you become aware of these psychic gifts within yourself, you can ask your Psychic Guide if there are any special tools for you to use that will help nurture this growth. Inquire about the crystal ball, tea leaf reading, cards, the I Ching, the Runes or even Palmistry. The crystal ball is directly useful for learning to disfocus your physical eyes while you stare blankly into it creating the opening for seeing with your intuitive or soul eyes.

You will discover certain tools work for you for awhile and then you will discard them for another tool. This is because as you grow, your needs change. Eventually you will discover that, it is not the tool that opens the doorway to your psychic input but your own openness and understanding of yourself that brings it about.

Developing the psychic or soul senses creates a better awareness and enjoyment of the spiritual world when you return to spirit after your physical death. The strengthening of these abilities opens your frequencies to the higher levels or the spiritual worlds when you soul travel in meditation or dreams.

Be careful of becoming fascinated with just the psychic phenomenon itself possibly seeing it as your goal. The psychic level of activity is simply a beginning to opening your higher intuition. As you focus upon your spiritual growth your psychic abilities will unfold beautifully.

Developing your psychic spiritual self develops your intuition. Intuition is your own inner knowing of the other realms and your own Higher Self. Intuition happens when you interact with the non-physical or spiritual worlds which is your birthright. Being intuitive is being whole, because you are utilizing your whole energy unit. Using your intuition takes you beyond your five physical senses and the limitations of the third-dimension. Once your intuition is trusted and your are using it effectively you become a mystic. A mystic is able to use the universal energy in his or her life to be able to live in happiness, peace and harmony because he has learned not to look outside of himself for his truths and answers. An illuminated mystic lives within the "Kingdom of God" right here on earth. I believe that table tipping and its powerful energy circle process is a potent tool that can directly help you to open and actively develop your intuitive awareness. Its process can help you evolve your soul's senses from the psychic level to the mystic level of function. The table tipping experience then can help you along towards your own mystic and mastered level of existence.

The willingness of the guides to help you is powerful and supportive. Their assistance is always available to you through the table no matter what the level of your progress.

All of your guides and Higher Self will work with

you patiently while you develop your spiritual gifts. They know that as these materialize they are the landmarks of your progress towards spiritual mastery. Developing psychic gifts in a directly spiritual manner, with the table as a communication link to guidance, will assure that you use them properly for the benefit and balance of the Universal All in this lifetime.

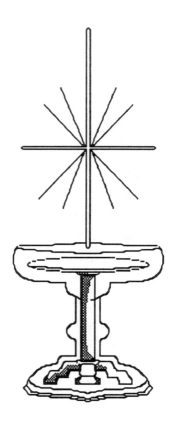

*"A STUDENT ON THE PATH OF SPIRITUAL
GROWTH - (INITIATION) MUST BE THOUGHT
AND EMOTION RESPONSIBLE TO A
CONSTANT DEGREE, FOR THOSE SKILLS WILL
BE THE TOOLS OF HIS SUCCESSSFULLY
DEVELOPED AWARENESS."*

CHRISTOPHER

CHAPTER ELEVEN

More Fun and Interesting Uses For Table Tipping.

A. TAPPING INTO FUTURE EVENTS

AS I HAVE MENTIONED before I do not favor asking for predictive material when addressing the guides. Nevertheless, there are several occasions when the guides will predict personal and world information. It always seems to happen when you least expect it. Maybe it happens because you do not ask and spirit feels free to share ideas without sensing they will interfere with your free will or intentions.

My experience has been that the Chief Guide will predict world events if they are something that will affect your personal life. I recall one time in which mine predicted the rise in the value of gold because our group was asking if it was in our best interest, due to the current economy, to save money or to invest it in a home. The guides showed us gold bullion and coins immediately. Within a week of the tipping session gold went up in value significantly and would have been a good investment. I always thank the guides for this kind of information but I do not request it even though there are times I am tempted to do so.

I am sure they trust I am not the type of person who constantly needs their point of view to make my decisions in life. That would be insulting to them and unfair to myself for I would be negating my God-given gift of free will. There are realms of life and God existence that do not have this beautiful power of free choice.

We have had incidents when the guides tell us of earthquakes, storms or potential accidents that may happen. These predictions have come through when we have asked questions about moving or taking business or pleasure trips at certain times. The guides often warn us if there will be storms or difficult weather ahead if we are planning to be doing some special out-of-door activity such as taking a pack trip into the mountains. They provide information about earthquakes or earth changes that could have any affect on us if it will happen near where we live or would be traveling. My sister-in-law has been warned about certain Southern California earthquakes and her guides would feel that their job of protection would be easier if she would move from such a high-risk earthquake area.

There have been instances when dolphin energies come on the table to warn of undersea earth changes which will effect the coastlines. The dolphins have been an active and reliable source of earth predictions.

We experienced having the Lord of Spiders coming on the table to predict an overpopulation of spiders to control the overpopulation of certain flying and crawling insects in our area. The Lord told us to be patient with his spiders while they performed their mission for they were meant to protect our plants during that time of pest imbalance. We cooperated and in a short time our pests were under control and the number of spiders present seemed to balance out as well.

We have had Lords of different bird species come

to predict the trade wind and jet stream current changes that would effect the weather. A Lord of Gophers came on to warn of the low water table in our area and to tell us to be conservative in our water usage. He told us of the offenders who were over developing the land far north of us. All of these predictions or statements were later verified in the newspapers.

There have been many sessions in which the guides have predicted information just to be helpful. One day a lady whose turn was next to ask a question simply asked if any of her guides had a message for her. Immediately, her Timing Guide moved the table for a **Yes**. He identified himself as a male named Robert. He insisted he had an urgent message. We all opened our minds and listened. He visually showed us some For Sale and Sold signs in our minds. He then showed us the sitter as a little girl with her father. The father's hand was extended as if he had given her something. The symbolic image sent looked as if it was a valuable piece of paper.

We asked Robert if his message was about something she should sell. He excitedly moved the table for a **Yes**. We then asked was it in her best interest to sell something her father had given her. Again we received an affirmative answer. Robert let us perceive the color blue. Then, he sent images of what appeared to be something like gambling chips. Next, he showed us the type of graph that would be typical of what businesses use to evaluate profits or losses over a year's time. We figured out that he was communicating about blue chip stocks. The lady was so surprised. She had almost forgotten that she had those old stocks her father had given her years ago. She told Robert she would get the stocks out and look them over. She said she would sell them if he perceived from his vantage point that there was good cause. We asked Robert to reaffirm if that was his message. He moved the table emphatically for **Yes**.

A few weeks after the table session she sold the

stocks and it was just in time. She had talked with her stockbroker who agreed she could sell the stock and get a good return on her father's investment. A month after the table session, the company failed. This turn of events reduced the value of the stocks making them almost worthless. The company was fairly old and established and none of us would have dreamed this company could ever be at risk. The lady sitter saved several thousand dollars by selling the stocks immediately as Robert had suggested.

On several occasions the guides have told us, in complete descriptive physical detail, which people would be effective connections for our business efforts. These types of comments come in response to our telling them about business trips and asking if they have any messages for us about them.

My brother-in-law was looking for a second car. He wanted an older Volkswagen. The guides came to the table and volunteered the information about a special little car that would be excellent for him. They said it was just a few miles away from where he lived. The guides described it as white with a light interior and dark accents. They said it needed some work but that it would be a good buy because it was a collector model. They even gave us the directions he needed to locate it. Surely enough, he found a little white VW beetle that was perfect for his needs just where the guides had said it would be.

My sister-in-law's Chief Guide told her she would probably be opening her own business over a year before she even considered it was possible. He eventually helped her find where to locate the business. He said he had helped in this way because he was excited for her to learn all the spiritual lessons that would be involved if she had her own business. She is very successful now in her business at the guide's suggested location and she has encountered many self-awareness and growth lessons along the way.

There are times when the guides will tell you about specific repairs you need to do on your vehicle for your own safety. These suggestions are usually prompted by a necessity, so we always act upon them immediately.

We have discovered that spiritual teachers will inform you about political movements and changes. These teachers tell us that our attitudes and the energy emissions that are produced by our negative thoughts and words produce many of the world problems we face today. They show us that in the spiritual dimensions like energy attracts like energy. So, if you become angered and send out that angry energy indiscriminately all day long, wherever you are, you are responsible for the dispersion of that energy and its results. If enough persons emit this type of energy, it collects in the atmosphere of the earth. Then this collective travels to and settles in an area that has a concentration of the same type of energy. This compounds the negativity already present there creating the potential for death and destruction.

Sometimes, teachers will tell us of terrorist activity that will be caused by a such a negative energy collective. We were once alerted to an outbreak of cancer among Americans that was to be the result of the public anti-American chanting by the Iranians a little over a year earlier. The clustering of that cancer outbreak occurred in a neighboring community within weeks after the teacher told us of the verbal outrage and the resulting powerful negative energy the Iranians had produced. These teachers let us see the gray clouds of negativity gathering and where on the earth it would have physical effect as well as in what manner it might manifest. I know they do this to teach us to be responsible for our thoughts and actions.

Each time there has been a prediction, it has been for our personal protection and well-being, or it has been for the purpose of helping us with our spiritual growth. We have been given predictions for the purpose of soliciting our meditative assistance to clean and balance energies for the earth, the solar system, the universe and humanity itself.

Whenever you are dealing with predictive information and the table, you must be very cautious and emotionally calm. Remember about the power of your lower will and its capacity to effect the table's movement. Your thoughts can be strong enough to create a thought form that can represent itself to you on the table as if it were an individual spiritual entity. There have been instances when I have witnessed a sitter communicate with his or her own fear thought form through the table. The situation can be beneficial if the sitter wants to understand the fear and work through it. But if the sitter is unaware that he or she is communicating with a personal fear thought form it can be treacherous and reinforcing of that fear.

The reason I mention this is that you need to understand there are also universal fear thought forms or layers of consciousness that are created from group and race fears. Often, frightening predictions about the future of our earth come through such a consciousness level. All through the history of humanity there have been doomsday seekers and seers. They create a definite layer of negative consciousness that is available to the table. Thus, if you receive fear reinforcing predictions, you might want to question the source of your information. Believe it or not, a fear consciousness thought layer will admit to you exactly what it is if you ask it about identifying itself.

Of course, we do live in an remarkable time of change for the earth and all of humanity. Change can be exciting and beneficial as well as transforming. This is a time of what humanity will perceive as miracles and tragedies, so be careful to qualify the source of any prediction. The guides will predict cycles of spiritual energy and the purposes for the present energies on the earth. In reference to those cycles, the guides have told us that the decade of the 1980's was a time of detachment on many levels and that the decade of the 1990's would involve learning egolessness.

When we enter the century of 2000 to 2100, humanity will need to evolve into a time of partnership, wholeness, unity and with a clearer awareness of the God within. The next eighteen to twenty years are especially critical for the development of the spiritual potential of the earth and humanity. It is our responsibility to create a bonded partnership with our own teacher within - our Higher Self. It is essential that we learn who we are and effectively balance our emotions and levels of mind. With this partnership and balance accomplished we will enable ourselves to unite with all humanity as a human family in love, peace and balance through living the spiritual laws here on earth. We will be citizens of the earth, working together and sharing what the earth offers us with respect for its living vibrations. This achievement will save and balance the earth for future generations of souls to use as their campus for higher learning.

B. CRYSTAL, BOOK AND CLASS SELECTION

In the Spirit Guide section of this book, I have already discussed the technique to use with the Crystal Guide and the table in determining which crystals are effective for your own personal use. But you may have concerns about the wearing of certain stones together on the body at the same time. This is another area about which you can consult the Crystal Guide. There are certain stones that when worn or placed together can have a powerful effect upon a meditation or a healing experience. My guides have told me to wear a ruby ring on my right hand and to wear an emerald ring on my left hand to amplify my spiritual telepathy in special instances when I am tired or just feel I need the extra power.

Early into my metaphysical career working on an arson case proved to be very difficult for me because of my fear of fire. Each time I would psychometrize a piece of the burned building, I would go back in time to the fire and be present in the burning building. At that point, I would become physically ill and unable to proceed forward into the vision.

I had great difficulty working on this case until I asked my Chief Guide how to temporarily get past my fear of fire. He called my Crystal Guide to the table. She told me to hold a piece of obsidian in my right hand and a certain clear quartz crystal with the piece of the building in my left hand. The result was tremendously effective. I was able to have the courage to move through the fire and see all that had happened. So, please be open to any suggestions about stone combinations that can help you in any way.

There are some metals that reduce or amplify the power of a stone. So whenever you wear stones always determine which metal works best with the stone's energy in combination with your personal energy.

You will want to ask about certain specialized crystals and their uses on the table. For example, if you are a crystal healer and have several crystals, you would be able to determine what areas of the body to place these stones as power points for the specific health problems that a client may display to you. You will discover there are receiving, transmuting, amplifying and sending crystals. There are some stones, that will give you more self-confidence when they are on your person. Some specific minerals will help to empower you to manifest your physical needs. There are special stones that can magnify your creative energies. So, when you find out that an individual stone or mineral is an effective enhancer of your energies, determine in what manner it is helpful to you.

You will discover that the Crystal Guide will not only tell you where on your body it is best to wear a stone, but will also help you to design a piece of jewelry combining the correct metals and stones to be beneficial to your energies.

Other communications given through the table will help you to determine if there are any objects that you have or should have that are power objects for your energy field. Your guides can help you design your own personal mandala, which is a symmetrical drawing that is usually circular in concept. You can use this mandala as a visual gateway focal point to facilitate an easier passage to deeper levels of self for more profound meditations.

Spirit can tell you if an amulet would be helpful for your energies. You can ascertain from them what types of materials to use for the specific design or form it should take. The guides will tell you where to place it on your body or within your home for the desired effect.

One of my spiritual teachers told me of a bracelet to wear that will have to be custom designed. It is to have specific designs on it. I used a piece of paper and pen to draw the design as I perceived it Clairvoyantly. I then put the paper with the drawing on the table for the teacher to verify my understanding, allowing him to help with any corrections of the sketch. The teacher described the type of metal needed for its construction, the specific stones that were to be used and exactly where in its design the the stones were to be placed. It is a balancing amulet to empower my whole being that is to be worn on my left wrist. The teacher said that this amulet will help me achieve the cycle of vibration I need to be in direct communication with certain angelic entities of the higher realms.

During various intervals of time spirit will suggest I wear Lapis Lazuli at my throat chakra, because it helps me to surrender to the higher will of the God force enabling me to establish my next level of Higher Self connection. They frequently tell me that I could wear pearls for balancing with my Higher Self. I regularly have copper pennies in my pocket for balance due to the suggestions of my guides. If you are starting a new facet of your study such as inspirational writing or channeling, ask if there is a stone that would assist in the enhancement of your vibrations to make these inter-dimensional connections effective. Spirit's suggestions may vary from time to time because your vibrational frequency changes as you grow.

Whenever you are preparing to take a class in the esoteric sciences such as Metaphysics, you can ask if it is in your best interest to vibrationally participate within a particular group. The guides will give you an honest answer. Also, feel free to ask for the reasons they have for their answers. Ask for suggestions about classes and groups. Sometimes, they are aware of a class that you do not know about which would be in your best interest to attend.

It is fascinating to inquire about books you have read or would like to read. If you have the book, you can place it on the table and wait a few seconds for the guide or teacher to evaluate it. The guides read your vibrations and know when you are ready for certain books. Often, they will suggest that you read a certain book. Sometimes this book comes into your life through the suggestion of a physical person. You will find out that it came to you because the guides have made sure that you physically have it. There are some books that they will say are inaccurate for you, meaning it could be a useful truth for someone else, but not for you. They will also specifically tell you what parts are inaccurate for you at this time. There have been times the table "walked" across the floor of the room in the direction of a book that was present somewhere else in the room just so we would take notice of it to discuss it with spirit.

Another area of inquiry can be about musical or meditation tapes. The guides can sense your vibratory rate very accurately so if you play certain music they will tell you if it enhances your energy. They can be specific as to the manner in which the music can be utilized. For example, maybe the music would help you to achieve out-of-body travel, a deeper level of meditation or a wonderful state of relaxation.

The guides will tell you that there are certain musical notes that will resonate with each chakra's energy. You could use a pitch pipe while at the table to determine which note is resonating with each of your personal chakra's vibration. You can then chant or hum the note in meditation while you are working through a clearing of that chakra with an increased effectiveness because the vibration of music resonates with your personal energy body vibration.

Feel free to explore the many uses of the table that are beyond those I have previously described. Be creative. Both you and spirit will love the adventure and the rewards of such a quest.

C. SOLVING CRIME CASES

The table is an efficient tool when working with crime cases. I have done crime work, but, I never feel emotionally comfortable with it so I usually do not take such cases any more.

Earlier I mentioned an arson case. When we used the table to obtain information on the case, some detective guides came to the table. They told us exactly how the man entered the building and described the pyrotechnical technique used. The guides said that when he left, the man had used an outside phone booth in the alley to the rear and left of the building about a half-block away. The guides told us the exact location of the door through which the man entered and exited. They described the man physically.

All of the descriptions and physical locations as well as the details of the specialized equipment the man used were verified by the fire inspector. The description matched the physical appearance of a previous employee of the present business located in the building. This was an exciting confirmation, because the fire happened in a city in an Eastern state that neither I nor my friend who was my table tipping partner had ever visited.

Besides calling in detective guides you can call in the soul that was involved in the crime if it included a death. However, the soul must be dimensionally available to cooperate. You may need to ask the Table Guide to locate the soul and bring it to the table if it is willing to present itself. Sometimes a physically alive relative being present at the table session is incentive enough for the soul to make its presence known.

An example was an incidence of the highway

death of a young girl. By analyzing the evidence found at the scene of the accident, the sheriff said it appeared she had been speeding and lost control of her car driving it over a cliff to her death. The family found this difficult to believe because carelessness or suicide did not fit the nature of this girl's personality or habits.

When the deceased girl's mother and father tipped with me, the mother's Chief Guide was able to locate the girl on the other side in the spiritual realms. When she came to the table, she explained that an old yellow truck swerved into her path racing head-on towards her. It forced her off the road making her loose control of her car in the rocks and bushes outside of the edge of the pavement. She tried to bring the car to a stop just as she realized that the land ended and dropped off sharply on the other side of the bushes. She described her anguish when she knew she couldn't correct the situation. She said time slowed down and she then felt she was watching her car fall to the bottom of the ravine. Suffering a cranial blow from the shock of the impact when she hit the rocks and bushes, she said she was out of her body immediately before her physical death. She rose above the scene of her accident and saw the driver get out of his yellow truck and look down the ravine at her car.

She said she could sense he was terrified and witnessed him get back into the truck and speed away. She told us that had he had the courage to come and help her body she might have physically lived. However, in her present state of harmony and happiness she felt no negative emotions towards the man. She knew her life's lessons as this personality were complete and that her soul and Higher Self had planned to end her relatively short life with this almost painless death.

The most validating message that came of this communication with the girl was that she saw and remembered the license plate numbers on the truck. The family turned this information over to the local sheriff. The sheriff's department discovered that a man did live in the area who owned the described truck with that exact license plate number. He had reported that the truck was stolen a few days before the accident occurred. The truck was never located again. This created insufficient evidence to involve the original owner of the vehicle. Also, there were no witnesses to the theft of the truck so the case ended there.

The family felt that they had satisfactory proof that the girl did not commit suicide and was not recklessly driving. They now know the incident was a true accident and that fact plus the knowledge of her spiritual peace gave them a special comfort.

Whenever you use the table for crime solving purposes call upon the help of your detective guides. They are closer to the frequencies of the physical dimension and having a sense of time and space they can be very specific in relating critical physical details that can help solve the case at hand.

In order to have success in crime solving, you have to have balanced emotions. You will have to act within a special format of indifference and be emotionally detached even though the victims or their family members are at the peak of their emotionalism. Working with the factual details demands that you keep your rational conscious mind thinking at bay in order for your intuition to open the way for the valuable accurate information. Crime cases are difficult work. However, they are an excellent physical plane area of spiritual search work to help determine your personal accuracy level in your communications with spirit.

D. LOCATING MISSING ITEMS AND PERSONS

Your guides are of direct help through the table when you have lost something. Ask for a guide who has a sense of third dimensional placement and time. You may want to call in one of the guides you already know who works with you within the mundane areas of life. You need to picture the lost item clearly in your mind and ask if they have a clear understanding of what the item may be. With that fact established, they might need to understand when you last remember having the item.

You will want to determine if the guides know if it is permanently lost to you and will not be found ever again for some reason. If they tell you that you will find it, then proceed with the following thoughts and questions. You can ask if the item is still in your home. Next, inquire if you lost it at work or in your car. Check with them about if you lost it at another physical place such as a store, a parking lot, the yard or a friend's home. If spirit says the item is in a familiar physical location such as your house or a building in which you work, then you can ask about the area checking it room by room.

Another method to use to determine the lost item's location is to ask about a cardinal direction: for example, ask "Is the item to the south of where I am now?"

My mother-in-law lost a delicate gold initial necklace that her husband gave her just before he died. She was very upset that it was not to be found anywhere. The guides told us it was in her family room. My pendulum guide wanted me to take my pendulum to her home and use it to locate the necklace because he was anxious to give me practice with the pendulum.

Once I was at Mom's house, the pendulum vibrated (as the guide had said it would) when I was at the general location of the missing necklace. The pendulum started this vibrating when I came close to the coffee table in front of her family room couch. At this point, Mom insisted she had looked there and taken the whole room apart but still could not find the necklace. Nevertheless, we moved the table and did not find the necklace on the carpet beneath it. Then I, too, was discouraged.

Upon returning to my home and joining a table tipping session, my Chief Guide came on and insisted the necklace was under Mom's coffee table and rocked our table vigorously with frustration to demonstrate that we would find it if we trusted and looked more carefully. I returned to her house once again. We moved the coffee table. Then we took up the large designer rug Mom had under the table and there was the necklace! I am so glad the guides are loving, persistent and patient with me and with all of us.

When you are looking for a missing person, you can use the idea of directionality again. Place a map on the table pointing to an exact location asking for a **Yes** or **No** response from the guide or teacher who is helping you. Spirit can be very specific. As I mentioned before, sometimes if the person is deceased their spirit will come to the table to tell you about their death or where their body is located.

In one case, the soul of a little boy who was missing for five days came to the table with an exact physical description of his location using child-like directions. He was frightened and confused about being out-of-body. But his soul, being separated due to the shock of exposure to his physical body at the time, was able to come to the table while he was physically alive. We were able to soothe and calm him. He gave us all a clear vision of what he could see in his surroundings. This information allowed us to tell his parents what it looked like where he was They recognized the location from the details we had and were able to find him.

E. TALKING TO THE SOUL OF THE UNBORN BABY

This is a fascinating use of the table. I have had such enjoyment with this process. The fetal energy is so delightful and joyously excited about its new upcoming lifetime that it is fulfilling just to have its energy come through on the table. The baby's soul will tell you all about its soul purpose and intents for coming into this life. It has full awareness and knows clearly the karmic relationship ties and the spiritual reasons it has for choosing these particular parents. It will disclose past life situational information that will help you to understand the soul as a child, including its soul intents, fears, achievements, karmas, spiritual lessons, talents and interests.

The soul will tell you of the genders of its past life experiences and why it chose its present gender. However, I am not recommending that you approach the baby's soul with the question, "Are you a boy?" or "Are you a girl?" That is a predictive question which critically lowers the energy of the situation. The baby's soul will tell you about its choice of gender when it is ready.

The baby's soul can share with you if it may have any physical weaknesses and why they are chosen. Sometimes the problems that could be present in this incarnation can be worked through with the soul while it is in spirit before the baby is born.

The child will be able to tell its mother of the preferences it has of what she does while it is in her womb. One baby greatly enjoyed it when the parents played classical music and another liked it when her mother read aloud to her. One soul loved it when his mother went for walks on the beach at sunset.

Sometimes, the baby is very specific about the name it should have in this incarnation because the name given

311

is the vibration that effects its expression of itself throughout all of this incarnation.

The parents can research their shared past lives with this soul. They can determine if there will be any personality conflicts between them. They may even be able to gain insights as to how to help the child to learn its lessons in this life time. Most parents find this very valuable in gaining the most from their life long relationship with this soul.

We have also experienced the soul of the baby coming to the table after it is born, when its physical body is resting, to gain insights into its present personality. This usually occurs when we have already spoken with the baby's soul before its birth. Once this process was very helpful when the baby's body became sick. Its soul was able to communicate why the body was experiencing its present difficulty allowing the parent the insight into how they could help correct the situation.

Communicating with the fetus's soul can share a clearer picture of its soul qualities and lessons than would be possible to obtain once the soul has experienced the dulled awareness of the veil of physical birth. When it enters the physical body the soul becomes less consciously aware of this spiritual information due to the activation of the conscious mind and the interference of the personality.

F. COMMUNICATING WITH THE SOULS IN THE SURROUNDING ETHERS.

There are many souls that are present in the space surrounding where you are physically. You might be interested to determine what, if any, effect they have upon the energies around and in your home, work place or any other physical area where you spend your time.

Sometimes there are souls who spend their time observing you and learning vicariously when you are working through a lesson. This gives them experience to fall back on when they have to work through the same or a very similar lesson when they come into their earthly incarnation. Souls preparing to be born are often doing this. It is interesting and fun to communicate with them. They are very excited about their upcoming life. Their freshness and compassion is nurturing. Sometimes they have a valid insight that helps you and you have information that helps them to better understand your actions.

There is an arena type etheric stadium that surrounds the earth and is within its aura that is often visited by souls from other dimensions and planets. These souls may have not chosen to experience the earth directly and can learn about it by watching humanity in their game of physical life. Recently I have noticed that this stadium has been filled to capacity because of the time of dramatic change the earth is presently experiencing. These souls want to witness how we handle our evolution. I find these souls are filled with compassion. They often will give energy in unison as they cheer us on in our endeavors.

Be open to communicating with these surrounding souls because you can find out much about the earth and how things can progress from their objective vantage point.

313

*"IF YOU ARE IN REMEMBRANCE,
EXPECTATION OR ANTICIPATION YOU ARE
NOT IN THE SPONTANEOUS NOW - THE NOW
IS THE PLACEMENT OF JOYOUS BEING AND
POWER."* CHRISTOPHER

CHAPTER TWELVE

Creating A Table Tipping Journal.

KEEPING DETAILED RECORDS of your table tipping experiences will help you organize all your information. We all think we will remember the names and other important data we are given in each table experience, but recording it stores it verbatim. Keeping records eliminates assumptions and simply forgetting about what was presented. The guides, teachers and other level spirits do not forget the material they have shared with you. They appreciate the efficient habits of keeping records, because that expedites your spiritual progress. Also, I have found that if I write down the information, it has a deeper degree of meaning and at times gives me a whole new level of interpretative observation. I have always been pleased when I have recorded something that is pertinent about the future because it is available for reference. It is especially helpful if I have recorded the original date of the forecast. With recorded dates and their sources you will have the fun of checking out the accuracy of your sources.

When you keep a table tipping journal, you will remember the guides' names and their positions more easily.

Referring to your journal helps you to notice any changes in your guides since sometimes, one moves on and a new one takes over. You will recognize when this happens more quickly and can keep record of how often it happens. You will want to ask them the reasons for this happening. You might be pleasantly surprised to find out that these changes occur because you are expanding your vibration at a rapid rate and the guides have to work on their vibrations to keep their level at the right placement (to serve you as teachers) for your growth.

I suggest that you create a **General Information Page** for each session. It should include: the names of the sitters, the date, the time of the day, the name of the table operator, where the session takes place, what are the present astrological phenomena, (if you are interested in their effects and are aware of them, such as moon phase, solar placement, planetary aspects, etc.) and the theme that is the purpose for the sitting. The general information page can be helpful when you want to overview your experiences for effectiveness and to evaluate the results achieved from each session. If ever there are problems with your communications, such as inaccuracy you may discover a common thread to the problem sessions through the recording of this page.

Next it is important to devote a dated page to Spirit Guides. With the information from chapter 7 make up a list of the Spirit Guide positions and then record the names you receive for each job. It is also interesting to record how you perceive each guide. If there is a vision of it, record what is seen. Always note if there is a specific color. Record any feeling you associate with the guide. The individually descriptive data you record will help you to feel comfortable with identifying this guide when you meet it again. The purpose of this sheet is not only to assist you in keeping records of your guides, but the energy of the act of filling it out in of itself, reinforces the trust you have in your spiritual friends creating a deeper bond with them. Also on this **Spirit Guide Page** include an an area to list your spiritual teachers by name and their descriptive identities.

You should do other Spirit Guide pages periodically, taking time to recheck the original list, in case there are any changes in your guides and their duties. I have copies of my Spirit Guide Pages which date back several years. It is interesting and lots of fun to review what was recorded. It is revealing and fascinating to note how many varied energies have worked with me. As time passes it is beneficial to review these pages for you will be able to reference them to measure your personal spiritual and psychic growth by what has developed and changed within your spiritual helper group as a mirror of your progress.

Create a **Session Experience Page** or pages. These pages are for you to gage your personal responses to each session and to record the overall effect the session had for you and your spiritual psychic growth. Through these pages you will be able to monitor energy situations that come up during sessions as well as keep record of the cross over work that you have done. You will have record of predictions spirit gives which will help you to determine the accuracy of specific spirits and the direction of your own energy. Items to record on your Session Experience Pages are: a list of which guides communicated with you and the general premise of their messages during this session, a list of any new entities you met including names and descriptions if received, notes of difficulties with any astral entities, state if you did any soul cross overs noting how many plus any interesting details about each case, record how you received your information - did you receive it psychically through Clairvoyance, Clairaudience, etc., note and describe any healings that took place stating whether they were on an emotional, mental or physical level, note any channeling that occurred and if there were any predictions given and by whom. Take the time to evaluate how the sitters felt on all levels after the session. Were they tired or energized? Tell who felt what. Record how long the session lasted.

You can also make a dated **Personal Information Page** for when you are working on yourself to develop a deeper understanding of yourself and your spiritual purposes for this lifetime. You need to note what spiritual intents you were told you chose for this lifetime. Write down any of the information you received about your spiritual lessons, especially if your have received details of what those lesson are and suggestions of how you can progress through them more easily.

You will want to record your findings about your past lives and what relationship roles you have played with your guides and present physical friends and family. From your notes you will be able to track your karmas, helping you to be prepared to work them through with an ease that comes with understanding why you are in a certain circumstance.

Through careful record keeping, you will learn; which gender you may have preferred in past lives and why, and who from this lifetime you have interacted with the most in past lives helping you to understand more deeply what your role is with them now in this life. As you look back over your Personal Information Pages, you will be able to find personality patterns and determine what past life blockages you need to release. You will be able to chart how and when they have restricted you from your free flow with the universe. Through the knowledge of where and what your blockages are you can release physical, mental, and emotional negative energy which allows you to heal yourself to live with less pain and struggle creating peace and balance.

Through recording your information you will become more aware of how much your psychic skills are developing by comparing your ability to receive information quickly and accurately as time passes.

Creating a **Universal Information Page** will help you to organize a universal quest. For example, you may wish to understand the concepts of; God, soul, Higher Self or what is in the spiritual realms. If you write the focused goal for your quest before you start your session, you will notice that spirit is directly aware of and prepared for your intended search. Writing out a need or a desire also physically activates the subconscious mind to open to spirit's input. On this page record who answered the questions posed as well as their information. Also allow space for any suggestions from the Universal beings, your have attracted because of your impersonal theme.

Many times I have referred to some of my notes from a year or years prior only to find I was given the same information then but I did not understand it at the time because I was not ready. Amazingly, I have discovered profound truths through assembling the information given by diverse entities. Due to their different vantage points you will receive more details to complete the answer to your question or quest. I know that writing down your findings can help you organize your sessions so you can derive as much information as possible from each of your table tipping experiences.

It is my hope that through the use of recorded pages you will be able to identify your life's path and who you are. I know that actively keeping a table tipping journal will help you to not only discover the spiritual or real purpose for why you are here, but enable you to enthusiastically live this purpose with a practical sense of wholeness and joy.

"ALONG THE SPIRITUAL PATH YOU MUST SLAY THE DRAGONS OF DOUBT, FEAR AND IMPATIENCE WITH SUCH CALM STRENGTH THAT THEY WILL NEVER AGAIN IMPEDE YOUR PROGRESS THROUGH THE CONSUMPTION OF YOUR PRECIOUS POWER AND FOCUSED ENERGY."

CHRISTOPHER

CHAPTER THIRTEEN

Advanced Table Tipping

AFTER YOU HAVE been accomplishing table tipping sessions for a considerable period of time, you will start to develop your psychic capacities to hear and see more easily and your intuition will flow more freely. You will better understand yourself, your spiritual lessons and be actively growing in awareness. You will apply spirit's guidance within your life and feel yourself in the flow of the Universal energy most of the time. It is at this point in the table tipping experience that the energy changes during your sessions. Spirit starts to work with you to grow at a faster rate. They expose you to new techniques and more expansive energy exercises to enable you to be within a higher level of self-confidence to get proficient at working with them without the table

A. CHANNELING

As your psychic capacity evolves because of your spiritual growth, spirit will start to perform what then seems to be an almost upsetting trick on you when you table tip. This is especially a common occurrence when the group is comprised of the same sitters who repeatedly work together.

Suddenly when a question is asked, spirit relaxes and does not move the table to reply **Yes** or **No**. The table simply moves over to someone's lap and rests there. Usually, that particular sitter will sense an energy difference. Many times there is a sensation of heat flowing up the spine. As I have noted before this is the Kundalini energy line within your energy and physical bodies responding to spirit. Spirit is working to raise and expand you energy at this time. When the Kundalini is raised so is the enlightenment opened for that person. The energy expansion may be necessary for you to meet with the spirit's higher frequency before communication between you is possible. Remember, spirit would not stretch your energy if you are not ready to safely experience such a frequency. If the sitter relaxes, there will be a spiritual bonding going on that creates a strong telepathic connection between the sitter and the spirit at the table. Then, the spirit will start a channeling experience for the sitter if they allow it.

Channeling is the term designated for the occurrence of spirit being involved with your energy within your mind and body. The amount or degree of spiritual energy that can participate with you is within your control. If you allow spirit to enter your whole body and take your conscious mind out of the experience you will be doing what is called unconscious or "dead" trance channeling; an example being the Edgar Cayce readings. There is another level of trance channeling in which there is a vague conscious awareness of the self through the conscious mind while the spirit is within your energy field. A third level of channeling occurs if you allow spirit to make a telepathic connection with you creating an awareness of its mind while you still have your full conscious mind awareness, this is called conscious channeling. The types of channeling that spirit offers you through the table can be conscious or trance, for the energy and the capacity to perform these levels is present.

I prefer to do conscious channeling. I am not an

advocate of "dead" trance channeling. I do not allow spirit to work with me through dead trance. It is my opinion that we, as a race of human souls, have evolved enough through our own spirituality to be consciously aware that we are channeling and have the mental discipline to not interfere with the experience or filter the knowledge coming through us. We humans have achieved enough ego-shedding evolvement to maintain our conscious mind awareness as a separate energy as well as to sense and receive from spirit's mind.

When a person is channeling they are obviously speaking spirit's message aloud and not needing the table's movement for a **Yes** or **No** for effective communication. Sometimes, spirit will utilize this process with each sitter at the table throughout the entire session. Then, of course, there is actually very little physical table movement happening during this session. But a great deal of information is shared through the concentrated spiritual energy circle that the beings both physical and spiritual collected at the table session provide.

If you should decide to experience the channeling process, notify spirit and they will cheerfully empower the energy circle to amplify your energies sufficiently to create a successful channeling bond. When the table stops tipping and lies in your lap or leans totally in your direction, the spiritual energy comes down and through the surface of the tabletop. This energy focuses into a beam of light aimed towards your physical body in readiness for it to enter through your energy bodies. The beam will usually will enter through the solar plexus, heart, brow, throat or crown chakras.

When I participate in the table tipping channeling experience, I prefer the crown or brow (third eye) chakras for placements of energy entry. I open to the sensing of the energy flowing into me through an infinity symbol formation and consciously share with spirit only a part of my head. I prefer the right half because the right brain is then activated with spirit's energy. After I sense its presence within my head, I allow it to flow down my neck and into my vocal cords allowing the use of my speech, but I ask spirit to remain only on the one side. I do not allow spirit into my heart chakra area unless I want to sense the spirit's emotion which is not essential to receiving accurate data. Usually I do not allow entry at my solar plexus because it is my personal will center. I prefer to communicate with a spirit who vibrates with my higher energy or spiritual level chakras.

The most beautiful and comfortable entity to channel is your own Higher Self. It should be your first choice to call in for it is your own higher teacher and Godself. Channeling your Higher Self bonds it with you permanently and raises your frequency to be able to tune it to it regularly. You will be able to resource it without using the table after the first experience of it raising your frequency. Having and maintaining a relationship with your Higher Self allows for its personal wisdom to flow within you constantly, giving you a new level of peace and comfort. This is an achievable and soul noble goal well worth pursuing through the use of the table.

Whenever you have any questions about the phenomenon of channeling, ask spirit so that through the table it can help you can fully understand what is taking place on all levels. **You have a right to feel completely comfortable with the experience. If you do not, tell spirit.** If at first the table does not move, take charge and require that the spirit respond so there is a better understanding about the channeling process.

B. UNIVERSAL TELEPATHY

Another change spirit can initiate during the table tipping experience is the type of movement that is performed. There will eventually come a time when it will seem that the table is moving but it is actually not physically moving. The sitters will be able to "feel" the table tip the answers and will agree exactly about what they felt. You will sense the movement for **Yes** or **No** in your hands and body and not see the table move. Spirit is allowing you to telepathically sense its answering movements. This is a special technique spirit will use to help you practice being open to receiving intuitively without the direct use of the table.

Occasionally, this "etheric movement" is the signature of a highly evolved being that is presently communicating. The vibration of the most advanced hierarchal beings is often not dense enough to physically move the table. In this case the being uses the spiritual power of the energy circle to connect with those seated around the table. It can communicate for hours with no apparent physical movement of the table. Sometimes these beings take the group etherically into special realms to learn information about their quest from an experiential vantage point. It feels like a group out-of-body experience which is remarkable to sense. These incidents are powerful for the whole group and are deeply memorable.

Sometimes, the sitters within a certain group are spiritually very connected and can be vibrating at the same frequencies within similar levels of evolvement. These sitters, because of their repeated work together, will establish a highly developed telepathic bond amongst themselves. Their minds will receive the same symbols and they will interpret them in the same way or receive very similar information. Such a bond is an uplifting and wonderful experience. This type of harmony will attract occurrences of highly evolved beings wanting to communicate. It enforces one's belief in the unison of the Universal All through practical experience.

There are friends with whom I tip that the only way our information is received is through "ethereal movement" and conscious channeling. We start our session with empowering our energy circle until we can feel it pulsing. We all visualize and feel ourselves expand. It is as if our spiritual selves fill the room. We focus upon the energy within our cells and sense it as the same energy within the air, the furniture in the room, the house, the city and the world - feeling it all as the God Force in action. We focus on this elevated sensation and feel its rhythm. Many times, we actually witness and vibrate with the rhythm of the Universe. With our hands on an unmoving table, we have worked out innumerable spiritual projects. The information received is always superior. We work through many problems and verifications of specific facts for others with these techniques as well.

Sometimes I will place the sitters and the table within a 6 ft. tall copper-tubed-pyramid a friend of mine made from specific spiritual dimensions given to him by his guides. We always attract the highest of beings and incredibly fascinating information from remote dimensions when we are within the special pyramid amplification effect of our spiritual energy circle. The pyramid intensifies the Universal telepathy experience.

You will discover that the advanced style of tipping is truly spiritual, psychic and healing. It raises the sitters' vibrational levels powerfully so that all of them will attune to the highest level energies possible at the time. It can be an ecstatic adventure. When you have reached this level in table tipping experience, rejoice for it is the reward you reap for consistent and devoted spiritual work.

C. MULTIPLE BEINGS

As you develop into an experienced table tipper with a balanced sense of energy, spirit will expose you to another interesting energy feat. Your Table Guide will allow more than one entity at a time to use the table to help the sitters without creating confusion. One entity can be answering questions at the table while another initiates a bond with a different sitter for a healing on a physical, mental, emotional or spiritual level. For example, in one class experience a lady was receiving a healing in her arm, shoulder and neck areas to remove the damage caused by an accident she had experienced a few years previously while another spirit - a Blueprint Guide - was moving the table to answer a different student's question about her purpose and path in this lifetime.

All of this activity is possible because spirit can separate or entwine its essence due to the nature of its energy. Thus, spirit can be in several locations at once or several spirits can be in one location simultaneously. Spirit is not subject to the physical laws of space and time because it is not limited within a form. Groups of spirits with a single purpose can focus their energies simultaneously and come on the table at the same time as a functioning group. Spirit has the flexible ability for multiple applications of their energies and at this level of table tipping you can directly experience them.

The more experienced you are with the table tipping process the more flexible the spirits become in the manner in which they use your table tipping time together. Be open to their innovative ideas and grow.

D. OTHER TECHNIQUES THAT CAN ENHANCE THE POWER OF YOUR TABLE TIPPING EXPERIENCE.

Now that you are an experienced tipper, you will want to take advantage of all the energy expansion that each session can offer from the highest of vibration spiritual energy that chooses to be present to assist you to develop you own inner balance and intuitive awareness. Spirit will support you with all that is available to it and you, because, this goal puts you into the position of performing as an empowered light being blending its role efficiently within the macro plan of evolution.

Most likely because spirit will continually urge you to meditate, you will discover that by now you are probably meditating successfully with some regularity. In order to advance spiritually with any balance of flow you will have to honor yourself and meditate. If you are meditating you will be able to more fully embrace the rewarding fun of advanced table tipping.

USING AN ADVANCED FORM OF THE PROTECTION PROCESS

As you grow in tipping experience you will want to use a more advanced type of grounding and protective process. One that releases any limitations to the most expansive session you can attract at your present vibratory level. Since you can now relax into the meditative state of the grounding process with a practiced ease, you will be able to deepen that state as a group by concentrating on your breathing in unison.

If you like, you could burn sweetgrass, sage or cedar at this time. Use it as a cleanser of the vibrational area of the session. As its smoke rises, call in spirit to help you to clear away all thoughts of your third dimensional problems of this life letting them go and seeing them as smoke or illusion that clouds your knowing of who you really are. Then, focusing on your spiritual self - be pure and open to spirit's higher truths. A representative for the group can monitor the burning for a moment and say, "We move through our illusions into Universal clarity knowing no harm can overcome us."

In the silence of the very beginning of the protection procedure, mentally request that Divine Spirit fill the room. Breathe it in and exhale surrendering the sense of the personal "I". Let go of all concern. Feel neutral. Sense a deep peace that has no desire or need. Feel a limitlessness. Sense the freedom you are creating by letting go of doubt and fear. Most of all feel a quiet restful strength and be still.

Once you are relaxed and seated in the normal grounding position focus your attention upon your heart center. Feel your comfortably relaxed heart beat and breathing rhythm. Visualize a white flame within your heart center. See it as bright as you can possibly conceive - much like a welder's white hot flame. Then sense that all around you is light by thinking about the active life force within the atoms of the air that surrounds you, as well as the furniture, walls and the building that you are in. Acknowledge that the light of your flame is the same light that is present in all the atoms that make up the earth and all third dimensional form. Feel akin to this light of life force as deeply as possible. Focus once again upon the flame within your heart enlarging it to this size of a basketball. Always maintain the brightness of the light. Continue to grow this white light flame until it is as large as your aura filling your entire body and your personal energy unit with its intense whiteness. Connect your whiteness with that of each of the other sitters and see it magnifying your energy circle connection. Then see this united light as one large white flame that includes the table, your energy circle, the room and the space high above and below it. Say, "The power and purity of our white light flame burns away all dissension and negativity and strengthens the bond of our circle to its greatest expansion of consciousness. The Light of God protects us - we are this light and protection. We are the Light of God vibrating in attunement with all the Light in the Universe." (See your circle and the white flame strong and watch it expand. Then see it vibrating and echoing its vibration outward into the universe) "The love of God enfolds us. We are this love radiating impersonally without end." (Take time to concentrate on feeling love - think of it and deeply be in love. Visualize the circle spiraling upward and outward with this love vibration. Then see the flame expanding and vibrating with the love in the universe) "The presence of God watches over us. We are within the presence of God expressing Its purity of intention to align only with Its Plan." (Visualize the circle and the flame vibrating with large ocean-like waves of willingness reaching outward to be open to the highest of beings that are available to you at this time.) With this completed you can say "We are united in the Light as a strong, loving force within the Heart of the Divine."

Anytime you perform this protection process you will create a special magnification of your personal spiritual power that can raise your vibration permanently. Without question, it directly aligns you with your inner teacher or Higher Self. It raises your consciousness to a level that allows you to receive answers from within with trust and accuracy. The effect of its use is long lasting. You will reach higher levels in meditation, recall powerful dreams and attract an awareness of a great deal of helpful spiritual interaction within your every day life. You will notice more instances in your daily life of you knowing you are performing within the Universal flow because you are following your inner knowing. When you do this you will feel a very special joy and contentment.

Repeated use of the energy circle at this advanced level empowers it to be stronger in each session as you and the group visualize it. You will notice that the ongoing growth and expansion of the energy circle will create a powerful new level of energy transmissions for communication and the healing process that are filled with a strengthened purity. Feeling and working within the unison of the power of the energy circle is great practice for the development of oneness, and as you observe your personal benefits you will deeply understand the Universal principle of oneness in action.

USING ASTROLOGICAL INFORMATION

Knowing your astrological natal chart moon placement can enhance your tipping experience because you will know the times when you are more intuitive. You will have much more psychic power when your moon sign is in active placement. For instance, my moon is in Gemini, so whenever the moon is in Gemini I can receive and send with much more power and ease the higher vibration energies.

There are certain aspects that enable you to more readily release blockages and fears or empower you to be more able to complete a spiritual lesson or karma.

The guides speak of the power released during sun flair activity and the importance of knowing about its energy and magnetic effect upon the earth and our physical body. They tell us to work with the phases of the moon when we are releasing or detaching and while we are goal setting for our manifestations.

I am not an astrologer. However, spirit has provided that I have a very special friend who is a spiritual astrologer that helps me to know when special planetary aspects which can directly effect my energy are occurring. A knowledge of astrology can assist you with the effectiveness of your tipping sessions.

SEVERAL GROUPS TIPPING WITH THE SAME INTENT

Another practice that has interesting results is for two or three groups to table tip at different tables and ask the same questions. Then, the individuals involved must compare the answers received. It is interesting how much more information can be provided in this manner. It seems that allowing more spirits to answer certain questions brings in a more well-rounded collection of knowledge about the subject discussed. This can be done in the same room at the same time or in different locations at different times.

TIPPING WITH THE SAME SITTERS

When you have been tipping with the same group for many sessions, there is a comfort between the sitters and the spirits. It should be noted that the spirits have to work together as well as the physical people in the table tipping session. If the same spirits work together long enough they become energy efficient and vibrationally connected with each other as well. The familiarity creates an ease and improved strength for achieving connections with higher level spirits.

ENTERING THE SESSION OPEN TO SPIRIT

When you know all your guides and are aware of most of your lessons and karmas your need to direct the session for personal growth lessens. You relax to a new level of surrender concerning the table experience. Amazingly powerful undreamed of experiences await you at this time. You can start your session with the following request. "We open the table and our energy circle to whatever energy wishes to speak to us from the highest vibration level available to us today. We open to receive any and all information that this level wishes to share with us at this time. Whenever you (the entity or energy) have collected your energy and are in vibrational resonance with us, please let us know by moving the table for a **Yes**."

Some of the best information I have received resulted from this approach to the session. Usually it is the only technique I use unless a client needs personal information. Most often this technique will result in either etheric movement of the table or channeling. The teachings I have received in this manner will be in my next book about practical personal energy management and how to live as your Higher Self.

FOCUSING IN ON IMPERSONAL QUESTS

Feeling more comfortable with who you are and knowing you are the co-creator of your pathway, you tend to use the table tipping session to ask impersonal questions. Usually you will want to better understand the Creative Plan or want to know all you can about God. You may wish to know the history of humanity or all about ancient civilizations, such as Lemuria. Whatever, when you are at this level of intention you can access the Akashic records of the planet, the solar system and the universe. Once you are familiar with this level because you have reached it in table sessions through the empowerment of the energy circle, you will now have the capacity to tap into it on your own without the table. This can happen for you in dream and meditation.

When your group in on an impersonal quest, you will automatically be talking with higher level beings and masters. They will have regard for you because you have shown an interest in the whole of the Creative or Evolutionary Plan. They will only communicate with you about energy lessons and the universe.

Often, these beautiful energies have the desire to allow you to participate with them in certain projects that are helpful to the whole universe. They have had us work with the water sprite devas in order to create balance which might produce rain clouds somewhere over the earth where it is suffering a drought when it does not interfere with karma or lessons.

They will give an account of negative collectives that will and often do create political problems. At times, they will give us specific details concerning group meditation techniques to do that supports the souls who are directly effected by strengthening them to learn their lessons. Some techniques help us to be united with these powerful beings in sending the needy souls positive energy for a consciousness raising. This can enable them to create new ideas and techniques to ease or rise above the negativity of the difficult conditions they are experiencing.

As you become a member of the team that is doing God's energy work here on earth, you gain an understanding of what it means to be a master. This understanding gives you the ability to perceive and direct yourself towards mastery levels. You might be asked to volunteer to do some special work that is fulfilling and interesting to complete. You will often be surprised that what you are asked to do is to honor the individual souls involved by giving them spiritual strength to grow through their experiences. You will not be asked to change their plight for they have created their own way to learn. Spiritual law respects their free will choice of the manner in which they wish to learn.

Some members of the Brotherhood of Light and a group of Starbeings came onto the table and asked some friends and myself to be involved in the work of opening a new earth vortex. These Light energies were very specific about the location for the initiation of this vortex. We used a map when table tipping to find the locations while the energies directed us. With their help we pinpointed the newly evolving power spot.

My friends fasted in a specific manner for several days, as they were prescribed to do by the spiritual group working with them through the table. They traveled by car several hours to the remote location shown on the map. They took their table with them in order to tip while at the designated area to verify with spirit the exact location for their work. They then created an energy circle at this location using the stones, crystals, copper and power objects spirit had requested that they lay out in the specific cardinal directions.

We were told that there was a powerful crystal submerged deep into the earth by an ancient civilization that had to be activated now through our combined ceremonious work. My friends meditated at the requested time and in the required manner from the special directions provided by spirit through the table. I participated in the meditation at home to send energy assistance. They worked on this process at this remote location for several days. I continued to work with them telepathically. Spirit used our energy work within their own special processes. We all must have done well for we received verification a few days later. Some well known out of town psychics went to the area and publicly claimed they found a powerful new earth vortex. They had no idea of our work, but we were excited anonymously. We are working on our masterhood and know that conquering self-importance is a major part of this type of growth.

BEING PERSONALLY BALANCED

Since one's personal state of balance effects the level of energy one attracts to the table, I am careful about my diet, atmosphere, thinking and emotions. I find it best to keep a less dense diet. I am not telling you that you should become vegetarian, but when I eat only fruits, grains and vegetables, I easily attract higher vibration beings to the table. I feel moderation is balance. However, there are times in my growth patterns when animal protein in my diet is too dense for my vibration. I do special fasts occasionally when I feel it is beneficial for my spiritual balance. When you are scattered and feeling unable to pull life together then it is best to take a day to be quiet and alone. Most often my only intake for that day is to drink lots of water. This pulls my energy in and allows me to empower it. I release all connections to anyone or anything in order to cleanse and be just my own energy. Then I am able to balance.

I am particular about the colors and the types of fabrics I wear when I tip. Positive colors attract positive spiritual energy. (White, blue, green, violet and pastels are positive colors.) Natural fabrics also have positive energy effects.

Eliminating negative thoughts throughout the day creates a positive mind. Listening to positive vibration music such as Vivaldi, Scarlatti or Mozart reinforces your positive energy. Thus, I use the positive vibrations of; color, sound, foods, fabric, thinking, speech and emotions to keep a special balance of in my life. These daily practices create the necessary energy within and around me to attract high vibration communications with an everflowing ease, with or without the table.

E. EMPOWERING YOUR ABILITY TO MANIFEST THROUGH TABLE TIPPING.

Being co-creators we have to decide what it is we need in our life and lay out the structure for our intended goal. It is our right to bring our goal into physical reality once we have thought and felt it through. Of course it is also important to allow the space for the intervention of the God Force because from Its macro vantage point of expanded existence It may fulfill our need in infinitely more abundant and perfect ways.

To bring our need from a thought level reality (a thought form) into the physical reality is called manifestation. Christ demonstrated manifesting hundreds of times in what was termed as miracles and said, "Do as I do." He was telling us that we, as spiritual energies, have the power to manifest. Looking at Christ's example, we witness that He saw only what was perfect, not seeing or focusing on the problem. He only saw the perfect answer. He saw it already answered and **had no doubt it was so.**

In order to manifest our good we must feel worthy, declare our need to be present in a loud confident voice that has complete trust that it is so. Declare what you perceive you need with a voice and intonation (Because the spoken word has great power!) that sound and vibrate with complete trust in the Universe and yourself. There can be no trace of doubt. No trace of the ego saying; "Can I do it? Can I do it well enough? Will I succeed? Should I do this?"

Manifesting is simple. We humans make it complicated. You only decree it **to be so.** Think of the Star Trek character Captain John Luke Picard on the Starship Enterprise who says to the crewman, "Make it so." The Captain trusts it is delegated and accomplished and moves on to his other leadership tasks almost forgetting about his declaration for he knows it is being competently taken care of. That is how simple

simple manifesting is designed to be.

When the request is presented, it is a statement to your own Godself that you need this or something better that is available in this matter to be so. If you whimper or doubt, your Godself and the supporting Universe will not take you seriously. You must feel with a deep enthusiasm that it is already so. This feeling of joy must fill your heart and solar plexus centers because then you totally trust it is so. You are aligning your own will with the higher will combining them with joyous enthusiasm and complete trust that this or something better is happening.

See the new desired condition as a means to allow your whole self to do your spiritual work in this life in a more empowered manner enabling you to be in service to others benefiting the whole of the Creative Plan. This could mean, for example, that you want to be in business for yourself selling ice cream. Visualize yourself as the best ice cream salesman you can be. Know and deeply feel that when you sell your ice cream you give your customers happiness and a sense of well-being. Then know and visualize that because you sell happiness and a sense of well-being everyone wants to buy it.

Using the table tipping experience to enhance the strength of your manifesting power is one of the most fun and exciting ways to use advanced table tipping. The reason the table is so potent in creating your manifestation is because we now have "two or more asking in His name." The established union of the oneness and the Universal consciousness created by the energy circle magnifies and magnetizes the energy of the manifestation. The table itself is round and when it stands on a single pedestal ending with three legs, as mine does, these three supporting legs symbolizes our personal trinity. This trinity is combined in a balanced union when the legs join with the single pedestal. The top of the pedestal terminates at the round tabletop creating the perfect symbol of a full circle symbolically demonstrating that - "what comes around goes around." The physical circle is symbolic of the completion of the spiraling of spiritual energy outward attracting to itself the returning of a like vibration energy - the physical manifestation.

It is helpful if each person at the table is united in the need for a manifestation. Maybe all of them need a new and better paying job or if each person concentrates upon bringing in their most expanded good that can be supportive enough. The emotional bond of the common need is not necessary, but it is a helpful for a magnification of the energy charging the manifestation.

When you have completed your advanced energy circle process, all of the sitters place their hands on the table putting their energy into it as a physical representation of their energy circle. At that time the operator can speak out loud a declaration for the manifestation allowing at any time verbal input from the others.

A suggested declaration example that I have found to be effective is the following: "We manifest at this moment a powerful input of abundance and creativity into our vocational path without limitation of doubt or lack of trust as to how it will come to pass. We have full faith that it is now patterned in the cosmic idea and will constantly grow into further abundance and serve us in our service. We empower this manifestation now with love, (Pause and take the time to deeply feel love.) joy (Pause and feel it.) and enthusiasm. (Pause and take time to feel it.) We send out our personal tones of vibration so that they who are aligned to this manifestation are attracted to us to give what they have to offer to resonate along with our energy giving us whatever is needed to manifest our highest and best pathway. All authorities, participators and renderers of this path vibrate strongly to hear and respond with empowered action for the fulfillment of this manifestation."

Now all the sitters hold hands saying, "We open ourselves like a beautiful Lotus to the fullness and limitlessness of this experience. We are open to all of its good whether it comes in appreciation, funds or in love and warmth. We are open to the exact fulfillment of our declaration or anything that is better. We see this manifestation only as an empowerment of our service that we give in joy and harmony as a spiritual being."

Now with hands still joined raise your arms upward and with great enthusiasm say, "We now release the power and the strength that we have built - we release it sending it outward freely to return to us. We release all pounding on Heaven's door, trusting that its return is swift."

All of you can say aloud, "Manifest! Manifest! Manifest! It is so. It is now!"

Take in a deep cleansing breath saying, "With the release of this breath we completely release this energy."

Now it is your important task **to not think about this need again.** Letting it go is releasing the energy to be pure and powerful to incubate the need into form. You must act as if the need is already here. The guides tell us that if you are in love - being and performing in the way a young lover radiates when he is in love for the first time - you will manifest love in your life. You must live this "in love" feeling with the great excitement of that young lover singing and playing joyous music. **Be in love and in joy and it is so.**

Only when you have physically experienced the manifesting process through the energy circle of the table can you describe the feeling of the unbelievable power that is created. It is astounding to witness the rapidity of the result as well.

EPILOGUE

As we flow through this gift of life we have choices. We can cruise in a neutral gear like a car that has its wheels free to roll with the ups and downs of the road's surface with no sense of direction, blaming the wind and the road conditions for our ride. While in neutral, we can just pass through life as helpless observers feeling bitter towards others because of what we feel they do to us. We can think we are victims of life and all the circumstances that surround us. We can also choose to slip into reverse gear and go backwards in our spiritual progression, criticizing others hoping they will change. While in reverse gear we can focus on others with judgmental hindsight, keeping ourselves busily concerned with other's problems so we can avoid working on our own self-awareness and improvement. There is a procrastinating safety of not having to consider the effort or risks of moving forward. The comfort zone of traveling over old known roads that have no change for us gives us a chance to feel a great self-importance and mental control in reference to others.

Each of these directions can make us feel alone, sad and small inside. They can be choices that pull down a blind which closes out the beautiful growth vistas that are offered outside the window of life's expression. We can choose to look and reach through the window to discover all the spiritual helpers of a whole friendly universe that is at home within and outside of us. We can welcome, through physical world challenges, the incredible inner knowingness of our true beauty and flow in God's Creative Plan which will balance, heal and place us in its perfect evolution through our own expanded awarenesses. That is the beautiful effect of going through life in forward gear or "drive".

I believe spiritual table tipping to be powerful as

an enlightening and helpful tool to use as one passes through the window of life's expression. It is a tool that can blend with meditation and other forms of opening your awareness to your full potential of beingness. The potency of the table tipping spiritual energy circle technique and its use will expand your consciousness with a swift and direct simplicity.

My goal for sharing the spiritual table tipping process with you is to create for you an awareness of the direct manner in which you can permanently connect yourself with your higher knowing, your Higher Self. This connection results in a bond enabling the perfect flow of its intuitive energy in action. This bond frees you to be all you are as a perfect spirit and enables you to never have to look outside of yourself for direction or answers again. I honor the table tipping experience as a spiritual process and a wonderful group teaching tool because it is a directly connecting physical bridge between spirit and physical beings to empower this noble bond to be used for personal-spiritual freedom.

In my opinion, the spiritual table tipping process is safer than many levels of trance channeling because the communicating spirit uses the table as the physical tool instead of your body and whole energy unit. This protects and reserves your physical body and your whole energy unit for your own soul and spirit. Gathering wisdom with the use of the table instead of your whole body allows for you to be consciously aware of both planes of existence while receiving information. This is an incredibly useful skill - an evolved skill. It is a skill we are more able to develop at this time in earth history. When you have achieved this other dimensional awareness skill with the use of the table and its energy circle, you will discover you will no longer need the table to receive information accurately. Since earth events will unfold quickly and dramatically during the next few decades, I consider the development of this skill vital to our existence individually and as a race. It is time that we allow ourselves to have the awareness that we are advancing daily and can now embrace our spiritual gifts as a race of progressed humans.

Your spiritual table tipping experiences enable you to better understand yourself because you learn who you presently are and have been. Your past life research allows you to study most of your personality patterns. This opens the way for learning about your karmas, spiritual intents and soul lessons to help you to better understand why you came into this life. Because the table session allows direct conversations with your Spirit Guides, Spiritual Teachers and Higher Self you now are enabled to understand how you can fulfill your incarnational plan effectively in this lifetime. This type of knowledge enables you to facilitate the power of your Godself. You will embrace a peace and happiness that is constantly growing within you because you consciously know who you are and why you came to earth.

Another level of inner security is found through table tipping sessions because you can now have a deep understanding from an experiential vantage point that we, as human souls, are eternal. We are more than a physical body, we do not die. The physical body experience is necessary for the growth of the soul so that it can expand and move on to other dimensional expressions of itself as an active spark of the God Force. You will learn that the earth is just a city on the path and that this life is just a script of an interesting and challenging opportunity to act out our lessons and karmas within our whole or holy journey through many worlds to become mastered God Lights.

I know that we can better enjoy this present expression of incarnated life with awareness of both the physical and spiritual planes. We can have full contact with our spirituality through our own Higher Self moment by moment actually living within it as a whole person. This ability makes us whole and fulfilled in a deeper manner than living separately within a physical world with no recognition of the spiritual realm. We never need to suffer the pain of loneliness, because we know we are never really alone. However, we have the free will choice to perceive only with our five physical senses or to open ourselves to the expansiveness of our true nature which is to perceive beyond these senses by opening and accepting our own soul senses of perception. This "whole" method of perception creates the expanded picture of what we truly are and why we exist.

Through this fuller perception, we can have and maintain an inner calm throughout whatever circumstances we encounter. This inner calm gives us a power to fully and completely experience the events of our lifetime. Within this perception you will feel and know with security that each of us is an incredibly beautiful piece of the All - a Light energy working within an immense Universal Plan of evolution.

I pray, with the power of unconditional Universal Love, that the spiritual table tipping experience opens all the blinds of every personal window for all of you beautiful souls. That it enables your personal spiritual growth and expands your knowledge about God and your role in His Plan. I pray that spiritual table tipping empowers you to be the director of your emotions and mind, to be in balance and to radiate joy while you travel in "drive" along your own created, free will chosen spiritual roadway. It is my dream that through your spiritual growth you will realize yourself to be, not just a part of, but **one with the All!**

Angela M. Mattey

CLOSING PIECE

345

BIBLIOGRAPHY

Clark, Adrian V., Psycho-kinesis: Moving Matter with the Mind. West Nyack, New York: Parker Publishing Co., 1973.

Garfield, Leah Maggie, and Grant, Jack, Companions In Spirit., Berkeley, Ca.: Celestial Arts, 1984.

Henkin, Bill and Wallace, Amy, The Psychic Healing Book, Berkeley, Ca.: Wingbow Press, 1978.

John, St., of the Cross, Doctor of the Church, Dark Night Of the Soul, translated and editied by Peers, E. Allison, Garden City, New York: Image Books, div. of Doubleday & Co.Inc., 1959.

PRODUCTS

TAM ENTERPRISES
"Producers of Products for Enlightenment"

1. Audio Meditation CD; with the *Grounding Meditation for the Table Tipping Protection Process that empowers the Spiritual Energy Circle necessary for White Light Communications.* (This CD contains two meditations: Track 1 has the basic meditation for grounding and protection for the beginning tipper which safely attracts personal spirit guides, angels and loving deceased souls. Track 2 has the advanced energy shifting meditation for grounding and creating energy expansion for the more experienced tipper which attracts Universally Advanced beings such as Archangels, Masters, etc.) **Price: $16.95 Plus $5.95 (S & H.)**

SEND CHECK or MONEY ORDER TO:
TAM ENTERPRISES
4050 CLOVERLAWN DRIVE
GRANTS PASS, OR 97527
OR: order on-line www.spirit-eagle.com

PHOENIX, ARIZ. 85078

OR WRITE TO TAM ENTERPRISES FOR INFORMATION ABOUT:

1. **TABLE TIPPING SEMINARS;** When and where they will be.

2 **A TABLE TIPPING NEWSLETTER** Containing the latest information received from current table tipping sessions about the earth and humanity's future - plus the most recently received new and exciting spiritual truths.

3. **OR** - To share the Universal truths you have received in table tipping sessions from the spiritual hierarchy.

ABOUT THE AUTHOR

Angela M. Mattey is an ordained minister, metaphysician, and philosopher. She was a teacher for 10 years in the Ohio public school system. She is an award winning professional artist who owned 2 studios in the Phoenix metropolitan area for eight years.

She had a proven psychic mother, an Irish-born maternal grandmother who shared her Celtic mysticism (Clairvoyance in reference to the human aura and the fairy kingdom) with Angela during her childhood and a paternal German-born grandfather, who regularly communicated psychokinetically with the spiritual dimensions.

Because of her own special talents and the influence of her inherited environment, Angela lives with a unique working awareness of both the spiritual and physical realms.

Angela is a graduate of the Silva Mind system. She studied hypnosis, psychic awareness and spiritual development at several Southern Californian metaphysical centers as well as the University of Humanistic Studies. Her extensive psychic and spiritual research has enabled her to understand in depth the subject area of Spirit Guides. The most effective tool she used to develop her abilities with intensity was table tipping in its spiritual form. Because of this, she researched it and used it with hundreds of students. She has been teaching and performing table tipping seminars and classes since 1981. She has taught table tipping, meditation techniques and psychic development for the City of Phoenix adult education program and for several metaphysical centers in the Phoenix metropolitan area. She has utilized table tipping to; find missing items and people, communicate with Spirit Guides and the Higher Self, as well as, to solve and harmonize various mysterious spiritual happenings.

Angela has seen and sensed her guides, Guardian Angel and other dimensional beings since her youth. She reads cards in the same manner as her mother did, auras as her Grandmother had shown her, consciously channels other's Spirit Guides or Guardian Angels in personal readings and enjoys table tipping with clients to solve spiritual problems like her Grandfather.